ONE WAY OF LIVING

¶ *a list of James Bridie's other books and of his published plays is given at the end of this book*

ONE WAY OF LIVING

BY

JAMES BRIDIE

The frontispiece is from
a bust of the Author
by Loris Rey

CONSTABLE AND COMPANY LTD

PUBLISHED BY
Constable and Company Ltd.
LONDON
·
*The Macmillan Company
of Canada, Limited*
TORONTO

First published 1939

PRINTED IN GREAT BRITAIN BY ROBERT MACLEHOSE AND CO LTD
THE UNIVERSITY PRESS GLASGOW

" This is the bell that never rang,
This is the fish that never swam,
This is the tree that never grew,
This is the bird that never flew."

Jingle on Glasgow City Arms

" Inertia is the property of matter by which it retains
its state of rest or of uniform rectilinear motion so long
as no foreign cause occurs to change that state."—*The
Dictionary*

" Well, British Public, ye who like me not,
(God love you!) And will have your proper laugh
At the dark question, laugh it! I laugh first."

The Ring and the Book

CONTENTS

ONE WAY OF LIVING

CHAPTER I

The First Five

In cellar sit I like a bin
But empty of good wine within
And hear around with horrid thump
The high explosives round me bump. . . .

. . . " *Ach!* " *I said, " I cannae write verse with that noise
outside and my face like a couple of boxing gloves and this
howling, whining pain picking out the branches of my
trigeminal nerve.*" *So I went to the Colonel and I said,
"Colonel, look at me."*

*The Colonel said, "By the Holy, you are a sight. Away
you go now, down to the Casualty Clearing Station and
have them out."*

*I took an ambulance and drove through the sleet and dark
for hours in such a temper that whenever the driver asked
the way and said he thought we should go to the left, I said
the right and was wrong. It was two in the morning when
we came to a horrid hut with only one patch of heat in it,
five inches from the stove. A dingy lout took my name with*

more of dumb insolence than I expected from a uniformed man and then took himself off. In an hour or so an angry M.O. in spectacles came in and said, " Vat de matter mit you? "

I pointed my swollen face and the chap said "Ach, Zo."

In an hour and a half I was in a cold bed and Sister Kerr was giving me an aspirin. Next day I went up through the snow to the château and sat me down in a dentist's chair while the two men filled me with gas till I rose in the air to the sound of tin trays being beaten together.

I looked down with some interest at the bloated, blue faced wretch with whom the two labourers were struggling. I said, " If you don't mind my mentioning it, I think you should lower his head and inject a twentieth of strychnine into his tongue. . . . Ah, as I thought. His heart has stopped beating and you have no adrenalin in your damned awful C.C.S. It is fortunate that he will not feel the cold in the mortuary."

I turned and went to the place I had to go. St. Peter was gey thrang. He had a map and a list and he was running his fingers through his tousled hair and shouting on us all to get back and give him room and give him time and stop all that noise. I was in no hurry and I leaned against the jasper wall and wondered that people thought themselves so important even after they were dead and done for that they should shove and shout like that.

A seraph said, " Hey, you! Come this way." So I followed him through a little sally-port.

" There has been some mistake," I said, when I saw where I was.

" Very probably," said the seraph. " We are that thrang we dinna ken whether we're on our head or our heels. Ye maun make the best o't. Bide here."

I was back stage at the Repertory Theatre. The dusty stage was lit by an amber float and Aristophanes was having

2

a row with Garrick over a script. The chill air blew through the swing door and I could see a queue stretching up to the Stage Manager's office. The A.S.M. came up to me.

" Listen," he said, " he'll take several centuries to get through that lot. Here is paper. There is a typewriter among the props. . . . Sit down and write."

" But I don't pretend to be a playwright," I said. " I'm a doctor, in point of fact. It's true I've written things for smokers and bazaars. But . . ."

" Put your explanations in black and white," said the A.S.M. " Can't you see we're busy ! "

Mrs. Centlivre went past and threw me a nod. I sat down to write.

" Scene One. A lounge Hall in Sussex—Surrey— Bucks—with french windows opening on a privet hedge."

" No, no," I thought. " That won't do. I must explain. Let me see. I am a Captain in the Royal Army Medical Corps, Special Reserve. I died of a couple of alveolar abscesses and the effects of nitrous oxide and ether at the age of twenty-six . . ."

" You got better of that," said Mrs. Aphra Behn. " Don't you remember? "

" Yes," said Colley Cibber. " You got better. Your war ended. You went home. You took up writing. They acted your plays, Stap, Rend and Pickle Me if I understand why. And here you are with the thousands and tens of thousands who have contributed to the degrada- tion of the Theatre. What are you doing? "

" I am writing my life," I said. " I must get it clear. How old am I ? "

" By your looks, I should put you in the fifties! " said Mrs. Behn, kissing her hand to Wycherley and moving off. The old stage creaked and swayed as my fellow country- man, Ben Jonson rolled across it. I turned quickly to the typewriter and wrote:

3

" The Lowland Scot is the fine flower . . ."
" To consider curiously the Scottish Character . . ."
" Whatever we may think of the general characteristics
of the Lowland Scot . . ."
I found I had put in the carbon paper wrong side up.
I tore out the sheet and began again.

The Lowland Scot differs from the rest of mankind
in that he has no Unconscious Mind. He is aware
and critical of all the levels of his consciousness, even
when he is asleep or tipsy. He is expert upon himself,
if upon no other matter.

He divides his consciousness, as a result of wary and
continuous observation, into three planes—the Intellectual Plane, the Moral Plane and the Physical
Plane. He makes no claim that this arrangement is
scientifically or philosophically just; but merely that it
is a good working scheme and that it explains many in-
consistencies in his conduct. He makes no claim that
the arrangement is valid for other human beings, but
only for himself. He has considerable evidence that
the consciousness of his neighbour is not so tidily
marshalled. His neighbours are orra bodies; queer
folk; all out of step but our Jock; amusing; even
partly explicable; but disordered and *abnormal*.

One result of this is that the Scotsman is a good
biographer but a bad autobiographist. His remark-
ably objective view of himself brings the recording of
his own acts and experiences out of the field of art and
into the field of mathematics. The story of an instrument of precision has poor appeal to the emotions.

I am a Lowland Scot. I am told that, on the distaff
side of my ancestry, there was an ancient scandalous
connection with the ducal house of Leeds; but this
I take to be fancy. My father's people came from
Aberdeenshire, Banffshire and Fifeshire. My mother's

4

came from the Mearns of Renfrewshire. So far as I know there is not a drop of English or of Highland blood in my veins. I am thus ill-qualified to write the story of my life or of any part of it.

Yet, there are reasons why I should. Perhaps the best is that I am fifty years old and fifty is ten times five. Five is a gallant number, with its swelling paunch and its little flag. It is the finest of all the multiplying numbers except seven. Any number multiplied by five gains an added grace, and so do the objects so enumerated.

> Five pounds.
> Ten Virgins.
> Fifteen Men on a Dead Man's Chest.
> Twenty Sonnets.
> Forty Days and Forty Nights.
> Forty-five Guardsmen.
> A Hundred Runs.
> A Thousand Chariots.
> Fifty Thousand Copies.
> A Million Anything.
> Five Million Red Corpuscles.

Fifty years is an interesting age, no matter whose age it is. On the third of January, nineteen hundred and thirty-eight, I was fifty.

I take a personal delight in all this because my life, when it has moved at all, has moved in cycles of five years. I have lived ten different lives and now is the time to turn back and survey them. When I am a hundred I shall be too old. My treacherous memory will have done me the last indignity and deserted me altogether.

I find myself at fifty in a pleasant and even enviable material position. I live in a comfortable house in agreeable surroundings. I have a wife and family of whom I am fond and who are fond of me. I have an

B

overdraft at the Bank, but my Bank Agent still smiles when I speak to him and I am able to afford many minor luxuries. I belong to some good clubs and have reached a respectable position in at least two difficult professions. I am under the orders of nobody except the tax-gatherers and the police. I have several friends and no enemies except one lady who writes me anonymous postcards. I sleep well. I have no troublesome illnesses. I have ten times as much leisure as anybody between the ranks of a millionaire and a tramp. I am in a position to turn round, to breathe easily and to take stock of my Past. I am the more in such a position that more than one reputable publishing firm has offered to pay me for my stock-taking. The market for Memoirs by butchers, bakers, candlestick makers, burglars, hill-climbers, street walkers, literary gents and their bullies, politicians, diplomats and soldiers has never been in better shape. I should be meeting a Demand with the utmost possible satisfaction to myself.

This History of a Happy Bourgeois and How he Became That ought to contain a Lesson; and no doubt one will emerge. The moral plane of my consciousness will attend to that. At this stage I am determined simply to set down such facts as will not offend those whose right it is to be offended and to set them down as far as possible in their proper order. I reserve the right to break the narrative with any reflections that seem pertinent to my purpose. I have promised my publisher that this book will contain no obscene or libellous matter. As far as possible I shall keep that promise. As far as possible, moreover, I shall be frank, open and candid with you. But you must remember that I find the character, whose life I am setting out to recount, a very attractive character indeed. I should be failing in my duty if I did not convey something of his charm to you. I am also pleased to think that he is respectable, in the best sense of the word. It may be necessary, therefore, to suppress certain passages which might militate against an altogether favourable impression. Any reasonable man and most reasonable women will understand this necessity. So much having been said, it is time to begin this record of experience and endeavour.

I have not re-visited my birthplace, but I understand that it was a flat in a decent, stone-built building in a residential district of Glasgow called Pollokshields. I never knew either of my grandfathers. A bust and some photographs of my father's father show a biggish man with a magnificent beard and a humorous but obstinate cast of countenance. He was ordained as a minister, but never, so far as I know, settled down to a parish. Instead, he conducted a school in Pollokshields. He married Mary Ann Bridie, the daughter of a Dundee Skipper. They had eleven children of whom my father was the fourth. My grandfather's name was James Mavor.

My mother's father had come in from the fields with cheeses and, with others of his family, had stayed in the town to sell them. I have only seen one photograph of him. He was a gentle looking man with a thick, dark beard and very deep-set eyes. Those who knew him spoke of him more with affection than with reverence. He had seven daughters and a son. His name was Hugh Osborne.

Hugh Osborne died in his thirties and James Mavor in his early fifties. They left their families no money but a good deal of character. My recollection of these families is clearest at the period when I was almost between the ages of three and thirteen.

The Mavor household was ruled by Mary Ann Bridie. She died when I was eight and there is a certain confusion in my mind between her personality

7

and that of Queen Victoria. She was a serious, plump, good-looking woman with a very long upper lip and a short, obstinate nose. She wore an elaborate lace cap and grey silk clothes except when she was ill—she had heart disease.

At those times she wore the cap and a Paisley shawl dressing-gown. She taught me and my brother table manners and arithmetic. She read to us, on Sunday afternoons, the *Tales of a Grandfather* by Sir Walter Scott. It was a surprise to me to find, later on, that the great novelist had actually composed this work. I believed them to be by my grandmother's late husband, whom I had never seen. Indeed, I reconstructed him from these stories as a hodden grey person in a Kilmarnock bonnet and little side whiskers. I made no attempt to reconcile this picture with the formidable bust in the lobby or the photograph beside the mantelpiece. I do not know at what time of life the child begins to be worried by irreconcilable conceptions. To me, even when I was supposed to be studying biology as a medical student, a cell remained a little dark room with some straw and a fetter in it. To this day the contradictions of theology which have set the world in an uproar do not upset me much. Perhaps there is a reason for this. The two households of which I am writing were so different that the words " grandmother," " aunts " and " uncles " seemed to have no common meaning; and I am a product of them both.

Of James Mavor's family, seven survived. James, the eldest, had just become a Professor of Political Economy in Toronto after a stormy career as a Lecturer, Editor of an Art Magazine and Socialist Candidate for Parliament. He became a very considerable figure in Canada.

In these days, when a Professor is indistinguishable from a stockbroker in appearance, it is difficult to evoke such an archetype as was my uncle. He was a lanky man with a conical bald head on which he wore a conical soft hat with a wide brim. He had a straggling, uncut beard and the short-sighted man's peering aspect. His coat, waistcoat and trousers belonged to different suits of clothes. This foible led to a story of which I am sure that he was the original.

He had a hole in his trouser pocket and became annoyed by the shower of coppers and silver which kept falling from him at odd moments. He therefore went into a slop shop and bought a new pair of trousers. Next morning, after he had left for his lecture, my aunt went into his bedroom to make the bed. She saw my uncle's trousers hanging over the back of a chair and at once leaped to a certain conclusion. She rang up the Gate Porter at the University and asked him, if he noticed anything unusual about Professor Mavor, to put him in a cab and send him home.

It was this lady who woke up in a *wagon lit* on the first day of her honeymoon trip and wished my uncle " Good morning." He answered her with a horrified stare and said: " Good God, Miss Watt, what are you doing here? "

He was a friend of Tolstoi, Kropotkin and William Morris. He loved Russia and wrote a classical economic history of it. He imported the Doukhobors to Canada.

He became the Grand Old Man of that Dominion and it was essential for visitors to be taken to him and introduced to him in his great library. He was a wit and, except for Mr. Bernard Shaw, the only master of the anecdote I have ever met.

My father was the second surviving son. The other children were Sam, Alfred, Isabella, Nan and Jessie. Ivan had been killed in an explosion two years before I was born. Alec, a chronic invalid, had died in boyhood. I know nothing of the others.

9

Sam and Alfred were romantic and terrifying figures. They were robust, athletic young men who had been everywhere and done everything. Alfred was not of the household, but he descended on it from time to time, a tall, stout fair man with a beautiful wife. He taught us single stick and boxing. I did not know him very well, but I could feel his almost gluttonous zest for life. His end was unhappy. Sam had been an officer in the Japanese Navy. He had had heroic adventures; but children as young as we were have not yet organised their hero worship. They can set up an idol so long as he ignores or placates them. My uncle did neither. His prestige made his jokes terrifying to us. We loved others who had less kindness and generosity because we did not understand his ways.

Isabella had been a missionary in India and was known as the Missy Baba. She had been sent as a child to school in Italy and used to quote with a seemly hilarity her schoolmistress's first report to my grandmother. "Your daughter is neither beautiful nor clever. Let us hope she is good." Her schoolmistress will be cheered in Hell to know that her hope was realised. The qualities of patience, courage, humour and loyalty seem to me beautiful; and to keep up a life-long weekly correspondence on equal terms with my remarkable Canadian uncle seems to me clever. But the goodness was not a matter of opinion. A drunken woman on a tram car was making herself a scandal to the passengers. Indeed, most of them got off the car at the next stop. While the conductor was looking for a policeman, my aunt took charge of the woman. She spent a couple of hours in this disreputable company trying to find the woman's lodging. As the woman failed altogether to locate it, my aunt took her to her own home and put her to bed until she was in a condition to be let loose on the street. That was in Glasgow where we are very keen on the conventions and that was the sort of person my aunt was.

Nan and Jessie were pretty girls with an enormous store of energy which is, happily, not yet exhausted. If they had a fault it was an insistent seconding of their mother's efforts to make my brother and me into little gentlemen.

The houses in which the Mavors lived had an atmosphere of dignity and good manners and a smell of old books and ink. They were full of interesting things which we were allowed to see and touch and play with under certain sanctions. The principal conditions were that we had to be good and that our hands were clean. Aunt Nan told excellent stories; Missy Baba read to us with fine feeling, accent and expression; Aunt Jessie sang to us very agreeably; and Uncle Sam made fun of us.

The Osbornes lived in Garnethill, where they had a small property. Garnethill was not then, as it now is, the Latin Quarter of Glasgow. It was quite a respectable neighbourhood. It is notable now for theatrical lodgings, a few nursing homes, ruined villas occupied by advertising agents and specialists in the growth of hair, sinister, lurking figures and occasional domestic fights in which foreign people are killed or injured. It contains the School of Art, a building still considered *outré* in Glasgow, though it is the mother of modern European Architecture. The School of Art was built by Charles Mackintosh.

Garnethill is also interesting because it is one of the seven hills of Glasgow which has been annexed by the Roman Communion of the Church of Christ. From its steep streets, you can see green fields.

When I had first visited the dentist, I was carried in a hansom cab, yelling with pain and fright, to 30 Rose Street, Garnethill, where I was received with the sweetest sympathy. My grandmother was a charming little woman who radiated a curious, still kind of affection wherever she was. She had over a hundred nephews and nieces who all loved her and came to see her and wanted to protect her. Her husband, a cheese merchant, had left her a young widow with seven daughters, a son, and his aged mother who remembered Waterloo. My mother was the eldest daughter. The others were called Jane, Maggie, Nancy, May, Mary and Edith. The son was called Hugh.

In the Rose Street days, Jane and Maggie were married. Nancy was a joyous, plump figure, full of talk and laughter, May was a Martha with a quieter sense of fun. Mary and Edith were schoolmistresses. Mary was a handsome, peaceful, cultivated young woman—she later married a missionary and went to India—and Edith was all fire and energy and cleverness. Hugh was not very much older than I was. He was a tough, well-knit fellow; an engineer and a skilful amateur soccer player. He had a square face, deep-set eyes and a gentle voice. Later in life he developed an extraordinary passion for the works of Turgeniev. Condescension was not in his nature and my brother and I were very fond of him.

Old Mrs. Fulton was very beautiful and alarming. Her strong, pink face was a map of wrinkles. She wore an elaborate snow-white cap like a barrister's wig and a great, soft, snow-white shawl. She was ninety years old. Her descendants to-day could fill a battalion of infantry. She spoke very occasionally and then in a Scots so rich and broad that we found it difficult to understand. Most of the time she sat thinking, like an old goddess. Once she talked of a gooseberry tart of which she had pleasant memories.

" You can't have one now, Granny," said my Aunt Nancy, " gooseberries are out of season."

" Ah, weel," said my Great-Grandmother, " we sadly muse on former joys that will return no more! "

. . . .

My father, Henry Mavor, was a tall, spare man with a heavy, ginger moustache and short beard, with darker hair with copper-coloured lights in it. He had a heavy stoop and long, thin hands and feet. His eyes were light blue, shaded with heavy eyebrows, the left with a humorous tilt. His cheeks were rather sunken, his forehead was high and finely modelled, his nose was lifted at the tip, his lips were full, and he had a small, strong chin.

He wore a blue morning coat, a white silk necktie and a bowler hat. His manners were courteous and often a little aloof and he spoke with a slight North Easterly accent. He had a medium pitched voice, which he knew how to use, and his speech had a tang of the schoolmaster in it without being pedantic. He was fond of the English language and abhorred slang and neologisms. He liked reading aloud and did it very well. Except Mr. Gielgud and Mr. Quartermaine, I have never heard anyone speak Shakespeare's verse with so fine a sense of its values as my father had. He wrote verse himself and drew and painted admirably.

He was born in 1858. Before he settled into his chosen walk of life, he was a clerk in a business firm, supercargo on a windjammer sailing round the world and a medical student. When I use the word " chosen " I use it in the Calvinistic sense. If my father had had any personal choice in the matter he would have been a Doctor of Medicine. He was only allowed to follow this ambition for two years. During that time, his Professors told me, he showed remarkable promise. Some observations of his on the movement of the ulna in relation to the radius, found their way into textbooks of Anatomy. As he was only a second year medical student at the time and, for all practical purposes, did not exist, his name was not attached to the discovery. As I do not, myself, understand Anatomy at all, I have only the haziest idea as to what the actual discovery was.

A financial storm drove him out of his course in 1882 and he began to be an engineer. He made the first electric lighting plant in the country in Queen Street Station. A little later the Corporation of Glasgow held a banquet lit by electric light. At the stage of dessert the light began to fail. My father left the banquet and ran across George Square. He found the stoker who fed the boiler that supplied the steam engine that worked the dynamos was very near exhaustion. My father took off his dress coat, rolled up his starched cuffs and stoked the boiler fires himself. He then returned in time for the speeches.

He married Janet Osborne in 1886. They were both adherents of Pollokshields Free Church of which the pastor was the Reverend James Wells. There was a curious nuclear quality about the church of Dr. Wells. For three generations everybody in Glasgow who was any good at all had been christened or married by that remarkable clergyman. It was he who was once subjected to an abdominal operation and insisted on being opened with prayer. His church, in a very austere period in the history of Scottish Religion, appears to have been the best club in the West of Scotland without abating one iota the reputation for godliness of its minister. In its social activities my father and my mother seem to have taken a lively part.

I find it hard to describe my mother's appearance. She had a magnificent head and profile—so magnificent that they would have been intimidating if it had not

14

been for the indescribable gentleness of her expression. Her hair was parted in the middle over a huge forehead and big, deep orbits. There was a Roman look about her finely cut nose. She had a strong, square jaw and a wide, compressed mouth. She always looked (and was) a little anxious. When her father died in his early thirties she was the only really effective member of that big family of girls and, from that time till her death, she thought and planned for them and for an ever increasing circle of all mankind.

Her sense of responsibility was sustained by a deep religious feeling. It was a grief to her when my father, who, in spite of his upbringing, was a born Rationalist, began to neglect the ordinances of public worship. He often went to church to please her, but the leading feature of the Scottish service, the Sermon, almost invariably maddened him. His sense of form and style was too often outraged by the mechanical rhetoric and perfunctory argument of the preachers. He would fidget and read the Book of Job. Once, at the end of a statutory sermon on the Conversion of the Jews, he stood up ostentatiously in his seat and passed on the collection plate without contributing his mite.

His impatience gave a sort of authority to my own Sunday miseries. I hated the dreadful smell of varnish and damp cushions and moth balls and hot pipes and the lavender and eau de Cologne on the ladies' handkerchiefs. I hated the unctuous wheeze and bellow of the organ. I hated the creak of the minister's boots on the pulpit stairs. I hated the evil, rheumy, sacerdotal beadle in his white necktie. I hated the parson because he turned his collar round the wrong way and put his humanity behind him with his collar stud. I hated the nippit faces and reverent bronchitis of the worshippers. I hated the abominable, snivelling voice with which the parson addressed his Maker. I disliked most of the hymns and practically all the Psalms. When, on a rare occasion, a hymn or a metrical psalm happened to have been written by a poet, it was a relief that only intensified the torture that was to follow. I hated the cruel, stone-eroding monotony of the sermon. It used to take three-quarters of an hour. I couldn't read the Bible when the man was talking. I used desperately to imagine myself an acrobat climbing up the organ pipes and swinging from varnished beam to varnished beam on the roof. The pew was uncomfortable; my Sunday suit was uncomfortable; the atmosphere was insupportable. I liked only the elders when they came round with the plate. Some of them, I knew, were pleasant men; and I had a sense that I was paying my threepenny-bit to get out of Purgatory.

When the time came when my mother asked me to join the Church these early terrors must have fought for me and I remained an outlier and a heathen in spite of all appeals to my honour, my religious sentiment and my affection.

My father and mother hit on a compromise when they joined the congregation of Dr. John Hunter of Trinity Church. Dr. Hunter beautified his church and his service and accommodated his doctrine to the restless minds of those whose pedestals had been shaken by Darwin and Huxley. For me, the horror remained and the Doctor's discourses were far above my head; but my father found an island where his mind and his soul could live together on respectable terms and my mother felt happier.

.   .   .   .

We lived, for the first five years of my life, in the country. The place was East Kilbride, near the birth-place of the anatomist, John Hunter. My brother Jack was born there, a year and a half after me. I met dogs, cows, ducks, geese, thrushes, blackbirds, sky-larks, goats and an occasional horse. I met a bearded gardener called Morris who called the earth the yird.

Visual and auditory memories of childhood are always sorted out and touched up in later years. We remember that we remember. Our memory pictures, like all acts of the will, are shamelessly dishonest. My own impression is that, before the age of three or four years, we form as many hallucinations as direct impressions. I am certain of two or three occasions in that period when I heard voices of people who were many miles away and saw persons and objects who were not there at all. I discovered from the aspect of those to whom I told these things that I had been mistaken. I became used to the idea that I was more often mistaken than not and, by the time I was five, I put hallucinations in their proper place and thought no more about them.

The discrepancy between the world which, by common consent, exists and the world of the primitive imagination, continued to torture me in dreams. For years I had terrifying and abominable dreams hinged on this very point.

I dreamed that I woke in a state of drowsy content. I looked at the bars of the Venetian blinds shadowed on the wall. I looked at the crack in the plastered ceiling—and it was going from left to right instead of from right to left! I was in the wrong world. I struggled out of my dream like a drowning swimmer...

Sometimes the dream went further—that was in the early days—and I was cheated into deeper waters of unreality. I was awake. I was in bed. It was my own room. But there was something wrong. I must get into the light and speak to my father and mother. They would calm my uneasiness and protect me from —whatever it was. I got up. I went into the corridor.

It was bright with gas-light but very quiet. I called out. My father and mother came out into the corridor and confidence flowed back into me to be stopped with a jerk. These people who looked like my father and mother were not my father and mother at all. They were strangers. They were malignant strangers. They made fierce hideous triumphant faces at me. The passage gradually filled with simulacra of my brother, my uncles, my aunts, my nurse. . . .

In some form or other this dream repeated itself again and again and it was necessary to find some antidote. I ran true to anthropology and invented two formulae. The first was pictorial, the second verbal. Before I went to sleep, I shut my eyes tight and saw a number of red devils in blue jackets dancing round a cauldron surrounded by leaping flames. From time to time I use this formula still. It is wonderfully effective. But I will tell you an odd thing about it if you have the patience to wait a moment for the second cantrip.

The area of hallucination is just outside the normal field of vision. It is a common experience to see a man approaching in the street and mistake him for someone else. *When we look at him straight* we find that he does not in the least resemble the person for whom we took him. This happens because we elaborate for ourselves the images outside our focal vision. In themselves they are crude and confused; mere suggestions, like a modern painting.

If you talk to a person with a disordered sense of reality—a paranoiac—you will learn that one of his favourite theories is that spies and other enemies are watching him from an angle. When he turns to confront them, they disappear. I knew one paranoiac who followed a lady into a shop and struck her because she had crossed his path at an angle of exactly forty-five degrees. He went back to the street afterwards and measured it. Now, the peculiar thing about my exorcising devil-picture is that I cannot nowadays get it into the centre of my field of vision, no matter how hard I try.

The second exorcism was a couplet, and I am sorry, for more than one reason, to tell you that I have forgotten it. It was an invocation to birds, beasts, flowers and Jesus. It came to me in a dream and I spent a waking day learning it desperately by heart. If I felt uneasiness and strangeness coming over me when I was asleep I had only to repeat that couplet and I woke, quiet and comforted.

The alternative method of waking—that of shouting myself up through two or three layers of waking consciousness left me sweating, exhausted and afraid to go to sleep again.

The invocation was a sovereign remedy against the incubus, the succubus, brownies and bogles, langleggity beasties and things that went bump in the dark. You will perceive that I had within me the elements of natural religion.

Hobgoblinism was not my only fear. Indeed, as I cast back in my memory, I find very few objects or circumstances of which I was not more or less afraid. I conclude this more from evidence than from clear recollection. I do not know how it is with you, but I retain real, material, physiological fear very dimly. I served through the 1914 War and was repeatedly frightened out of my five wits. Yet, while the *mise-en-scène* remains to me fairly clear in each instance, I have great difficulty in reconstructing the emotion. This is not because any emotion is difficult to reconstruct in the memory. I can remember pain, anger, spiritual exaltation, love, embarrassment, and feel them again almost as powerfully as at their first impact.

People were the only things in which I took any real interest and I was afraid of them—of all of them. My brother Jack used to approach entire strangers with the greeting,

" I'm Jack. Would you like a sweetie? "

But then, he is what used to be called an extrovert. These manœuvres of his gave me a red face. I was a great believer in human dignity when I was five. When Jack and I went to a Ladies' School in Dennistoun with that leaden dragging of the feet that afflicts the young on such journeys, he used to excuse his lateness with the oafish and childish excuse that he had a sore leg.

" And what is the matter with you? " the Head Mistress would say.

" I am sorry to say, Miss Carter, that I had a severe cold," I would reply, purple with misery and offended *amour propre*.

I was often ashamed of Jack, but I had, as often, to admire his courage. Once, just after he had learned to walk, he and I leaned on a fence watching a goat tethered to a post. We were discovered a little later. The goat was rampant at the end of its taut chain, making threatening weaving motions with its head. Jack was stoutly toddling in its direction. I was on the sensible side of the fence encouraging Jack, in an agony of vicarious terror and curiosity.

" Nearer, Jack," I said. " Nearer yet. It's all right. Go *right* up to the goat, Jack! "

My mother beat me for that. My father never beat us. He only hit people of his own size, or bigger.

My father was very active physically, but he was not very strong. He suffered from chronic bronchitis, chronic dyspepsia and bunions. These disabilities did not impair his physical courage. A navvy stood on his bunion in a tramway car. My father damned the

20

navvy and the navvy replied in kind. My father struck
the navvy on the head with his umbrella and the fellow,
after a moment's hesitation, left the tramcar. I have
another memory of my father speeding the departure
of a drunken jobbing gardener with kicks and blows.
This habit of violence among the respectable middle
classes seems to have disappeared with my father's
generation. Except in a set fight, I do not recollect
striking anybody since I was sixteen years of age and I
find that this is true of most of my friends. It is true
that I once hit a policeman, but this was under great
provocation. When I was at College I wished greatly
to see Mr. Asquith who had been elected Lord Rector
of my University and was arriving by train at the
Central Station. I was dressed as a Wrecker with false
whiskers, a petticoat and an alarm clock, and I climbed
over the barrier with the idea of getting a view of my
political hero. A large Inspector of Police lifted me
like a puppy by the back of the neck and heaved me
over to the public side of the barrier. I then hit him
as hard and as often as I could. I only succeeded in
hurting my own knuckles. I did not even make him
angry.

I noticed this habit of laying about them under what
seemed to be mild provocation in the parents of my
companions. It seems at first sight an odd characteristic in a generation which dressed itself in tight clothes
and starched linen; but, if we remember that the
soldiers of that day wore pipeclayed straps, scarlet
tunics, helmets and bear skins, leather leggings and
stocks; and that they were distinctly more courageous
than the soldiers I had a chance of observing in the
War, we may find a line of investigation likely to repay
our efforts. That line I shall not pursue. I wish
merely to let you know that my father was a brave man.
To-day we set great store by moral courage, holding it

to be a much superior kind of courage to physical courage. My own observations lead me to believe that moral courage is extremely common and physical courage extremely rare. I have found, moreover, that the two kinds of courage are usually found in the highest degree in the same person. I think there is a good deal of nonsense talked about moral courage. It is much more often a function of stupidity and insensibility than physical courage. A moral coward is a person who respects the feelings and prepossessions of his fellow being. The most courageous people in the sphere of morals I have ever met were people who had no conception of what morals were. The bravest men I ever met had a very clear idea of what would happen if they were hit by a shell or a bullet or swamped in a sailing boat. My father had both kinds of courage and both kinds of imagination.

. . . .

I began my last passage with some reflections on childhood memory. I must not lose sight of the fact that I have set out to convey to you at least a proportion of these impressions. The devil of a thing is to find the best way of doing it. A sort of telescopic language like that invented by Mr. Joyce or an obscure Glasgow poet of the eighteen-seventies called Thomson might be the most effective way. These memories sing in one's head in bewildering patterns like the notes played by a piano-tuner. To arrange them neatly in any sort of sequence must give a false impression. I could tell you that my parents moved to the country before I had any skill in gathering impressions at all. I could tell you that we lived at a cottage called Rosemound in East Kilbride where my brother Jack was born. I could tell you that we then moved to a villa in East Kilbride. From there we moved to Glasgow to a flat in Dennistoun, spending from spring to autumn at Kilcreggan on the Firth of Clyde. In town I went to a kindergarten. At the coast I attended the village school. The house in which we lived at Kilcreggan was called Thornbank, and my brother Eric was born there. This is the correct sequence of events for my first five years and it is no more interesting than a railway time-table. Events that were significant enough to be remembered do not arrange themselves in any arbitrary chronological order.

I tried some time ago to write an essay on Kilcreggan with the following unsatisfactory results:

" I was standing in the roadway with the little Sayers girls when a lady came running in all the hot panoply of ladies of the period, and, following her a great lolloping Newfoundland dog. She said, ' I've got to catch the boat. I am going to miss the boat. Do take this dog home. Don't touch him or he'll bite you. You'll know the house. The garden is full of midges.'

Mary Ann sleeping in the lea of a patch of bracken and bramble, the contents of her basket scattered around . . . A boy, blubbering, with a bleeding nose, his mouth masked with lappered gore. The terrible Mr. M'N., high on the box of his wagonette with his great red beard and his dangerous whip . . . The more terrible Mr. M'C., the schoolmaster. My brother and I went to school, and went in continual fear till we found that we and a farmer's son were immune from M'C.'s rages. We wore boots. These talismans, we thought, preserved us when M'C. raved round the school lashing right and left with his strap. ' He had a skalled head and piled beard, and of his visage children were afeared.' I am told he was a learned man . . . We found out in his school that some people, and among them Willie Todd, are able to put pins through their toes without shedding blood, and I found an easy method of doing addition sums. During the meal hour we fought in a combat called The Champagne War. The bigger boys entrenched themselves in the shed and piled up road-metal ammunition. A dozen medium-sized boys, armed with sticks, were appointed officers to the enemy. We, the smaller boys, were the enemy and we were driven into a withering barrage by the sticks of our officers. Those of us who survived the barrage were hurled back into the roadway by a sortie and fled weeping for miles.

There was nae-banes-the-day-John, the soprano butcher. There were swamped rowing boats and a lug sail that fell on our heads. There were the Man Rock and the Ship Rock. There were two long-shore bullies who beat and tortured us and terrorised us into silence and taught us the grand national virtue of hatred. There were humiliating, dressed up afternoon tea parties . . . Pate Fleeming or somebody else had taught me to smoke and I boasted to my father of this ; so he gave me a pipe of tobacco and I became very ill—so ill that I could barely crawl to the porch to see the little *John* of Kronstadt carrying my favourite uncle to Lake Baikal far away . . . ''

This is what happens when I try to pick out of the jumble impressions related by time and place or by anything else in the universe except the jerky and confused development of my own sensorium. Yet there was a sort of order in the things that happened to me during the first five years. Perhaps the schema can be suggested by one of the earliest impressions of all. I remember that I was compelled to walk while my brother rode in the perambulator. This happened for the first time and filled me with horror and a vista of rocky roads in the years to come. The negative poles of my being seem always to have craved this curious kind of disembodiment, this " being carried ". It took a long time before I could appreciate the fact that there were joys even in the weariness of the flesh.

Every good Calvinist knows that a child is born fully equipped with Original Sin. Every good Catholic knows that Sin is composed of seven elements. The names of these elements are Accidia, Luxuria, Invidia, Avaricia, Superbia, Ira, and Gula. Accidia is my master Sin; but Accidia is in herself a composite character. The element in Accidia that ruled my life was sloth. Depression played its part but sheer simple physical sloth must be given the credit for building the admirable character it is my task to describe.

Any inventive faculty I possessed in my first five years was bent to the device of methods of getting from place to place with the minimum of exertion, or preferably, to the device of methods of avoiding getting from place to place at all. I decided to be a Doctor because the Doctor with whose children I used to play owned a brougham. My father, the engineer, had no brougham. He had not even a governess cart or a dog cart. I longed for a donkey of my own to pull me about in a governess cart. I came near to content at the sight of the rump of my uncle's mare illuminated by gig lamps as we jogged down the road to Ballochmyle on one of a series of pleasant visits. Nothing else in the holidays at Ballochmyle carried such satisfaction. My uncle owned a creamery on the field where Burns wrote " Man Was Made to Mourn." He also owned a stable, a pig sty, a little forest, a mill dam and an engine room. The place was an everlasting garden of delights for an active boy. I was not an active boy but I could see the possibilities of these pleasures and even experience them in some degree. I should have been a sloth indeed to take no interest in the swirling churns and the beating of gigantic pats of butter with huge wooden spades. It is difficult to watch landscapes or machinery for any length of time without a very specialised taste for such things. Such a taste may be acquired, although I for one have never fully acquired it, and the sight of moving and changing objects may be sufficient in itself without some sort of story or philosophy to animate it and give it an extraneous value. The happiest people are those who love things for their own sakes—the London crowds who gape at gangs tearing up the streets without wondering why ; the scientists of Japan and Germany ; makers of documentary films. Superbia, too, has a hand in this habit some of us have of making ourselves Gods and creators of sham universes.

One of my friends once formed the theory that I was a heathen God who had lost his tribe. I sometimes think there is something in this. Boys who bullied me and school masters who failed to appreciate me were smitten sooner or later with blains, blights, dropsies and ruin of the spirit without conscious intervention on my part ; and I liked being transported from village to village. And still like it. In any case, I had a very strong feeling that I was a person of much more importance than people realised. It took several five year cycles to get this last out of my head.

Those who were responsible for my education were fully aware of my Sin of sloth and did their best to deal with it. They used to watch lovingly for any sign of movement in that curled-up slug, my mind. My father was delighted when I told him, at a very early age indeed, that I wanted to be a doctor ; but I did not tell him why I wanted to be a doctor. He took me for walks in the country and tried to teach me Botany. He tried to get me to keep a herbarium. He took me to marshy pools to collect any animalculae and bring them home to the microscope. He dissected rabbits, rats and corncrakes for me. He took me to museums. In one of them I saw the head of a little girl cut in vertical section and preserved in a glass jar full of spirits. She had been run over by a stage coach in the time of William the Fourth. These excursions were very exhausting and I longed for sleep. A primrose by the river's brim a yellow primrose was to me, and it was nothing more.

When my father found that I could draw, he took me to picture galleries. He drew and painted very well himself and was a friend of many of the painters who formed the famous Glasgow School. Mr. Lavery, Mr. Walton, Mr. George Henry, Mr. Macaulay Stevenson were shown my pictures and asked for their opinion. As my masters were the artists who created the Pink Kid and Weary Willie and Tired Tim in *Comic Cuts* and *Chips*, these great men were unwilling to make prophecies about my future. My father did not allow me to study these journals, but where there is a will there is a way.

At about the age of four I developed a literary style. I am sorry to disappoint the professor. I do not know from what it derived. I think probably Shakespeare had something to do with it. The writings of Shakespeare were the only good influence in my early life to which I did not put up a sturdy and mulish resistance or, to put it another way, to which I did not oppose my heaven-sent inertia.

Be that as it may, the first thing I remember writing was a Drama on the life of King Robert the Bruce. One complete scene survives:

" *Scene : The English Camp. Enter the Earl of Pembroke.*

The Earl of Pembroke : I wonder what these devils of Scotsmen are up to now.

(Exit the Earl of Pembroke)."

27

Sometime after I had written this *King Robert the Bruce*, I saw my first Play. It was the tragedy of Macbeth. I liked it very much. Macbeth was dressed as Rob Roy and much was made of the Witches.

As soon as this stirring appeared in me, my father began to read aloud to us. He read Carlyle, Emerson, The Authorised Version of the Bible, Shakespeare, Robert Louis Stevenson, Tennyson, Browning, Coleridge, John Ruskin, Charles Darwin and the Arabian Nights. In some of these works I delighted. Others were agony. As my father was a little irritable when he was reading and insisted on attention and no fidgeting, the others were probably a useful discipline.

I wonder whether discipline, apart from the discipline that inculcates good manners, ever is useful. I was taught to pretend to pay attention to Emerson but not to listen to him. When, in later life, I was compelled to hear lectures, I seldom listened to them. I do not think I developed the habit of listening to lectures till I was over thirty.

I remember that, in my first five years, I heard *The Cloister and the Hearth* and Isaiah with pleasure. I was taught to read by my Aunt Mary when I was four and read with some pleasure Hogg's *Brownie of Bodsbeck*, the interesting bits of the *Pilgrim's Progress*, the interesting bits of Shakespeare (*Draws. They fight. Hotspur dies.*) which were all printed in italics, a book of fairy tales which included one about tubs of blood, the more morbid writings of Hans Andersen, and some horrifically restrained stories by Juliana Horatia Ewing. That is to say, I suppose, that I sublimated my nightmares. I did not read for information. I was invincibly ignorant and liked it.

That was why, when I left the country to live in Glasgow, I didn't carry much of it with me. When I was told that we were to live henceforward in the town,

my heart nearly broke. But it was a vague kind of
nostalgia that possessed me. I remembered the terrier,
Sweep ; the greyhound, Kelt, who once leapt over the
garden fence pursued by Fritz, the black cat. I did
not love anyone in the country particularly except Ann
Pann, the serving maid. The country itself was a haze
of greens and browns and yellows pervading a general
sensation of fatigue.

. . . .

At about the end of my first five years my younger
brother, Eric, was born. While he was waiting to be
born, Jack and I were sent to Skye with Seonaid.
Seonaid was tall and fair and ample and kind. She had
the West Highland accent which seems to the imperfect English ear to be so like Welsh and does not resemble it in the smallest degree.

We journeyed in the *Claymore*, the mightiest ship
we had ever seen. I think we left in the early evening
and we must have seen some splendours going through
the Kyles of Bute, but I do not remember them. I do
remember the Mull of Cantire, the Scottish equivalent
of the Bay of Biscay. We had been told of the terrible
Mull, with its waves mountains high and its tossing of
great ships like corks. We lay awake waiting for it,
but it was a disappointing storm after St. Paul and
Robinson Crusoe.

The astonishing thing was the disintegration of
Seonaid. We had never seen a human adult wrecked,
ruined and abandoned to misery. Seonaid had been,
even to the eyes of our unsexed infancy, a beautiful
object. More still, she had been informed in all her
speech and actions with the fine dignity of the Highlands.

When we retired for the night, we were instructed
to keep our faces to the walls of our bunks while

Seonaid removed her upper garments. This we politely did and when we turned round again, Seonaid was in her upper berth and in an uneasy sleep. We lay awake and waited for the Mull.

After a space of time, the ship began to pitch a little. We did not wish to wake Seonaid, but we asked each other if this were indeed the Mull at last and doubted if it could be. There was no roaring of the wind or crash of falling rigging. No foul-mouthed boatswain was rebuking his passengers. Our cabin, at least, was not shipping it green. There had been more excitement on the rocking horses at the village fair. There was so little noise that we could have heard the frightened crew at their prayers, if they had been frightened and at their prayers.

There was a sound from overhead. Seonaid was at her prayers. She was praying in Gaelic and the flow of her orisons was interrupted by retching. Without any perceptible increase in the force of the storm, there was a rapid deterioration in Seonaid's condition.

" Mo thruaigh, my pain and my sorrow! " said Seonaid, rolling from her bunk and reeling dejectedly to and fro in the narrow space. So must the mobled Queen have looked when Priam's limbs were minced. Her hair was like corn dishevelled by a waterspout. Her face was distorted and begrutten and coloured like a map of the British Empire. Hardly enough was left of her passionate modesty to keep her damp and stained nightclothes about her.

I do not remember that my brother and I had any sympathy with our friend and sweetheart in her desperate plight. We stared and stared as might tourists at Mount Etna—with which the spectacle had something in common.

When we woke in the morning, the cabin was clean and tidy. Seonaid was dressed, calm and reserved.

Her beauty and dignity had returned, but she was lily-like and tragic.

We came to the harbour of Tobermory where Mr. Boswell, after deciding to behave himself ten times better in return for his life, came all alive like Antaeus, gaining new vigour when he touched land. So did we; for, to tell you the truth, we were sick of the voyage.

The great Mr. Boswell—I might digress here on Mr. Boswell, who was a personification of his native land besides being an immortal genius ; but I shall leave him till later on—the great Mr. Boswell said of Tobermory that it was really a noble harbour. I recall that it seemed so to me and that the sailors drove a herd of cattle down a gang plank into the sea and that they swam ashore, herded by men in boats.

We did not land at Tobermory, but its charming name and delightful appearance refreshed our spirits. The sky over the dark green land showed either sunrise or sunset, I forget which. It was scarlet and gold and peacock blue. Mr. Boswell says . . .

I cannot get Mr. Boswell out of my head. Wherever he has gone, what pleasure he must derive from our opinion of him! I do not think he is laughing. I do not think he ever laughed very much. His was an unfathomable sense of the incongruous that burned like the heat in the centre of the world and could not have burst into flame without destroying. This demoniacal sense belongs, in some degree or other, to the Scottish nation alone, though never has it grown to such magnificent proportions in any individual as it did in young Auchinleck. Urquhart is his only rival in the world of letters, and when Urquhart laughed it killed him.

To call Boswell's pervading master passion a sense of humour would be as much an understatement as to say that Tintoretto could recognise the two ends of the

31

spectrum. He records with some satisfaction Johnson's opinion that a Scotsman cannot see a joke. *A joke!* . . .

Boswell took an enraptured interest in his own idiosyncracies, but he decided that his own personality was too recondite a subject for the masterpiece he had it in him to write as his crowning pleasantry. He chose the local demigod and lavished on him the affection that Pavlov must have lavished on his favourite laboratory dog. He stroked and tickled him into reflex action, playing all the time with exquisite virtuosity the part of an adoring simpleton. Only once did his demon really get the better of him and he took his learned hippopotamus for a tour of the Western Hebrides; but with what grace does he conceal his real motive and keep his terrible and devilish delights to himself! Paoli strutting on his little island, the grotesque Wilkes, the exuberant Frederick who so caught the fancy of a later Scot, they were nothing to this in breadth and subtlety. There was more richness in this specimen than in all of them rolled into one. He chose with care, he demonstrated with genius, he hugged to his bosom his immense wicked satisfaction. The world has accepted him as a great man without for a moment suspecting in what his greatness consisted. So much for him.

As for us, we came at length to Skye. We sleepily heard Seonaid talking the Gaelic to the kind innkeeper of Broadford ; we ate and drank ; and we went to sleep on a bed that still surprisingly heaved a little.

In the morning we drove fifteen miles or so in a gig to Seonaid's croft. It seemed to us a long journey and we looked with some concern at the prospect of coming back the same way. The road was rough and the scenery severe and bare. There were no trees. It rained a little, but not much—softly and mournfully.

When we got to the house we were disappointed. Seonaid, in her poetic Highland fashion, had led us to expect wonders which far surpassed what we actually saw. I was five years old and my brother was four. We said roundly what we thought. The truth of the matter was that Seonaid's people were very poor. They lived in a roughly-built cottage of two apartments, roofed with thatch. The smaller apartment was the sleeping room. It had two box beds and a small window. The larger had a fireplace in the middle of it, dug out of the rough stone floor. Some of the peat smoke passed out through a chimney hole in the roof. The rest fogged the living room and swam into the bedroom when the wind blew. The stable and byre were at the end of the house. The sanitary conveniences were a roughstone wall and a tin jordan under one of the box beds.

Seonaid's parents were prematurely aged. Her father, the bodach, was a silent man with a grizzled beard. Her mother, the cailleach, had jet black hair and a wrinkled face. She was not silent. She had no English and seemed to us to be in a perpetual state of anger. Seonaid told us that this was not so ; but her voice was loud and harsh and her high-pitched vocables sounded abusive. After Seonaid had reassured us, we were not afraid of her and tormented her as much as we could in our uninventive childish way. There were other faces in the household, but Alec stands out in my memory.

He was a boy of about sixteen, as handsome as Seonaid and full of gentle dignity. He worked very hard, but he could always find time to take us in the boat ; to show us the seagull with the broken wing ; to find us clubbydooes and mussels ; to give us rides on the plough horse ; to teach us how to milk the cow ; to tell us stories. When he was out at the fishing the days were very blank.

The blanks were filled up by driving Seonaid's

33

mother to frenzy and by visits. One visit was to Aunt Barbara. We were filled with nostalgia, for Aunt Barbara wore a bonnet and had a carpet on her floor. Another was to Sandy, who wore a shirt made of a potato-sack and whose white hair poked out of the holes in his bonnet. He gave us a little branch of fir root with a head on it like a fox's head and a shank like the barrel of a pistol. We cherished this object for nearly a year. Sometimes it was a pistol and sometimes it was a sort of doll, wrapped to the neck in a red spotted handkerchief.

After a day or two it began to rain in earnest. Jack and I complained and whined continually. We objected to the whole island, but most of all to Seonaid's house. We were told that if we were good we should be taken upstairs to see the second storey. It had a Turkey carpet on the floor. It had a grand piano. It had a parrot in a gold cage and a canary in another gold cage. It had a portrait of the Queen and portraits of the Prince and Princess of Wales and one of Mr. Gladstone. The wall paper was covered with a design of pink roses. There was plush on the chairs and on the sofa and presents from everywhere on the tables. Jack stopped whining and his eyes sparkled with expectation and longing and determination to be good. A big raindrop fell on my head. I looked up and saw another oozing its way through the damp, smoky rafters.

When we left, Alec cried and so did we. The Cailleach was glad to get us off her hands and us not having fallen over the mighty cliffs a hundred yards from the house. I remember the warmth in the pit of my stomach when I saw the broom at the doors of the Hotel at Broadford. It was the first plant higher than heath I had seen for two or three weeks. I remember no more of the journey.

We arrived back in Kilcreggan where we stayed with our Aunts till Eric was born, which he was on a bright June morning.

. . . .

The Reverend John (Whaur's your Wullie Shakespeare noo) Home of Edinburgh approached and looked over my shoulder. I rose politely. He told me to be seated. I told him I was trying to rake together a few memories to enable the Recording Angel and others to form a fair estimate of me.

He said, " Like John James Rousseau? "

I said, " No. On the whole, no. No, certainly not."

He said, " I am glad of that."

He said, " From the department of Paradise in which I find you, I presume that you are a dramatic author? "

I said, " No. Not yet."

He said, " I hope when you become one that you will realise the importance of making your Stage a rostrum for elevated sentiments."

I said I would.

He said, "And that you will eschew licentiousness and vulgarity. I trust, moreover, that these will be absent from your Memoirs. It is a great temptation in compiling Memoirs to insinuate vulgar incidents."

I said I knew that.

He said, " Lofty aims are the safeguard. I trust your aims are lofty."

" My aim," I said, " is to prove by my own life that it is possible to exist pleasantly on a minimum of personal endeavour. Work is a waste of time. It is the Curse of Adam. The sweat of the brow leads to acne and a consequent counter-irritation over the frontal convolutions of the brain, where, we are told, lies the seat of Reason."

At this he looked at me severely, shook his head and passed on. I was angered by this. It was the duty of a

35

clergyman to accept my gambit. Army Chaplains had wrestled with me nobly from dusk till dawn and I had always felt the better of it. I began to feel what is, with me, a very rare sensation—that of mounting rage. My head began to swell and red mists gathered before my eyes. There was a roaring in my ears. I struck out furiously and barked my knuckles on an army button. Somebody was fumbling in my mouth with a steel instrument.

A North of Ireland voice shouted that I was coming out and to give me more. There was a suffocating blast of cold ether and I was back before my typewriter, furiously thumping the crazy keys.

CHAPTER II

The Second Five

AT SIX I HAD become a solitary and a snob. The noise
and vastness of the City drove me to it. All my
life my shape has been determined by my environment.
I wish I were a better hand at describing my environment. If I were, you would find it easier to visualise
my hero. Material things do not reach me in detail as
I have already told you. I found that a disadvantage
when I came to study anatomy. I find it a disadvantage
now.

We went to 101 Armadale Street in Dennistoun in
Glasgow. It was a groundfloor flat in a red sandstone
tenement, and I remember nothing else about it except
the patch of seedy grass in front and a ferocious policeman on the beat. From this place my brother and I set
out daily to Miss Carter's School. Miss Carter was
frightening. Miss Mary was the most important.
Miss Augusta was the nicest. The prettiest girl was
called Ivy, because she had ringlets. The bad boy of
the school was called Willie Taylor. The most terrific

D   37

day was when he was whacked by Miss Carter with a
carpet cane. When it was found impossible to get Jack
and me to the school in time, a nice boy called for us
every morning and took us there. We did not join the
dancing class and my father filled me with embarrassment by writing on one of my lesson books:

> You may learn to read at eighteenpence a week
> At the excellent school of Miss Carter;
> But if you'd educate your feet
> You must pay a guinea a quarter.

I thought this in bad taste and dangerous, though I
liked my father's jokes in a general way.

Half of the year we spent at Kilcreggan on the Firth
of Clyde, whose shore was crowded with Italianate
villas. I have told you that the memories of Kilcreggan
were confused, but they were crystal clear to those of
Armadale Street, Dennistoun. We were sent to the
village school and, for the first time, made friends of
our own age. The best of these was Peter MacFeat,
the son of our landlord. He was an active boy, but
very gentle. He was with Admiral Kolchak almost up
to the time that admiral lost his head, and is now in
China. I recall that he was allowed to read the comic
papers we were forbidden.

It was at Kilcreggan that I met my first Roman
Catholics and my first pro-Boer. It was very strange
to me that people should be Roman Catholics or pro-
Boers. I have lost that feeling about pro-Boers, but I
still feel a little odd in the company of Roman Catholics.
These were children, looking, roughly, very like me.
There were slight differences in their speech, but I
didn't mind that. I found foreigners and most Jews
very delightful. I do not recall that they had been attacked in my hearing. I may have been told to avoid
saying anything that might offend them. I had been told

that, quite unnecessarily, about many different kinds of people. I thought none the worse of them for that.

It was a great mystery. They had eyes, but whatever it was that looked through those eyes was something different from the observer behind mine. For a time I had intimations of this foreign, dreadful phenomenon in animals. I was afraid to touch them because they were alive and yet had no identity with me. They did not think by the same processes as mine. I still sometimes find it difficult to persuade myself that it doesn't matter.

I think that this fear would make me cruel to Catholics if I were inspired by mob suggestion. I should pull down the symbols of their mysteries as my fathers did before me. I should not, however, shoot priests. I like Roman Catholic priests better than any other kind of priest. They are very expert in the art of living. There is no pleasanter exercise in the world than to argue with one of them. I have found no strangeness in their way of thinking.

It is not impossible that facts and theories taught by authoritarian methods warp or distort the mind—perhaps to a shape more pleasing to the Almighty. I do not know. It seems a strange shape to me and causes a reaction in my pilomotor system when I meet it. So might Mr. Chamberlain find with delighted surprise that Herr Hitler was a human being, though the sight of one of the more earnest of his disciples busy at some patriotic duty might make him sick.

I round off this faintly offensive digression in the habitual fashion. Anyone who has been parading his vulgar distaste for Jews, Germans, Irishmen or Frenchmen puts himself right with his conscience and the world by saying that he has known intimately several splendid and charming members of the sect. I have many close friends of the Roman Communion.

Talking of authoritarianism, what an abominable place a School is!

The first real School I went to was the High School of Glasgow which is a hundred years older than Eton and gave Great Britain two Prime Ministers and many better men. It was a sad-coloured place of enormous size through which bearded men, gowned like clergymen, walked solemnly. I tore the little red button from my Kilmarnock bonnet in my fright.

I was spared the Big School apart from drill on the cement playground under Sergeant MacNeill who had fought in the Crimean War. He, too, had a beard. I was taught in a little overflow house which held the Junior School. There I read aloud with such feeling and expression a certain poem that I was placed with the older boys for the study of English and with my contemporaries for everything else.

The poem began as follows:

> In a sunny alpine valley
> Neath the snowy Matterhorn
> Sat a maiden by a chalet
> Playing with a Gemsee fawn. . . .

I must have read this drivel with a certain contempt that gave me confidence. The school-books of my day kept alive bad poems, like Settle's numbers. It was a curious sort of limited immortality for their writers.

My year at the High School was broken by measles, and on the following year the family fortunes must have improved, for I was transferred to the Glasgow Academy for the Sons of Gentlemen. This excellent school was fifty years old when I first walked into it. For some time it had dropped its interesting sub-title and the success of its scholars in after life is very largely due to the fact that they never worried whether they were the sons of gentlemen or not.

It is a large, square, hideous building on the banks of the Kelvin and, if there is a fog in Glasgow, it is wrapped in that. The classrooms are, however, lighter than those in the High School. At that time the boys wore plain blue caps with a white badge. The High School boys wore, I think, magenta caps, but the colours of that school seemed to be in a perpetual state of flux. One of its Rectors forced a kind of tartan cap with a necktie to match on his suffering charges. The colours of the High School are now mud-colour and yellow. They look very formidable on the football field. The Academy wear two very tasteful kinds of blue.

There was one enormous advantage in going to the Glasgow Academy of my day. One could confidently look forward to a respectable social position in the city of Glasgow; but there was something more remarkable about the place. Field-Marshal's batons seemed to be served out regularly to one in ten of the boys. The peculiarly assorted names of James M. Barrie, John Reith, Walter Elliot, A. D. Lindsay, Louis Grieg, Jack Buchanan, Guthrie Russell, Jim Mollison, Charles Warr, D. Y. Cameron, William Ramsay and a Negro king whose name and kingdom I forget all appear on the class rolls. Well over sixty of them have played for Scotland at rugby football, which is perhaps more important. A number of them have become Professors and Judges and Generals and V.C.'s and even Proconsuls; but the principal common feature of its old boys seems to be that their souls remain unspotted by ten years' secondary education and they are confident enough to grab a hundred per cent. of their value if not more.

My first Rector was Donald Morrison who was very like Abraham, but more prolific of remarkable sons. He was a very handsome, aloof, devout person with a bushy white beard. Every class from the top to the bottom of the School was instructed in the Scriptures by him at least once a week.

One day we were herded in to a junior class room to take part in this exercise. This kids' room was surrounded with pictures illustrating the Ape, the Ass, the Dog and the Cat and the Ox. When I joined my companions I noticed that the pictures had been turned back to front. I didn't think this particularly amusing, but I laughed because the others were laughing.

I had no sooner taken my seat than the Rector came in. His mild but somehow dreadful eye swept the room. He did not laugh. It was obvious that he was angry. I do not know why he was angry. I think he probably composed himself for an act of worship before he came into the room and that this monkey trick disturbed him. He dropped his terrible eye to sweep the urchins in the seats. There was a silence. Then the Rector spoke:

" Who did that? " he said.

There was a deeper silence still. I, for one, began to sweat with fear. The eye rested on me.

" Did you turn those pictures? " said the Rector.

" No, Sir," I said.

" Come to my room at eleven," said the Rector.

" We will now read the word of God as it is written in the seventh Chapter of the Epistle to the Corinthians."

At eleven I went to that room. The ruins of Corinth, where the Corinthians lived, were opposite me. The room had a heavy, leathery, inky smell. The tall, beautiful old man wrapped his gown round him and towered over me. If he had sat down it would have been better.

" Now, my boy," he said, " think well before you speak. In the excitement of the moment and probably because you were afraid you denied having committed that act. The act in itself was trivial. But a LIE is not trivial. A LIAR is a pariah among his fellows. He dare not look his companions in the face. None of them trust him. None can be his friend. He has an evil mark on his forehead. In a very little while he does not know whether he is speaking the truth or not. He has debased the currency of human intercourse. It were better for him that he were dead.

" You are fond of your parents? They are very good to you. Some day you may have children of your own. Think of the unspeakable horror of finding that you are the father of a LIAR. Before it is too late, take thought and spare your father and your mother that shame and misery and degradation.

" If you have committed an offence, then, admit it like a man. Do not fear punishment. To be afraid is to be a coward and a coward is always a LIAR and a LIAR is always a coward. Did you turn round those pictures in Miss Wright's room? "

I was in tears. " Yes, Sir. I did," I said. The Rector patted my shoulder.

" I knew you had done it," he said. " Let us pray."

We knelt down, the Rector and I, and he prayed that I should be preserved from becoming a liar; that I should be a credit to my parents and grow up a God-fearing, self-respecting and useful citizen.

He had not made me believe that I had, in fact, turned the pictures; but he had exhibited Hell fire to me and I thought a lie was a small thing to break the growing impulse to throw myself into the gulf. I should have gone mad if he had tortured me for another moment. He was a very eloquent old man. When he died we were given a half holiday. It was the custom when we got a half holiday to cheer all the way

43

down the stairs. We began to cheer and then something stopped us suddenly.

He was succeeded by Edwin Temple, who ruled for forty years. Dr. Temple was very unlike Dr. Morrison. He was an Englishman. He was a little above middle height, but his huge head made him look shorter. It was a very remarkable head. It was set on a thick neck well down between his shoulders. It had a broad, low forehead above heavy supraorbital ridges and protruding blue eyes. All the facial bones were immense, but the nose was somewhat pointed. He had short, black, wiry, untidy hair and a smile that looked cruel till one realised that it was more a nervous grimace than a smile. He horrified us by wearing a bowler hat to school and knickerbockers at the playing fields. All the headmasters in the different departments of learning professed at the Glasgow Academy wore silk hats. This differentiated us from the High School.

He continued the tradition of instruction in the Scriptures, but his lessons had about them a whimsicality that was absent from Dr. Morrison's. He used to swing on his chair as if it were a rocking chair and to roll his pencil with a cracking sound over his signet ring.

" . . . And she brought him butter in a lordly dish. A lordly dish, MacKinnon. . . . Then Jael, Heber's wife, took an hammer in her hand, and went softly unto him, and smote the nail into his temples, and fastened it into the ground: for he was fast asleep and weary; so he died. Capital. Put into Latin all of you: ' I think that the enemy will be conquered.' *Victurum iri*. Stand up on the form, you miserable fellow. Play Football? In the Corps? Ah, you wretched boy. . . . "

Of the Corps, he approved. Football, he fostered. In his more heated moments he introduced us to two

44

strange conceptions, Good Form and Bad Form We weren't clear about the difference between them and didn't think much of either of them.

I think he destroyed some of our privileges and gave us new ones. For one thing, he appointed the Captain of the School himself. When he came first, we used to vote in the Captain of the School—all of us. We assembled in the Writing Room with the Rector in the Chair and a member of the Fifteen said, " I beg to propose Mr. Arthur." And we all cheered, though we would rather have had one of the Russells who could so heftily bash and kick our enemies.

. . . .

I must be careful about this second Five or it will run over the edge. In it the World was not odd and new and I had not yet taken my place in it. I was harried a good deal and I wasn't very well. I took to wearing spectacles. I developed a heavy, scholarly stoop. I mooned about a good deal and was frightened by everything to an extent I never experienced until the Great War.

My parents put me under the care of a Dr. Somerville, a large, hearty volunteer Colonel who made a hobby of physical training. At his house a series of healthy young women knocked me about till I was more exhausted and bored than I can tell. I was sent, also, to dancing school and, what with the one thing and the other, developed a sense of sex inferiority I have never entirely lost. The few little girls I had known, who had cried and told tales and cheated at games and cared about their clothes, faded and were replaced by strong-willed, strong-bodied, graceful, clever Amazons who belonged to a superior class of being to mine. I was afraid of them and hated them more than I hated the snivellers. I had one manly

virtue, however, that saved me from utter humiliation
I was as obstinate as a mule. You remember the story
of the man who had taken refuge from his wife under
the bed?

"You may thrash me," he said, "and you may
bash me. But you'll not break my manly spirit.
I'll not come out."

I defied all efforts to teach me to dance. When I was
forced to go to parties I read comic papers in the cloak
room. When I became old enough to smoke, I took
my pipe with me. They should not, I determined,
bully me.

Other people bullied me in this sad period. I
seemed to attract bullies. Every now and again I see
or hear of one or other of the poor little sadistic
wretches who made my life a Hell. Their unstable
nervous systems brought them sooner or later into
trouble, sickness and degradation. None of them has
ever made so much as a decent living.

I must have had some prevision of this at the time,
for I never took much delight in the terrific scene in
the school story when the bully is thrashed by the
plucky youngster. I disliked the plucky youngster
even more than I disliked the bully, and I knew something about bullies. The poor bully was an unhappy
lout always lounging dangerously near to some
miserable defeat of his self-respect. Nobody liked him
except the other bullies. The small fry cringed to him
but did not respect him. The Masters made fun of
him. On the other hand, the plucky youngster—
"the fine, manly little fellow"—was pampered on
every side. It was not enough that he was as hard as
nails and could run and jump and fight. He had to be
sicklied over with the adulation of old and young.
He had the best of everything. If he failed to escape
punishment his beatings covered him with glory and

his executioner apologised to him. He was held up as an example. Poor devil, his last state was often little better than the bully's.

My early schooldays were what I suppose they always are to a dreamy, lazy, unpunctual, feeble-bodied, introspective little boy. They come back to me as a time when I was compelled to sit still and silent for an hour at a time on a hard bench, suffering agonies of tedium mitigated only by apprehension. It wasn't that my Masters were stupid or inferior men. Some of them were or became very distinguished persons indeed. If it had been possible, in the circumstances, to interest me, they would have done so. Later, I found much in their personalities to amuse me. But what a torture the round of school is! It is worse than a convict prison. To adults it would be unbearable and their perceptions are blunted and their urge to activity diminished. When I saw my elder son square his shoulders and march through the iron gate through which I had often crawled, I felt as Abraham would have felt if there had been no ram in the thicket. I felt worse than Abraham. He at least had confidence in Jehovah. I felt I was offering my child to Moloch, a deity of whom I disapproved.

I was not without my pleasures. I was passionately fond of food—except chicken, boiled mutton, rice pudding and porridge. In this connection, my brother Jack made one of his worst gaffes. I was in the Third English Class. My brother was in the First English Senior. I returned to school in the afternoon. Under the regulations my brother did not; but my father arranged for him to have an hour's prep. from two till three. He and one or two other little boys used to sit in the front seats and do their sums and learn their verses while we, their elders, were being taught grammar. The master was the terrible Melven, who

47

had a long spade beard and an intimidating voice. I shall have more to say about him later.

Be that as it may, Jack trailed in late, when Melven was telling us never to begin a sentence with a pre-position. Melven stopped and followed him to his seat with eyes very like those of Lord Kitchener in the recruiting posters. When Jack was seated, he said: " Well? Why are you late? "

Jack was rapt. He was not afraid. He spoke in the rich, full voice of one who has seen visions:

" Please, Sir, we had two gentlemen in for dinner . . . and a fine big dinner it was! "

Now, apart from everything else, he should have said " lunch."

. . . .

I am sticking to my narrative. The two gentlemen are types of one of my other pleasures. When we moved to Glasgow, my father was able to see more of his friends and to some of his talk with them we were allowed to listen. The most entertaining of his friends were not the engineers but the artists. Glasgow was rich in artists in those days. The Glasgow School had been in existence for nearly twenty years and its members were ripe and confident and wearing haloes. Many of them visited my father's house.

It is necessary for teaching purposes to " derive " authors, poets, philosophers, musicians and artists from their predecessors. This makes a nice, orderly, properly divided lecture course along which we may take our students link by link. A disorderly sequence of men of genius would upset them. A disorderly Universe would be a bad example to the young. This being so (and who can doubt it?), the Glasgow School " derived " from the Barbizon School of Paris.

I gather that the Glasgow School were lively men from Scotland, England and Ireland whose mouths watered when they saw colour. The first of them were Walton, the Yorkshire Quaker, Roche, another Englishman, Lavery, the Irishman, James Paterson, E. A. Hornel, George Henry. To them were added Macaulay Stevenson, Arthur Melville, W. Y. MacGregor, J. E. Christie, David Murray and MacTaggart. Later in the day came the great etchers, Cameron, Bone and MacBey; but this is not a history of the Glasgow School. It will suffice to say that they excited Paris, " attracted attention " in London, and were reverenced in Glasgow. Some of these rough-haired men came, as I say, to my father's house and talked about Whistler.

I was even taken to the studios of some of them. I saw Harrington Mann taking my father's likeness. I saw George Pirie painting a Highland bull. Frew, who practised medicine and painted skies, was a favourite and so was his wife, Bessie MacNicol, the best woman painter of her time in Britain. Fra. H. Newbery, who looked like Rembrandt, who wore sugarloaf hats, was the head of the School of Art; and we went to his house and saw more giants. We saw there, too, Mrs. Newbery, very dreamy and witty in green serge with purple embroidery, her lovely yellow-haired daughters and their friends, the Walton kids, brimming with precocity, brains and ability. On Sundays we walked out to a place called Robinsfield and saw Macaulay Stevenson, the Scottish Corot, in the farmhouse he was gradually building up into a castle, paying his joiners and stone masons and praying plumbers, as often as not, with delicate sonatas and symphonies and songs without words done in misty paint. He was, and is, the most majestic talker in the world. Above his fireplace he carved:

Suffer me a little and I will shew thee that
I have yet to speak on God's behalf.

49

He told us of the temperature induced by the wave-lengths of the different colours and why red was hot and blue cold. He told us how to fry eggs. He explained the weaving of tweed. He informed us by what route the radicals were going to Hell. He told us stories of his kinsman, R. A. M. Stevenson. He envisaged the perfect State when artists should be honoured and, better, subsidised. He extolled the Poet Keats and recited his poetry. He told us how he sat up all night with Whistler in his bedroom in a London Hotel and what they talked about. He told us about Paris and poverty and food and wine and religion and his father, the Calvinist, and his brothers, the millionaires.

As for me, it was natural that I should want to be an artist. I met, in this phase, the two most important Scottish men of letters since R. L. Stevenson. They were Neil Munro and R. B. Cunninghame Graham. I liked Mr. Munro and I was bowled over by Mr. Graham. But to be an artist and to paint on canvas and to talk was the thing. I drew—not very well for my age, but with plenty of enterprise and a steady undertow towards caricature. My father showed my drawings to his friends. Some of them said I would be an artist. Others said I wouldn't. My champion was Newbery, but then he thought everybody should be an artist. My father said:

" I shall teach him a trade first. If I don't I have a suspicion what sort of an artist he will be. I do not want him to spend his life drinking and telling blue stories at the Art Club."

It was a great joy to him when I decided that I would like to be a Doctor. I had my reasons. As they would not have commended themselves to my father, I never told him what they were. The children with whom I played in the dingy gardens of Royal

Crescent—we had moved to a flat in Kelvingrove
Street—were the children of a Dr. Carswell, a distinguished Glasgow alienist. Their father had a
brougham. I decided that it would be pleasanter to
be carried about from place to place in a brougham
than to walk to a Works. Besides I did not like
the Works. I liked the workmen and had, from
time to time, breakfast with them. But the Works
were noisy and dangerous and smelt of oil. The
Moulders' Shop was charming, I admit, and it had
a heartening smell of burnt sand. I didn't get tired
of seeing the molten metal run into the moulds and
the tidy neat motions of the moulders' hands. I liked
the thumping on the boxes with fists and to see the
finished miracle. I was fond of the Smith and his
steam hammer with which he flattened threepenny bits
for me. I liked to see metal being cut into delicate
hard ribbons by the lathe. But I knew well enough
that to be a Smith or a Moulder was not the life for me.
I thought I wasn't good enough for either job and I
was quite right.

If I was not to be an artist—and I did not wish to
give my parents pain in the small matter of a career—
I should be a Doctor and have a brougham. My
father was very pleased, thinking that the idea that
would have made a really great Doctor of him if he had
had the luck had been reborn in his son. He took me
to see his Doctor friends and, among them, Cocky
Young.

Cocky Young was Keeper of the Hunterian Museum
and Professor of Zoology at the University. He was
a fierce little man whose fancy it was to look like
Shylock, ragged beard, elf-locks and all. He wore
either an immense wideawake hat or a square fur cap.
Once, when he was travelling by ship to the Marine
Biological Station at Millport he came up suddenly

from below, causing a Highland deck hand, who did not know him, to exclaim, " The Duvvle! "

" How did you know it was me? " said Cocky with a dreadful chuckle.

Three Cocky stories used to be thought funny. They can be most rapidly told in dialogue.

First story:
At a viva voce examination in Biology. DR. YOUNG *hands a* STUDENT *a square glass specimen bottle. A piece of stamp paper is pasted over the label, but the formalin has spilt and the stamp paper is quite transparent.*

DR. YOUNG: What do you make of this?

STUDENT: I see from the label, Sir, that it is an amphioxus.

DR. YOUNG: Go in peace. Thy faith hath made thee whole.

The second story:
A Class Room. Cocky has just made a remark offensive to his students' sense of the fitness of things. There is a thunderous tramping of feet.

DR. YOUNG: Will that idiot stop knocking his head against the desk?

The third story:
Cocky is delivering a Magic Lantern Lecture to a Society of Women Undergraduates. The oil lamp goes out. Darkness and confusion. The Professor begins frantically to try to strike matches on the wrong side of the box.

A LADY: Try the bottom, Professor.

COCKY: The very thing. . . .

(Cetera desunt.)

But perhaps he was shown at his best when he went to the Veterinary College to present the prizes at the end of the Session and to deliver an address on, I think, " Comparative Anatomy as It was Practised Among the Ancients." He had been invited to deliver this address on a beautiful sheet of vellum notepaper embossed with the name, title and qualifications of " Principal MacColl, F.R.C.V.S."

The Vets gave him a hearty welcome. They blew on police whistles and sirens. They stamped with their feet. They shouted. They even shot at their guest with pea-shooters. Cocky stood for some moments fingering his manuscript and glaring at them. He then turned to the Principal.

" Principal MacColl," he said. " In the Name of God, *Principal* MacColl! "

He then thrust his address into his oxter and strode out and away.

Such was the man who stood in front of a large open fire-place listening to what my father had to say about me. I was very young, but my father believed that a boy should shape his course early. He himself had suffered by not being able to do that. He had not, he said, observed many signs that I would develop into a great Doctor, or even into a very competent one. I was a poor naturalist and I was clumsy with my hands. On the other side of it, I was a determined boy and I had made up my mind. He was glad that I had made up my mind. What did Dr. Young think?

" Poor little devil," said the Doctor. " If he wants to go into medicine, he is soft in the head. Discourage him. Your way is clear. Discourage him. It is the last and worst profession in the world. The last profession in the world. Make him an engineer; or, if he is no use, a Parson."

" What do you think? " said my father as we walked home through the frosty streets. " Of course, he is a Doctor; but he doesn't practise. He would even rather be called the Keeper of the Hunterian Museum

E   53

than Professor of Zoology. I don't know that his advice is good. Would you like to be a Parson?"

I said, "No." Parsons wore a very peculiar type of collar and had to learn Greek and Hebrew. My brother and I used to play at being parsons with a pulpit and *Jesus, The Carpenter of Nazareth* for our book of sermons. We deeply admired certain parsons in their private capacity; for example, one Dr. Reith, an extremely handsome man with curly hair and whiskers, who took us on his knee and gave us threepenny bits, and who was minister of the College Church, who was later to win glory. On the other hand, we had no inclination to be parsons. Apart from everything else, parsons had to be good. Adult life was, to us, a glorious vista of unrestrained license. Nobody would dare to tell us to behave.

What form this licentiousness would take, we had not yet decided. I do not think we considered the possibilities in detail. A reasonable amount of destruction and gluttony no doubt played their part. My own daydreams at this stage and for some time later were animated principally by the Power motive.

I became a gentleman called Foscor. I had a heavy moustache and was growing slightly bald on top. I combined a heavy, rather lethargic frame with prodigious strength and intense activity. As a boy, long before the Relief of Mafeking, Foscor invented the Boy Scouts. They wore blue uniforms, they were exceedingly ingenious, and they fought battles with weapons that did not, at first, hurt. After I had fired an air-gun for the first time, they took to air-guns. After I had fired a shot-gun, there was no end to the lethal weapons they used.

Foscor grew up and became a Schoolmaster. I am sorry to say he was a Sadist. He had the finest collection of canes in the world and used them till the blood came. Perhaps it was because Foscor was such a brute that I have become a person who hates and contemns corporal punishment even more than my father did. I think that a boy who is assaulted judicially by any-one stronger than himself is justified in killing his enemy by whatever means his cunning can devise. I am ashamed of Foscor as I am not ashamed of any other of my incarnations and I should not mention him at all if it were not that his subsequent develop-ment had points of peculiar interest.

As a Scout, he had used his little army mainly in rebellion against constituted authority. When he became constituted authority himself, he misused his power shamefully. His next step was in the direction of Welt-politik.

He borrowed a wonderful white horse from a circus. He had other horses—bays—who used to race railway trains, leaping over seven-foot fences, cottages and mill dams when they came in the way. They were marvellous beasts and sometimes they beguile a dull railway journey for me still. Thirty or forty miles at a stretch is nothing to them.

He gathered an army of picked men. They were organised to the last detail. Their object was to place Foscor at the head of the Government of the British Islands . . . as Dictator. This entailed a good deal of galloping about on horseback; hill-fighting; sabre duels; street fighting; desultory shooting; and, above all, a brilliant collection of uniforms suitable for every kind of battle.

What Foscor proposed to do with the Government when he attained it was a matter he had very little leisure to consider. I need not tell you that his Army was invincible. They became trained to such a pitch that they took over the majority of the hand-to-hand combats and gave Foscor more time to develop high

strategy. It was no longer necessary for him to fight
duels with anyone under the rank of Commander-in-
Chief. Traitors in his own Army, however, he dealt
with personally. He was developing magnanimity.

In due course his efforts and those of his Army were
crowned with success. Wearing a dazzling white
uniform and mounted on the white circus horse, he
rode into Westminster Hall and up the steps. Queen
Victoria and the Prince of Wales were very glad to see
him. If Lord Salisbury had any reservations in his
mind, he wisely kept them to himself. Foscor made a
furious speech against the enemies of Great Britain,
who included the French, the Germans, the Russians
and the Turks. He announced that he was raising an
Army of ten million men and that the rest of the
population had nothing to do but be happy and cheer.
He created himself a Duke and a Field-Marshal and
made his friends Marquises and Earls. He proposed
to teach the rest of the world the might of the British
Flag. He closed his peroration with the ringing
words: " Are you with me? " The answer was a
pandemonium of full-throated " Hurrahs."

When he became Emperor of the World with
nothing left to do but make speeches and hold cere-
monies, Foscor tired of life. He was a lonely figure.
He had no intimate friends and I do not think he ever
so much as spoke to a woman. So far as I know he
never died. He dissolved from inanition. A sense of
humour might have saved him, but he had none. He
was a man of action and beyond that nothing.

. . . .

*Nothing! Apart from some lime salts in my skeleton
there was as little left of the inhabitant of those five years
as there was of the Emperor Foscor. This struck me as a
sad thought and I fell into a mood of melancholy. Tears*

sprang to my eyes. I shut them hard and opened them again. In front of me was a large stained-glass window. I remember noticing it when I sat down in the dentist's chair. It represented cherubs flying about in a vine with cherry-coloured ribbons blown by a thoughtful wind into decency-preserving convolutions. An odd thing was that the window was now in neutral tints. I was colour blind. This was only for a moment. The vine became green, the grapes purple and the modest ribbons blushed again.

My jaws ached and I felt horribly ill. I was transferred to a stretcher and carried down to the ward.

. . . .

I did not visit the Celestial Repertory Theatre for another two or three months. We had moved from Arras to the Somme Area. I was in charge of a billeting party. The train pulled up in the inhospitable town of Amiens. A young gunner and I had an inferior meal at an Hotel. We then went to view the Cathedral by moonlight and saw little but sandbags. We developed a longing for bright lights and a band, so we stopped a French Officer and asked him what entertainment the town had to offer. He pointed to the pavement and told us that there was a War on, even if we filthy English didn't realise it. He had gone before we had time to argue the point. We loitered palely through the dark streets till suddenly somebody began to bombard us with green apples from a top storey window. A direct hit on my companion brought high screams of girlish laughter from above. He shot through a dark entry and up a crazy staircase, I following. But the house was silent now. We found nobody. Nothing.

We went back to the railway station and dossed uncomfortably in the train. I lay for a long time and reflected. I had a very strong premonition that I was going to be killed on the Somme. In those days we laid great stress on

*such premonitions. They were infallible. I fell into an
uneasy sleep and up I went again.*

*My ricketty plush chair was occupied and a gaunt
figure with a sad mahogany face was sitting at it. He got
up when he found me standing behind him.*

*" Please," he said, with great civility offering me the
chair.*

" Not at all," I said.

*" I was only amusing myself," said Ian Hay, for it was
he.*

*" I didn't know you had stopped one," I said. " I
gather I have just been killed on the Somme, but I don't
remember how."*

*" I haven't been killed at all," said Ian Hay. " The
Time Space Continuum has got a little mixed since our
mutual friend Priestley took it in hand. Actually I am a
General but, at the moment, I am also plain Mr. Beith of
Fettes College and I should be very interested to see what
you make of your schooldays."*

*" That is very kind of you," I said. " Descend on me,
bright spirit, with those of Talbot Baines Reed and Judge
Hughes and Mr. Wodehouse."*

They did not so descend.

CHAPTER III

The Third Five

I WENT INTO THE Senior School in my tenth year. I had done fairly well. In each of my classes in the Junior School I had won second place and received two valuable prizes bound in calf and bearing the school arms and an inscription in Latin saying how good I had been. The books were *Discoveries and Inventions of the Nineteenth Century* (what clumsy looking things they did invent) ; and the other was *Eric ; or Little by Little* by Dean Farrar. I was not old enough to deride this book. I should like to think that I felt uncomfortable when I read it. I didn't. My mother, my brother and I wept over it. It was sadder than *Tom Brown's Schooldays*, but there was no denying that, apart from the purple passages, the story was better told. Pure story-telling is little enough prized nowadays, but when it appears it makes its author's fortune. With all his faults in taste, the Dean could tell a story. That is one reflection called up by *Eric.*

The other reflection is that a certain kind of coarse

59

assertion can make us ashamed of liking the things that, in our hearts, we like. Those sophisticated little cads, Stalky, MacTurk and Beetle, spoiled the poor Dean for many of his worshippers. Eric Williams was much liker a real boy than any of the urchins at Westward Ho. His masters were liker schoolmasters. His adventures were more exciting than the sordid, childish banditry of the Kipling juvenile gangsters, who could not even talk English. But Kipling was a great genius and his brutal, snobbish, literary-jargoning gutter-snipes came disgustingly to life and jeered us out of our plain judgement.

The Senior School was a broad new world. The forms in it were called the First to the Sixth Latin Class and we consorted with people like R. S. Stronach who was later to play for Scotland and break the World Hurdles Record. We had an enormous gravelled playground which was not enveloped in red dust in summer and deep in mud in the winter like the Junior School playground. We met, too, the Headmasters in the different departments of learning. They were not Brobdignagian to our juvenile eyes alone. They were extraordinary men and I shall have something to tell you of them.

I entered the Senior School with some confidence. I looked on myself as something of an intellectual. I had three or four friends who felt as I did about them-selves and about me. Among them were Tom Lind-say [1], Face Miller [2], George Holms Reid Laird and Haricot Hunter. We were somewhat bitten by Stalky and made fun of the athletes. Tom Lindsay was a sort of perpetual Dux. Face drew pictures of soldiers. Laird had had a poem accepted by a local journal. I

---

[1] The brother of the Master of Balliol.

[2] The Keeper of the National Gallery of Scotland. I put these things in to add to the importance of this book.

had the deadly gift of caricature. I could turn away, if not wrath, at least the exhibition of it, by drawing my enemy's picture.

My conceit was reinforced in a peculiar way by one, Snubs. Snubs taught Mathematics. He was a little man with a bald head and a beard. We made game of his Scots accent. We ourselves talked a filthy hybrid called Kelvinside English. A Glasgow poet has fixed that dialect in a poem that begins :

> Summer's over, Cousin Fenny
> From the Coast et lest is beck,
> End she doddles down Bichenen
> Street with hendsome Cousin Jeck.

Snubs, on the other hand, opened his vowels like a man and gave every consonant its full value with a bit thrown in for discount. One day he made the following speech :

" I was talking to a guntleman last night. He had just come back from South Africa, and he said that the thing that impressed him most were the oaxen. They pulled the big Cape carts, ye ken, over the veldt and through the muddy river-beds, plodding away. And the native drivers whupped them with big whups and shouted at them and kicked them, but on they went, plodding away, never altering their pace, plodding and slow, paying no attention to the noise or the whups, plodding and slow, plodding and slow. And suddenly I surprised him by shouting out, ' That's Steviston and Mavor! ' " [1]

The little sycophants in the class burst into merry peals of laughter, but Snubs silenced them with a glance of his boiled eye.

[1] The traditional Scottish way of pronouncing Stevenson. Beefy Stevenson, the boy in question, had a personality and played forward for Scotland.

"You may laugh," he said, "but Mavor's got the best head in the class. In fifteen or maybe sixteen years, you'll hear about Mavor. He'll beat ivery one of ye. Even the great Mr. X." And he mentioned the permanent medallist.

You will agree that this was a very dangerous thing to say. As I was as near the bottom of the class as makes no matter and as Snubs had no acquaintance with me outside professional business, his words had the air of inspired prophecy. A hush fell over the room. The promise that I should beat Mr. X deeply impressed those competitive-minded Scots. It was almost as if he had said that I would one day play for the first fifteen. For me it had the force of an annunciation and I cherished it in my heart. It bore me through many humiliations. When a wing three quarter said to me : "Do you know, if you weren't looked upon as a sort of village idiot, you would get a Hell of a lot of hammerings," I smiled in a superior sort of way.

"Guid gi'e us a guid conceit o' oursel's," is the Scotsman's most earnest prayer ; and God's emissary, Snubs, gave me that at a time of my life when I most needed it. I had a poor physique, a chronic catarrh of the nose, and a sluggish and "nerveless" mind. I was tongue-tied and oafish in my social relationships. I did not, for a time, play games. I was a coward, though consciousness of my high destiny sometimes led me to turn and fight with varying success.

My parents were anxious about me. Till they died they were anxious about me. Although my conduct was, on the whole, blameless in a negative sort of way and remains so, I showed very little capacity for the battle of life. To my father it did not appear that I was interested in the things that should interest a proper man. To my mother, my lack of any kind of method, my carelessness, my policy of drift tempered by obstinacy seemed to give poor promise of any kind of reputable future. And, with the best will in the world to cut a respectable figure in company, I cut a very poor figure indeed.

To build me up physically they sent me to the swimming baths. To build me up socially, they sent me to dancing school. At the swimming bath I spent most of my time in the hot spray. I did, indeed, learn to plug along for a length or two with an unspectacular breast stroke, but I never used the travelling rings, climbed the rope, or dived from a height.

The dancing school was misery. I began to go there, as I have told you, towards the end of my second cycle. I continued irregularly for two or three years. There was nothing I hated more. I can hardly bear to speak of it. It will serve, however, as a pretext for " disengaging the erotic motive," as Max Beerbohm so delightfully describes the process in his parody of George Moore. Between ten and sixteen the conditions of puberty arrive and must be sternly faced.

I may as well warn you at this early stage that this book will contain very little about erotics in any shape or form. I am sorry, but I am determined. This Age appears to me, in one of its aspects, as an age of Peeping Toms. Our readers of biographies, autobiographies and novels have become, will they nill they, an audience of hedges and bedroom windows. We are all scientists nowadays, and the branch of science most easy to master in its elements is the science of the Psyche. I found this out when I was trying to master Ehrlich's Side Chain Theory and picked up the Journal of Mental Science by mistake. It was featuring at that time Professor Freud. I read a great deal of Freud and Jung before they had got into the Sunday papers. This, I thought, was the stuff for me. It had a fascinating touch of magic and, given a start, could be spun out of one's own head by the yard. It satisfied also my natural appetite for smut in what appeared to be quite a nice way. I am anticipating. It was at the beginning of my fifth cycle that I discovered Freud. But it is necessary to anticipate if I am to make myself clear.

It was only a matter of time before the enthusiasm for this branch of science should become general. The basis of all thought and behaviour on sex was a lovely simplification and its corollary, an earthly Mohammedan paradise, a pleasing prospect. The new Gospel swept the world. There appeared a tremendous and open interest in operations and relationships that for many years people had agreed to regard as private.

Fondness for pornography was not new. Pornography had appeared in the classics. It had for long been associated in the British mind with French literature. There were passages in the Bible which were not generally read at diets of public worship. There was an enormous word of mouth collection of verses and narrative in common circulation. But it was not held reverence to have it set down . . . or it had not been so held for a century and a half. When smut became science, the taboos were lifted. Literature and polite conversation were granted a licence.

Here is an odd thing. Our old dogs in learning new tricks have kept some of the Victorian taboos. Simple coupling and its variations may be discussed in novels and text-books, but certain details must be left to the imagination in novels and expressed in Latin or Greek words in the textbooks. In the theatre, over which a rigid censorship is exercised, reference to fornication and the unnatural vices is permitted freely if the manner of such reference is sufficiently playful and the explicit words describing these pastimes are not used. Even in the most emancipated and earnest society, certain words and phrases which are common knowledge are not used in conversation when both sexes are present and sober.

House trained autobiographers, anxious to be in the movement but conscious of sanctions, have five or six stereotyped ways of describing their experiences, asserting their normality and satisfying the purely scientific curiosity of their readers. All of these seem to my prudish mind to be faintly disgusting.

None the less, exhibitionism must have played a part almost equal to that of the hope of gain in inducing me to write this book and a sop must be thrown to it. In the cycle of which I am writing and in the succeeding cycles, I had a very definite attitude to what is called Sex and you may as well have it in as few words as possible.

From ten to sixteen I was a romantic. From sixteen to twenty I was a misogynist. From twenty to twenty-five I stood in front of fire-places preaching this doctrine in the language of the gutter from a heart racked with the intimations of several grand passions. From twenty-five to thirty a grand passion burst on me with full violence, but the War mitigated its most devastating effects. From thirty to thirty-five I was derelict until a grander passion came to my rescue and I got married. From thirty-five till to-day I lived happy ever after.

I must try, in each chapter, to keep within the limits I have set myself ; but sooner than weary you by dragging this boring little brat step by step up to his sixteenth year, I shall tell you some stories about my schoolmasters.

John MacLaren was the eldest. He was the Writing Master. I do not know whether any of his profession survive. He was also the conductor of the Glasgow Academy Choir. He had beautiful silvery white hair parted in the middle, and a white moustache.

He wore a grey frock coat and a grey silk necktie. His teaching of penmanship was mostly a joke, though I have recollections of writing repeatedly the word " Fanfaronade " with heavy downstrokes and light up-strokes and of the word " copperplate " and of the smell of ink. He was really a Minister without port-folio. He taught us manners. His own manners were exquisite and he had a savage humour.

When he dismissed the writing class he used to say, " The handsomest man go," indicate the fattest boy in the class and give him a present of three pen nibs. The oldest man was the next to be dismissed. I was always that. I could not understand why, because I was the youngest boy in the class. There was one boy called Ian Wilson who shaved when he was in the Third Latin. After the noisiest, the most depraved, the silliest, the most noble-minded, the boy in the ugliest kilt and the spottiest boy had gone, he would order the riff raff to stand, stand out and proceed quietly down-stairs.

He worked, from time to time, a harmonium at one end of the Writing Room and taught his sopranos and altos how to sing in harmony and not to slur. It was in one such practise that a large pink boy committed an impertinence by singing, instead of " And from her wintry bed bid drowsy Nature rise," the words, " And from his wintry bed bid drowsy Mavor rise." This I resented. But I do not think I fought him till many years later.

No matter how great our need, it was no use saying to John MacLaren, " Please Sir, kinaget downstairs? " If we said that he first pretended not to hear and then told us that the proper way to say it was, " Please Sir (a pause) ; *may I* go downstahs? " He insisted on refinement in speech and deportment, but occasionally shocked us by his own liberties. When Watson said

66

he was feeling a little sick, John MacLaren said, " Go away, then. Don't vomit here."

He was at his best when the Writing Room was being used for examinations. Or, again, when he invited members of the Choir up to tea at his house.

" I once saw a man hanged," he would say. " I played truant from school to see him. The executioner put a white linen bag over his head. When they touched him off I could only see his head and his shoulders twirling round and round and then swinging like a pendulum on a clock.

" The last man who was hanged in public was Dr. Pritchard. I knew him well. I should have dearly loved to see him hanged for that man cheated me. His sons were at the Academy. When his house was set on fire they came to school and told us that the molten gold plate was running down the front door steps. What lies!

" A vain man, too. He insisted on being hanged wearing gloves. Black gloves."

The Glasgow Academy is a large square building overlooking the River Kelvin. It has a noble flight of steps leading to its front door, but that is reserved for the Rector, the Masters, the Governors and the Parents and, at night, for the Debating Society. The boys sneak in by a little side door and find themselves in a sort of alleyway between the main building and the new building which houses the chemists and the artists. Through a gloomy, cold shed, they pass into the main well of the building, a concreted expanse surrounded by loose-boxes in which hats and coats are kept. At one end there is a clock and a large bar where cakes and a peculiar kind of coffee are sold at stated hours. My eldest son told me once that nowadays the elder boys are served with whisky and soda, but I can hardly believe that. The other four sides are surrounded by a gallery with ornamental railings of polished wood and painted iron. At one end there is, or was, a huge bust of Pallas Athene. The second floor still opens on the well and is surrounded by glass cases in which such objects as alligators' eggs, the autograph of J. M. Barrie, foreign stamps, coins, photographs of James Wordie exploring the Arctic regions used to be displayed. On these cases, looking over into the seething pit below, James Wood and William Robertson used to lean.

James Wood was the Headmaster of Mathematics. William Robertson was the Headmaster of Classics. James Wood was short and stocky. William Robertson was tall and burly. James Wood was neat and tidy. William Robertson was not. James Wood wore a tight little black jacket and merino trousers. William Robertson wore a vast grey morning coat with baggy trousers of the same material and, I grieve to say, sometimes brown golfing boots. James Wood's ginger hair was parted in the middle and he had a smart little curly moustache. William Robertson wore a henna-coloured wig with a visible black elastic band on his occiput. He had a grand puffy face like that of a Roman Emperor. It was usually pale, but it flushed bright red when he was angry. He was called Big Bob to distinguish him from Lanky Bob, whose name was also Robertson.

We had a feeling that these two were superior men— superior to the Rector, superior to the great Melven himself. Lionel W. Lyde, who left for other fields shortly after I reached the senior school, was, we felt, the only master who could talk with them on equal terms. I do not know how on earth we knew this, but there seems to be no doubt that it was a fact.

Jamie had been a Don at Cambridge. He was an Aberdonian. He came from Cambridge to Glasgow to assist Jack, the Professor of Mathematics. His ambition was to become Professor of Mathematics in his native Aberdeen. This he nearly became ; but, after a most satisfactory interview with those who held the appointment in their hands, he went out into the harbour in a small boat on the Lord's Day. This impious act lost him the Chair and, in a blind fury, he cast aside ambition and accepted a mastership at the Glasgow Academy where he stayed till his death, making no further contribution to the Science that had rejected him. I do not think he turned out any first-rate mathematicians from the mill to which he chained himself. He was too ironic a man to be inspiring to the young. We were too much alive, in those long dull days, to his entertainment value to be afraid of him and his curious cat's smile ; but, afterwards, when we had gone out into the world conquering and to conquer and came to display ourselves to our old dominie, there came the chill of realising that perhaps he despised us.

One of his favourite stories was of a callow, loutish, half-baked sort of a fellow with his mouth still sticky with his mother's milk who threw himself down on a saddle-backed sofa on which Jamie was taking his ease at his Club. The oaf said, " You don't remember me, Mr. Wood." Jamie agreed. The oaf said, " Many's the flogging I've had from you."

Jamie, who could not understand why he had been interrupted in his siesta, began to fear that he was the object of some sort of vendetta. He said, weakly, that he hoped it had not done the oaf any harm. " No," said the creature, and he gave a great laugh, " it has made a man of me."

The youth could not have had many floggings from Jamie. When his rage mounted up to the point of physical violence he had a convention of pretending to lose his keys. In those days we were beaten on the hand with a strap and every master kept such an instrument in a locked drawer. The locks were often picked and the strap cut to pieces. If the drawer was carelessly left unlocked, the strap was always and immediately cut to pieces. Be that as it may, Jamie could usually avoid acting as executioner.

I recall one occasion when he found his keys. He ordered the cringing boy to hold out one hand and then another. He regarded the proferred mitts critically.

" K——, " he said, " in simple justice to the next boy who is to be flogged, I must ask you to go downstairs and wash your hands."

On another occasion he found a dead mouse on his desk. For some reason or other, he flew into a passion and shrieked for the name of the boy who had done this thing. The culprit, a rustic humourist called Rose, at once confessed and was soundly beaten.

There had been a plague of mice in the school. Rose, himself, had killed seven. We felt that here was injustice.

On the following morning, Jamie entered, beaming, and made the following speech :

" I have been looking into yesterday's incident. Fully. I have traced the history of the wanderer whose body was yesterday discovered in such an unsuitable place. Witnesses inform me that that was not its first appearance.

" Last Thursday it left its snug little home in the basement beside the heating engine. The Red Gods were calling it. It took a tearful farewell of its wife and its multitudinous family and set out to discover the North West Passage to the Dining Hall—a land flowing with milk and honey—and scraps.

" Making its difficult way up the precipitous steps to the first floor, it was seen first by observers in the

English department. It braved and passed the perils of the Rector's Room and struggled down the East Corridor, the strange sounds of foreign languages thundering in its ears. There was another struggle up and over moraines and crags and then the Masters' Room, cold, mysterious, menacing. It kept a stout heart and pressed on and upwards. It passed the Latin and Greek Classrooms and faced the long, arid Gobi desert of the Writing Room. It seemed that nothing could live in that eternal waste, but our explorer was made of stern stuff. He traversed the void and came at length, exhausted and well-nigh spent, to a door over which it saw written the characters MATH I. Naturally associating the higher sciences with magnanimity, generosity and hospitality, it entered, nothing doubting. It found itself in the hands of the Vandals . . . and the Goths. It perished at the hand, or rather, at the foot of Rose.

"Not only that. Following the barbarous custom of their kind, they exposed his little body brutally and ignominiously to the common gaze.

"Perhaps in the basement his brown wife is hoping against hope. More probably she knows the worst and is tearfully receiving the fruits of a subscription of cheese rinds and cake crumbs and consoling herself with the thought that her little Franklin will be suitably commemorated by a MOANUMENT! . . . But enough of these sad matters. We will turn our delighted attention to the Binomial Theorem."

In the class presided over by Snubs we were taught to intone our propositions in Euclid in a sort of litany . . .

"Let us sup-POSE for/ argument's/ SAKE . . ."
"Therefore we/ HAVE been/ WRONG in sup/POSING . . ."

Jamie Wood would have none of this.

"Yes, yes," he would say. "Let us suppose it for the sake of a peaceful argument to prevent any un-

pleasantness or rancour. Now get on with the proa-
position."

The same Rose who killed the mouse suffered more
lightly from this impatience of Jamie's when he interrupted him in a "proablem" he was dictating. It
appeared that a Fox was pursued by a Grey Hound.
She took so many paces per minute and her pursuer
took so many paces per minute. When would he
overtake her?

Rose said that that was wrong.

Jamie said that the error had escaped him.

Rose said that the Fox ought to have been a vixen.

Jamie said : " Rose, in the early part of last century,
gentlemen might have been seen carrying heavy-
looking walkingsticks of an appearance quite out of
tone with their dressiness in other matters. Crude
looking sticks. Dull looking sticks. Stupid looking,
bucolic sticks. Suddenly, when the man's assailant
expected it least, out flashed a rapier. Oh, yes, Rose.
Come in the afternoon after school. Join the Cronies'
Club. You will find pleasant surroundings and congenial company in Blank and Dash and Soandso. And
in the interval of writing out in a fair round hand
Problems 12 to 18, you may snortle and chortle and
coddle and coo and crack your merry jokes to your
heart's content. That's true Cronyism."

These bits of eloquence pleased us very much ;
not because they were amusing (and I still think they
were), but because they held up the tedious business
of the day. We were also glad to have our attention
distracted by Jamie's odd way of pronouncing " O's,"
short where we pronounced them long and open when
we pronounced them closed. Wit has no immediate
impact on schoolboys. Church and I thought it far
funnier to count the number of times Jamie said " So
that! " in an hour, and Miller drew soldiers.

It was of Church that Jamie said : " You are worse than you were last year, Church. And I said that last year too. And the year before that. And the year before that. You must have been a wonderful baby, Church."

It was of Miller he said, when he was reading out the results of the monthly examinations:

" Miller : Geometry, twelve per cent. Algebra, fourteen per cent. Trigonometry, five per cent. You are strongest in Algebra, Miller."

Church and I scored one point for each time he said " So that." Two for each time he said " Easee." Five for each time he told a story we had heard before from him. He made a large number of points with the story of the Coallie Doag. When the Coallie Doag's master, the shepherd, told it to gang furrit it came in ahint. When he told it to come in behind, it went forward. It, Jamie said, was consistent. We sometimes upset all his calculations by obeying him.

If I have failed to evoke Jamie, I do not know how I am going to manage with Big Bob. Stories of him cannot convey the immense dignity which tempered and etherealised the fantastic pieces of buffoonery in which he took part. If you hark back in this book to a passage about Boswell and Dr. Johnson, it will be easier for me to explain what I mean. Johnson, you see, was unconscious of Boswell's Scotch derision, but his essential nobility of character conquered his horrible biographer and shone through the devilish pages. We were all morally Boswells ; but none of us had his capacity as an artist. While we openly derided Big Bob, it has not been given to any of us to tell how much we loved and admired him through it all. You must picture for yourselves this large, noble, ugly, slovenly man and despise as much as you like the leaping fleas in his mantle. The flea, apart from its incapacity in description, is at a further disadvantage. It was impossible for him to know Big Bob intimately. He could delight in his host, but he could never know him. Big Bob was too shy. Many of us, after we left school, were drawn irresistibly to go back and talk to him. He would never talk to us. He would blush, stammer and dismiss us. He had all the outward marks of a friendly man, but I do not think he had a friend in the world but Jamie Wood. I do not know what they talked about, leaning on the glass cases. Probably they shared their misery. We all supposed, probably wrongly, that they both drank heavily in the evenings ; but not with one another. Every afternoon Big Bob caught the four ten to Ayr. We believed that he sat from five fifteen till closing time in the Poet's seat in the Tam o' Shanter Inn. No one knows what he did. I am told that he used to bet a great deal on horses.

During his working hours we tormented him steadily. The cruder spirits tormented him brutally, the finer spirits more subtly. We flung our foolish little banderoles and watched them hook themselves into his great flanks and heard him snort and saw his red eyes roll in bewilderment.

" I cannae conceive of a fullah doing a thing like that," he would say, and it was perfectly true. " It's staggering," he would say.

If he was staggered out of his ordinary solemn good temper, he used to get as red as a beet ; and one day he boxed Robin Brown's ears. He fell at once into an agony of contrition.

" Sorry," he said. " Sorry. Dirty thing to hit a fullah on the ear. Only did it once before. Never do it again. I apologise. I'll dream about this to-night. I apologise."

His more regular punishments took the form of

detention. He had always the same formula for pronouncing sentence. He would throw out his chest and abdomen and crook his right forefinger at the level of his shoulder.

"Observe!" he would say. "Take up your books. Back seat. Four o'clock for an hour. I'll be there. So will you . . . Yes, I will . . . No, I won't . . . Yes, I will!"

We used to chant the formula after him, like congregations in the Church of England. One day when the Class was struggling more or less silently with Unseens (from "a wee book full of racy stories"), a boy was dividing his attention between his work and the novel *They Call it Love*. Big Bob came down the aisle with catlike tread and looked over his shoulder.

"They call it Love?" he said. "I call it cheek. Take up your books . . ."

CHOIR : "Back seat!"

BOB : "Four o'clock for an hour."

CHOIR : "He'll be there!"

BOB : "So will you . . ."

CHOIR : "Yes, he will. No, he won't."

BOB : "I will."

CHOIR : "He won't."

BOB : "Toch! I've got to catch the four ten. Besides, it's no prison when it's raining."

CHOIR : "You'll have to forgive him."

BOB : "I'll have to forgive you."

Another scene seems to me memorable. Thomson is construing the Fourteenth Ode in the Second Book.

THOMSON : "Alas, Postumus (ahem) Postumus— please, Sir, Postumus twice—the flying years slip ; nor will piety bring custom . . ."

BOB : "Stop, you. Where do you find ' custom '? It is not in my version."

75

THOMSON : " Please, Sir, ' moram.' "

BOB : " Staggering. You haven't learned it."

THOMSON : " Yes, Sir, I have."

BOB : " You give small evidence of it."

CHOIR : " Give him a chance."

BOB : " I'll give him a chance. ' Piety bring custom! ' Do you think Postumus was running a Department Store? "

THOMSON : " I don't know, Sir."

BOB : " I may be wrong, but it is my impression that you know nothing at all about the Ode."

THOMSON : " Yes, Sir."

BOB : " You couldn't answer ten questions on it."

CHOIR : " Take him on, Thomson."

THOMSON : " Yes, Sir. I could."

BOB : " So be it. In what metre is the Ode written? "

CHOIR : " The wee Adonic! "

BOB : " Be silent. This is between Thomson and me. Besides it's not the wee Adonic. I couldnae conceive of anybody thinking it was the wee Adonic."

THOMSON : " It's the Alcaic. The two first verses are the Greater Alcaic, the third's an Archilochian and the fourth's a lesser Alcaic."

BOB : " Gibson told you."

THOMSON : " No, Sir. He did not."

BOB : " I'm sorry. I shouldna have said that. I apologise."

THOMSON : " Granted."

CHOIR : " Thomson, one. Robertson, nothing."

BOB : " What's ' ter amplum '? "

THOMSON : " He had three bodies." (Cheers.)

BOB : " Who had? "

THOMSON : " Geryon." (Cheers.)

BOB : " Who was he? "

THOMSON : " The giant. The son of Chrysaor and Calli- Calli- Calli-rhoe."

76

CHOIR : " Thomson, four. Robertson, nil." (Loud cheers.)

BOB : " ' Unda compescit '—What waves? "

THOMSON : " Please Sir, the waves of the Styx."

CHOIR : " Thomson, five. Robertson, love."

BOB : " Toch! "

CHOIR : " You're stymied! "

BOB : " I'm bunkered! "

It was an exciting contest. I wish you could have seen the challenge, the determination, the slyness, the grimness and the ultimate despair chasing each other over Big Bob's countenance. Under them was a suspicion he was too honourable to entertain, that Thomson was being prompted. Indeed, he had written his facts down on the margin from the notes in his father's Horace at home and Gibson was not guilty.

Nor could anyone better than Thomson have been chosen for the protagonist. He had a hesitating voice and a maddeningly innocent look. He is now a Commissioner in Lunacy.

Now that I come to think of it, is gossip about schools and schoolmasters of general interest? I seldom hear any except on appropriate occasions. I admit to some uneasiness and a slight sense of superiority on the rare occasions when I listen to chatter about other schools; but I don't find it without interest. As to the Glasgow Academy, though I usually avoid the Old Boys' Dinner, I eat once a year regularly with my own contemporaries and find pleasure in seeing separate lives being done up in parcels and sadness when the parcel is tied and sent away.

How capricious is the advance of middle age! Thomson, for all his eminence and in spite of a few grey hairs, would create little comment if he suddenly stood up in Big Bob's old room and began to construe

My cousin, Wallace, who used to be known as Thor, has finished his life's work in India and retired into the country to shoot little birds and running beasts; but, if he shaved off his moustache, he would show no change from the bulky silent youth he was when he was fourteen. Glassie, the Solicitor, had an aged, wizened, quizzical appearance when he was twelve. He has not changed. So with two or three others. It is like a dream to see them sporting about among the bald, fat, sententious elders the rest of us have become.

It takes a little time and alcohol before we can exploit the nostalgia that brought us together. For one thing, the social hierarchy has been upset and rearranged. The Dukes and Earls are no longer International Trialists. They cannot run. They cannot jump. They pursue a smaller and meaner ball on golf courses. The brainy ones have not fulfilled their earlier promise and are nearly all ill-treated by the world they advanced so confidently to conquer. The nonentities who walked like shadows, silent and vague in outline, through our corridors, are now solid men with huge bank balances and a say in how the country should be governed. The bucks are tarnished. The wits less witty.

On the whole, this levelling up has been a great improvement. Beauties of soul, acutenesses of observation and comment, livelinesses of thought, talents that were blanketed by the snobberies of our little State can now be seen and appreciated. It is not merely that they are now in flower. They are beginning to wither. They were there all the time.

To this dozen or so, the Masters were great men and are still. Their foibles are as fascinating as those of Mr. Gladstone, or Disraeli, or Wilde, or J. M. W. Turner, or Jowett, or Dickens, or Lord Kitchener would be to a larger circle. They recreate the more than life size figures who are dead—and they are nearly all dead. Lanky Bob, a tall, dark, morose man in our day, is still alive and in retirement. J. C. Scott is as lively as a cricket. He left the Academy to be Rector of Hutchesons' Grammar School. Became a Doctor of Laws. Retired. Was elected to the Glasgow Corporation and the University Court. Became a Bailie. Mixed himself up in politics. I met him the other day in Edinburgh when I was collecting my sons from the Cally Hotel to take them home for their holidays. He was as vital as when he used to run along the touch line with a flag protesting against the conduct of the High School fifteen. His moustache still bristles. His voice still resounds. He is as talkative, dogmatic and explosive as ever.

Perhaps the dining dozen are not under illusion after all. If Scott is a Personality at an age when common men are helplessly drooling and dithering towards an unmarked grave, he was a personality forty years ago. And there were others more gigantesque. There was the terrible Melven of the piled beard of whose visage children were afeared. We built him into a tremendous grotesque, but the structure was there to begin with. He was mocked behind his back by a series of writings called the MELVEN DIARY. These were read out from day to day in the horse boxes and showed our hero going through various degrading and absurd activities. He was supposed to run an old clothes shop as a side-line. The diaries were a compensation for a good deal of healthy terror. He had a voice that congealed the marrow.

" Herbertson," he would ask, " what were the characteristics of Queen Elizabeth when she came to the throne? "

" Please, sir, she was young, good-looking and affable."

" And what does affable mean, Herbertson? "

79

" Please, sir, I think it means she was fat."

And we dared not laugh.

Then there was Barbé, the French master, a Channel Islander who called us " gentlemen." We were conscious that this was absurd. We were bourgeois and proud of it. On his last day at school Glassford Alexander ran round the roof of the verandah and shouted in at the open window of the French classroom, " Gentlemen, you are cads! "

Barbé, whatever we might be, was a gentleman himself, and he took no notice. He had written a book on Mary Queen of Scots and a Jubilee poem on the Glasgow Academy. Like other of his colleagues he despised us.

MacKay MacKenzie, the Scottish historian, was another of these men. He was a furious Highlander with waxed moustaches and, from time to time, vented on us the humours of his combative spleen, as in days to come he was to vent it upon those who took the academic view of the battle of Bannockburn. I cannot do justice to these men or to Snubs, whose name was Andrew Muir. It was he, by the way, who was met in St. Enoch Station by an evangelist when he was on his way to a foursome in Troon. The evangelist asked him if he had met his Saviour. Snubs replied that he had met a most impertinent fellow.

Scott is the test. I make no apology for presenting them as remarkable men.

If you would like to know what I was doing all this time, I will tell you. For most of it I was playing a game called DAB CRICKET. George Laird had taught it to me during the earlier cycle. He was a keen cricketer, though he wore thick spectacles, and left our little Derision Club to play for the second eleven. The game, as you will probably know, consists of closing the eyes and dabbing with a pencil on a chart marked with numbers of runs and ways of getting out. It was a favourite game in my time but nobody developed it to the extent to which I did. At the end of a season my leading batsman had played as many innings as Hayward and Bobby Abel themselves, and I carefully compiled their averages. This took up a good deal of time and I stopped getting prizes.

In retrospect, Dab Cricket appears to be an almost entirely worthless occupation, but I cannot bring myself to believe that it was so. It rested the mind. It prevented my "intellects" from being destroyed by education. In it I created a much more civilised kind of world than the world of my earlier fantasies. It was a world of pleasant people, neatly dressed in white, engaged with great concentration on a harmless pastime. Their personal qualities were strictly bounded by the rules, regulations and idiosyncrasies of the game; but within these limits there was a great deal of variety. Vine would take an hour to score four; Jessop would knock up a hundred in forty-five minutes; Tom Richardson's bowling would puzzle the batsmen. I saw very few of the characters in the flesh and did not read much about them. I preferred to invent them for myself; and when, on an odd occasion, a few of them visited Scotland and I went to see them play, I was startled to find how correctly I had visualised them. I even went so far as to invent a village cricket team capable of giving Surrey and Yorkshire more than a good game. I played for this team myself, and was first in the bowling and second in the batting averages at the end of the year. In winter the village team played Rugby. It never suffered a defeat.

It is possible that the only time that is ever wasted is that spent on unprofitable work. My theory about Dab Cricket and Imaginary Rugby is that they tamed an imagination at once unruly and imitative and enabled me, in later years, to scratch a living in the easiest and pleasantest way hitherto devised by mankind.

In the world itself I did not do very much. I was bored to madness in my classes and played feebly the games of Rugby football and cricket. At the beginning and at the end of the cycle I tried my hand at journalism. I produced two lithographed magazines. The early one was called *The Kernel*, the later *The Tomahawk*. *The Tomahawk* was not very good, but it was so much more mature in every way than *The Kernel* that one is led into speculation as to what happens between the ages of twelve and sixteen. We grow suddenly into different beings without noticing the transition. *The Kernel* was a blameless periodical, completely without originality or any kind of intellectual content. There was enough in the *Tomahawk* to bring upon its editor the rage of the Rector. He sent for me and addressed me in the following terms :

" Why did you let yourself go like this? It is a shocking exhibition of bad form. It is a blot on the school. Did you write the description of the High School match? Did you write the personal notes? "

My brilliant improvisation was that I was responsible. I had, of course, written these things.

" The only good thing about it," said the Rector, " is that it is the last number. Go away! "

I went away with my head touching the stars. It was the proudest moment of my life. There was born within me an ambition to annoy others, and in a larger field.

The family fortunes were improving and we moved to a place which was then called Windsor Circus. It was a large oval at the back of the Botanic Gardens, and contained terrace houses on one side, villas on the other and trees in the middle to separate the sheep from the goats. The grass border was ornamented by large flints which contained the natural chalk in their crevices. With one such piece of chalk I scratched the panel of a horse tram-car and was arrested by the conductor. It was a dreadful experience and has kept me out of trouble since. The conductor held me firmly on his platform as the car jogged on to Botanic Gardens station away from my home and I knew not to what dungeon. My brother ran all the way beside the step weeping loudly and begging for mercy for me. My misery was too deep for tears. I thought of the disgrace it would be to my parents. I thought of the horrors of prison. At the station I stood in the middle of the little crowd while an inspector took my name and address and two old ladies investigated the damage I had done. I waited for a week, trembling every time the bell rang, but no policeman came. The panel cost nine shillings to repaint and my father thought it too much.

Ten to fifteen is said to be the formative period in a human life. It is for that reason that it is the most difficult period to convey in anecdote or reminiscence. Bairns and fools should never see a bit of work half done. I was very distressing to myself and to my parents at this period. The barrier between a boy and his parents shoots up in those years to an unprecedented height. He cannot believe that they understand him and that his jostling multitude of new ideas have ever occurred to anyone before. It may be the realisation of this that causes parents to send their sons to those ill-conditioned monasteries called public schools. The transformation from a son and a disciple to a shy, unapproachable stranger would be unbearable to them. A regimented school-boy, with a fair idea of what is expected of such an automaton during the holidays is at least a recognisable type. He has survived man's first death and returns, not as a ghost but as a decently ordered spook, rapping tables and talking through trumpets in accordance with the rules. From this point of view there is much to be said for public schools.

From any other point of view there is very little to be said—so little that I could put it in a few sentences. The question exercises the mind of the Scottish parent a good deal. The English parent who can beg, borrow or steal three or four hundred a year has, of course, no alternative but to send his son to a public school or something like it.

I went into this question rather fully some time ago with the idea of helping my fellow countrymen in Scotland to come to a wise decision. The general problem is : how the little Glasgow bourgeois may be fitted to take a distinguished part in the Drift South which appears to be his destiny ; or, alternatively, if he is unlucky enough to have to stay at home, how he may be taught suitably to impress the other natives. The most popular method is to send him to an English public school. It is presumed that in these places he will make influential friends and become tough in his physique and genteel in his manner and speech. Several substitutes for the English public school have been instituted in Scotland and staffed by English university graduates ; but it is rightly supposed that these, or most of them, are far from being the real thing. I have known boys who had been educated at the most expensive boarding schools who still retained traces of a Scottish accent—a very unsatisfactory return for all that expense.

During my investigations I found quite a number of Scotsmen who had made what is called "good" in England without a public school education of any kind whatever. I found an Archbishop, three or four baronets, seven knights, four persons who had made themselves noblemen by their own exertions, seven right honourables and many acknowledged leaders of the Church, Big Business, the Bar, the Stage, Literature, Politics, Medicine, Sport, Aviation, Engineering, War, Art, and Homeopathy. There appears to be plenty of room at the top for a Scotsman who has *not* been to an English public school. Why is this? I am afraid that our Scottish parents do not quite understand the English Caste System. It works out something like this in practice. The theory would take too long to explain.

Residence at Eton, Harrow or Winchester entitles one to become a Foreign Secretary, a Governor-General, a Chairman of Directors.

Residence at Rugby, Marlborough, Uppingham, Oundle or Charterhouse entitles one to become an Under-Secretary of State, an Editor, a Managing Director, a Leading Actor.

Residence anywhere else entitles one to a post in the Civil Service, the Army, the Navy or the Air Force ; a branch managership ; or a job with the films or in the advertising business.

This system makes things very easy for the Englishman. Whoever bears the Hallmark is quite simply allotted to his pigeon-hole. The Englishman generously allows any Welshman, Scotsman or Irishman who is able to pay two hundred a year for a workhouse diet, casual supervision, Gothic sanitation and a monastic or totalitarian regime, to become a Putative English Gentleman and take his chance in the appropriate queue. In the case of foreigners under the Flag, who remain unstamped by the Hallmark, his task is not so easy. He gets over his difficulty by thinking imperially. This means that the uncouth Colonial, with his strange American, Australian, German or Scottish accent, is often taken *pro magnifico* and actually given precedence over the Etonian himself. A very good thing.

My thesis being correct—and a very perfunctory study of *Who's Who* will show you that it is—it is obviously a bad investment to send one's child to Greystones or St. Bude's simply because of the pretty blazers and neck-ties they entitle him to wear and the beautiful accent and off-hand manners with which they endow him. When he grows up, it is true, he will have a certain advantage if circumstances compel him to remain in a Scottish city. That is to say, he will enjoy the society of other synthetic exiles of his grade, he will be able to speak to enormously rich people without embarrassment and he will have opportunities of taking part in the best kind of dancing and shooting available in his district. He may even collect a specimen or two of the Scottish Toady ; and of all toadies, none is so satisfying, abnegatory and complete at every point as the Scottish Toady. But, after all, these are but shallow satisfactions compared with a house in Park Lane, a Tudor residence in Dorsetshire, one's name in the papers and a good balance at the bank. For of such is the Kingdom of Heaven.

Apart from the reasons at which I have hinted, I can think of no other respectable reason for sending one's son to a public school. In Scotland we do not regard a person as belonging to the sweeper or untouchable caste because he has been educated by an Education Authority. On the other hand we do not rate highly the Scotsman who has succeeded in becoming an Englishman, unless his Rugby is exceptionally good. We are too apt to search him too closely for signs of affectation; and in Scotland alien affectations are treated very harshly indeed. We are kinder to our own. A foreign gentleman in Argyle Street, Glasgow, asked of two citizens the way to the Municipal Buildings. One citizen said to the other,

" What's he saying? "

The other replied,
" I'm jiggered if I ken."
The first citizen said,
" Ca' the perisher's feet frae under him! "
My father still laboured with me. There were two
things he said and repeated that made his task more
difficult and were very offensive to me. One was, " You
will realise when you are older . . . " The other was,
" No really first rate intelligence ever argues." We
used to argue the latter point at great length. We still
went for long walks and I was not so exhausted as I had
been in the earlier cycle, when the sight of a bus or a
tram in the fading light was like a sail to a mariner
adrift on a raft. We were pathetically anxious not to
bore one another. I know now that I must have bored
him more than he did me. He was a man with a richly
stored mind, and he could not help being interesting
even when he was at his most instructive. My mind
was an imbecile rag-bag, and yet I dared to criticise
him. We walked a good deal to Macaulay Stevenson's
house, Robinsfield, and once out to the Mearns where
we saw Neil Munro playing on his chanter. In the
evenings we played chess or billiards.

Sometimes my uncle Alexander Osborne came round
to play billiards with my father. He was a bailie, and
one of the noblest looking old men I have ever seen.
His picture by Guthrie is in the City collection, with
the paint on his beautiful white whiskers gradually
growing black, because Guthrie's paint merchant did
him a bad turn about that period. He gave me a respect
for bailies which it has taken me years to lose. Indeed,
I have not yet entirely lost it and still call bailies " sir "
when I speak to them. He was my mother's uncle and
was the head of a firm of cheese merchants of whom I
have already told you. He ought to have been Lord
Provost, but the weight of that office entails stooping

under certain low lintels, and my grand-uncle never stooped.

I am groping desperately for memories and can find nothing but the click of the billiard balls when I was falling asleep. There was something voluptuous about the continuous broken rhythm of the sounds—like modern verse. I liked verse at that time and even wrote a little. Whether it was Beetle or whether it was my father who was responsible Browning was my favourite. I did not know what he was talking about, but I found him intoxicating. He never let me go to sleep, syllable after syllable he kicked me on ; and while I appreciated the rosy coma induced by Swinburne and Tennyson, I liked the other sort better.

I was under the impression that I was a very cultivated kind of youth. I felt it my duty to open new horizons for a neighbouring lad, an early Pictish person of narrow interests. We used to walk out to Anniesland while I expounded to him the beauties of English literature and illuminated them with my own reflections. He was an earnest fellow. In six months he had read all the books that I had read or heard of, and when he began to discourse to me on the novel *Rasselas*, by Dr. Samuel Johnson, of which I had only heard in casual conversation, I answered him flippantly and was rebuked by him for taking these grave matters too lightly. It was a lesson to me. One should never teach the tiger cub to fight.

My relations with Foreign Powers grew in friendliness. I met with fewer affronts to my dignity and began to think well of myself. Even members of the fifteen would sometimes walk in the street with me. I felt a little concerned, however, about my brother Jack. If I came on a howling mob in the playground, I could be almost certain to find my brother in the narrow internal circle, fighting. He fought badly with wide sawing motions of his fists. He was stronger than I was, but I could usually beat him in our private fights. He got angry too soon.

I thought these public flailing exhibitions highly improper. Like most school fights outside fiction they ended in a draw and I had not the consolation of looking upon Jack as a sort of hero. He developed also at this time a vein of buffoonery very distasteful to me. He would even eat lavatory soap for a bet. He retrieved himself a little by winning the under fifteen high jump but not before he had done serious damage to my *amour propre*. My own friends erred if anything on the side of stateliness. They included a youth who called himself Lord Brown of Polmadeerie, though his father was the minister of St. George's Church. Lord Brown's humour had a grandeur not untinged with malice. One night the College Church went on fire and was burned to the ground. The son of its pastor was John Reith. At the school devotions in the morning Lord Brown turned to Sir John and said,

" Arson is a pretty serious matter, John. I hope your father finds himself properly compensated under his insurance policy."

The later part of the third cycle crackles across the years like thorns under a pot. Apart from Dab Cricket I seem to have spent a good proportion of it in laughing.

" You have a silent chuckle," Jamie Wood once said to me, " don't do it. The silent chuckler usually finishes his career with the detective's hand on his shoulder."

But, indeed, there seemed to me to be many boys who were very excellent drolls; and nowhere more than in the congenial atmosphere of the Cadet Corps.

The Cadet Corps was a product of the Great South African War. The intolerable conduct of President Kruger came to a head in 1899 when I was eleven years of age. The very foundations of the British Empire were shaken and it became necessary to make a demonstration. This necessity found me wholeheartedly on the side of the Government. I collected little celluloid buttons on which the photographs of great generals and even colonels were ingeniously printed, often on a background of the Union Jack. I followed the manifestations of their strategic and tactical genius with the deepest interest. Among them was Sir Archibald Hunter, a Glasgow Academy boy, who helped Sir George White to defend Ladysmith, and who was later to encourage the Cadet Corps to the extent of appearing in a cocked hat with feathers and a blue frock uniform to inspect it in the playground. I remember his speech.

" Boys, you are brave and strong. I know that you are strong because I look at your knees. I know that you are brave because you are Scotch boys. My word to you is the word given by Nelson to one of his midshipmen. ' Fear God, honour the King and hate your Nation's enemies like the very devil.' "

In the years before we heard that speech we already hated our Nation's enemies, and particularly President Kruger ; for, indeed, he had a hateful face. It was the type of face I was later to associate with LARGE WHITE KIDNEY, but I had never seen a kidney except on the breakfast table. *Tous connaître est tous comprendre*— and yet there was no excuse for that hat or for those evil whiskers growing from under the chin

I was deeply disturbed during those dark days of General Buller's superhuman efforts to reach Ladysmith. My sportsmanship was daily outraged by the methods used by the Boers to impede him. Great British victories are won by laws, written or unwritten, that were dreadfully traversed by these unclean and bearded men. I cannot say that I ever lost faith in

Buller though, as the months rolled on, I could not help thinking that if he shaved off his moustache and grew whiskers and a top hat he would compare almost unfavourably with the Dictator of the Transvaal himself. No one, of course, could accuse him of cowardice and we could and did accuse Oom Paul of that.

My interest in the war was passionate yet detached, as if I had been reading of a test match in Australia. The war was played principally by professionals and did not touch very closely my immediate circle. We had from time to time visits from colonels of Engineers and lieutenants of Artillery, but there was very little blood in their stories, and most of them had never seen a Boer. My cousin, Ronald Bridie, was an officer in Kitchener's Horse. He was a great friend of Jack's and mine and had even been to the Glasgow Academy. When he came back at the end of the war we hoped for better things, for he was a real fighting man. Unfortunately his experiences consisted mainly in going about from place to place on horseback, and he could have done that without going to a war. The bursting of a lyddite shell, he said, turns surrounding objects a yellowish-green. This, of all he told us, is the fact that stands out most strongly in my memory. It was pleasant, however, to go into Princess Louise's Convalescent Home at Rosneath with Ronald and see the wounded soldiers stand to attention when we entered.

A further recollection of the Boer War is a concert organised by my aunt for the War Fund. I wore a khaki felt hat turned up at the side and sold programmes. There was a real bugler from the barracks. Mr. Craighall Sherry, who was to become a star in the silent films and to create brilliantly several parts in my plays, recited " The Absent-minded Beggar."

On Mafeking night some of my father's younger and more ebullient friends hired a landau and my brother and I went with them down to George Square. Curiously enough I remember very little of what happened. I have one picture of a group of young men standing on a window sill of the Anchor Line offices in St. Vincent Street. They saw our Academy caps and waved huge planks of wood they had torn from somewhere and cheered for the old school. It was a proud moment. Tears came unbidden to my eyes.

The War petered out in some sort of unsatisfactory fashion in 1902, but we had learnt its lesson. The boys of the Glasgow Academy realised that they must train themselves to defend that Empire which had so recently escaped away like a bird from the fowler's snare and broken the teeth of its formidable foes. I was fourteen now, and was quite grown up. I had embraced the principles of the Liberal Party. Nevertheless I rushed to the colours. The authorities did one damned silly thing that tarnished the gilt on the gingerbread. When it came to designing uniforms for the Corps they devised a heather-mixture tunic with the idea that it might later be transformed into a civilian jacket for use with the kilt in those happier days when swords would be beaten into ploughshares and spears into pruning hooks. We should have preferred khaki. Our rifles were no Boys' Brigade tin guns, but real D. P. Lee-Metford carbines, which could fire blank and be fitted with a Morris tube. Our officer was Peter Couper, a strong-faced man who taught English on rather stereotyped lines. Our instructor was Sam Stewart, the gymnastic master, who was said to have led Lord Roberts to Kandahar. Our non-commissioned officers were recruited, not from the nobility and gentry of the school, but from those who took the amusing business seriously. There was thus little interference with our simple pleasures. The leading buffoons had a perfect *mise en scene* and a fine clear run for their money.

When King Edward VII and Queen Alexandra came to Glasgow (Queen Victoria must have died in the interval, but I cannot remember the incident) the Cadet Corps lined the road somewhere in the Maryhill district. Alfred Roemelle, one of the nobility and gentry and a German on his father's side, made me ill with laughing and I had to relieve my feelings by dropping the butt of my carbine on the toes of needy urchins who tried to push past the cordon. The King and Queen looked more like huge wax models than anything I have ever seen in Madame Tussaud's, but the thought that they were the descendants of long lines of princes was very moving, and my hand trembled as I clasped my carbine to my abdomen in their honour.

Then there were the field days. These were of two kinds, private field days and public field days. The private field days happened in the estate of Sir Archibald Campbell of Succoth—no, in the estate of his mother, Lady Campbell of Garscube—and they were incredible affairs. It was usually arranged that the buffoons should be detached from the main action on some pretext or other. Lord Brown organised them into shoots, and we brought down hundreds of brace of imaginary winged creatures with our blank cartridges. If we were drawn perforce into a battle, as sometimes happened, Lord Brown and Roemelle used to stalk Sam Stewart, instructing each other in harsh whispers to hold their fire till they saw the whites of his eyes. When they had done the deed and fired at him point-blank at about five yards range they heeded neither his rebukes nor his orders on the ground that he was dead, and they took no orders from casualties. These were beautiful days under shaded pastures and beside trotting waters.

93

On the public field days we fought with the first Volunteer Battalion the Highland Light Infantry, who were our guardian angels, and whose tartan we wore. These were sterner affairs and were fought over moorlands somewhere in the coal belt. We carried twelve rounds of blank and advanced by short rushes. We finished at the railway station with pies and lemonade, which were very welcome for we were very tired. The public field days were a serious matter. They contained some of the realities of war. A small proportion of the enemy got drunk and had to be carried to the train by their scarlet coated comrades.

We showed further consciousness that we had a part to play in adult life by forming a debating society. The forces of derision were strong here, too. James Rose used to write his speeches on enormous rolls of toilet paper, and Roemelle, during a political debate in which he was Chancellor of the Exchequer, had to confess that he did not know what the Income Tax was.

" But," he said, " I know more about politics than these bloody Liberals. All they can do is to sit there in a row with their mouths open like Chick France at the international."

The intellectuals were all Liberals. Their leader was Boyd Henderson, who regularly scored a hundred and ten per cent. in all English examinations. He was supported by Lord Brown, whose family was of a Liberal tradition, and by Tom Lindsay. This little cave was in the fifth. The sixth were all solid men. The President was the captain of the Fifteen, and the expulsion of the buffoons was an easy enough matter. The buffoons were also in the fifth. My own speciality was local option. It seemed to me a typically Liberal measure, with all the principles of enlightened and democratic compulsion at their best and going full blast. On a broader basis I was a Whig because, while the Tories in their foreign politics were accustomed to bully and destroy weaker nations and truckle to great ones, the Liberals courted and idealised weaker nations and were always ready to fling the whole might of the army and navy against nations qualified to give them a decent fair fight. The revolution of puberty had, you will notice, brought me disillusion about the South African War. Nothing could exceed the contempt I felt for Mr. Balfour or my hatred for Mr. Chamberlain. Puddock Carruthers, the captain and a Tory, went with me to hear Mr. Chamberlain open his Tariff Reform Campaign in the St. Andrew's Hall in Glasgow.

The hall was packed to the ceiling ; the organ was playing ; the Arthur Balfour Choir was singing patriotic songs. I stood like an icicle beside the glowing Puddock and despised it all. When the great Joe Chamberlain appeared on the platform, orchid, monocle and all, I sneered. I should not have sneered, for I was a polite little boy ; but if I had put up no barrier against those billows of emotion I should have dissolved into my component parts. I hated Mr. Chamberlain with all the energy of which I was capable. I was delighted to find that he was not a very good speaker. His voice was monotonous and commonplace, and his gestures dull and theatrical. I thought the orchid and the monocle stage properties and the rigid shoulders and iron stare an assumption intended to give impressiveness and courage to an essentially timid man. This was the judgement of a boy of fifteen, and I do not know how far it was correct.

. . . .

"*It was incorrect,*" *said Ian Hay.* "*And I am not surprised that it should be so. You were not, in any accepted sense, a schoolboy at all. If you had been to Fettes, I cannot help thinking we should have made something more tolerable of you.*"

" *You would have knocked the conceit out of me?* "

" *By no means,*" *said Ian Hay.* "*We never attempted the impossible. But we should have made you more conscious of a comity and more convinced of the necessity for action.*"

" *Gracious Heavens, what do I keep telling you blokes?* " *I said testily.* " *I am trying to prove that there is little or no necessity for any more activity than is provided by physiology and the instinct for self preservation. How can you see things if you go rushing around?* "

" *I cannot find much evidence that you have seen anything at all,*" *said Ian Hay,* " *or heard very much except a few very ordinary jokes.*"

" *You pedagogues,*" *I said, not liking his tone,* " *arrange matters so that your charges may see or hear as little as possible that is likely to interest them. Now, when I went up to the University . . .* "

" *I hope that when you went up to the University you had a good time and that you will be able to convey it,*" *said Ian Hay.* " *In the meantime I must leave you. I may not give the impression of being a busy man, but I am one.*"

CHAPTER IV

The Fourth Five

THE FOURTH FIVE BEGAN when I was still at school, but
in the early months of it I had already made prepara-
tions for the change. I sat my preliminary examinations in medicine. I got through French by reading
The Three Musketeers and *The Miserables* in bed at night
with a dictionary. I got through English by making
it up out of my head and bluffing the examiners as I had
bluffed the neighbour lad. I got through Mathematics by the grace of God. I do not know how I got
through Latin.

I had found a delightful equilibrium. I had even
found a kind of Rugby that I could play, in the third
fifteen at the back row of the forwards. My practice
with caricature made me sufficiently feared to be
immune from insult. I had a good many friends.

My father took me to the university to see his old
friend and teacher, John Cleland. The professor was
a man of great age and the largest head in Britain. He
was professor of Anatomy. He had a large mop of

sheep's wool on his head. It was said that this was
kept in position with the fat of human corpses, for,
while he was demonstrating, he would frequently
run his fingers through his hair. His large bearded face
was like that of a faun. I shall have more to say about
him. His advice to my father was that I should start
with practical anatomy and let everything else go for
six months. He was confident that he would make an
anatomist of me.

The next visit was to the banker. My father opened
an account for me, I left a specimen of my signature
and took away a cheque-book and a pass-book, and the
privilege of drawing anything up to five pounds a
month. I was to buy books and clothes with this. I
asked permission to smoke and was granted it. I
bought a pipe and a packet of Murray's Belfast
Mixture. Life had begun in earnest.

. . . .

I promised in the first chapter that I would make my
hero as attractive as possible. I showed the earlier
sheets of this work to my brother Eric, and what he
said shook my confidence that I had been successful.
He told me that I had fortified the impression he himself had of me in these early years, namely, that I was
a self-satisfied, spoilt, indifferent little devil, with no
gratitude in my composition. He said that I got the
best of everything and that my brothers had to be content with the leavings; he said that I gave no sign of
appreciating these benefits. Like most truths, these
opinions, baldly stated, were very unfair. To a pre-
judiced eye I was an anaemic little emperor, languidly
receiving gifts from my betters, choosing some
capriciously and tossing others aside, taking it all as a
right and appreciating not at all the labour and loyalty
that had won these gifts for me. If this is the light in

which my childhood and boyhood appear I do not
know how you are going to take the next period. I
must correct the impression as far as I can.

I was not indifferent. I was an affectionate creature
—so affectionate that the extraordinary sensations in
the pit of my stomach used to overwhelm me and make
me feel quite ill. I feared them. I feared even more
the certainty that if I pushed up pseudopodia of
sentiment towards my fellow creatures they would
certainly be trodden upon sooner or later. I looked
like an ape and muttered and mumbled in my speech.
I knew that and did not expect to be liked. I did not
take the affection of my home circle for granted but I
knew I could count on it. The trouble was that I was
afraid of it too. I was afraid it would make me cry,
and I shunned it in all its demonstrations. I secreted
a shell and retired into it.

I do not think I was ungrateful to my father and
mother, though a survey of my behaviour and actions
certainly suggests that I was. They saw very little
return for the intelligent care and loving kindness they
expended on me and of the gifts they would gladly have
given me I utilised very few. But I can see all along
the line unexpected places where the things they taught
me have stopped a bullet or held me up in a quagmire.
My father did not make me a scholar and a scientist,
but he gave me a curious code of honour which I have
seldom transgressed, and a faculty for enjoying the
manifestations of greatness, goodness and workman-
ship whenever I meet them. My mother did not make
me a good or a methodical man, but she taught me
tolerance and loyalty. In my first twenty-five years
appreciation, tolerance and loyalty kept breaking out
in spite of me. I may have been repulsive, but I was
not bad. Please remember this.

.   .   .   .

The University of Glasgow is a hideous building set on a magnificent site. It stands at the top of Gilmorehill and looks south over the river, with its tall derricks and its moving masts and funnels. On either side of the river are smoking slums and beyond it green hills. The neighbouring hill to the east contains noble terraces, built on the Blythswood estate by the merchant princes of Glasgow. In the valley below and between these hills is the Kelvingrove Park. From the top of the tower one can see the Highlands, and, on a clear day, Ben Nevis. The building is arranged round two dingy quadrangles. In one of these the authorities have recently erected a dirty army hut and they have closed the open end of the other with a memorial chapel of somewhat perfunctory architecture. Neither the hut nor the chapel was there when I went to the place first, and only about half of the buildings which now disfigure the hill were built.

I put on a new four-and-sixpenny bowler hat, stood in a queue at the Registrar's office, registered myself as a medical student and bought a matriculation ticket and two tickets admitting me to the lectures in junior anatomy and the dissecting room. I then went over through smelly catacombs to a dingy little building at the north gate and joined the Union. I also joined a different kind of union called The Christian Union, partly because an old Academy boy immensely senior to me and an ex-member of the fifteen had come specially to my house to canvass me.

After an interval of a day or two I attended my first lecture. The anatomy lecture room was like most other lecture rooms of the day, a large, cold, tiered, dirty uncomfortable place, with a sort of bar at the foot behind which the professor would shortly appear. It was full of students, all older than me, for the class of anatomy was seldom taken earlier than the second session. They were singing a hymn, shouting and throwing balls of blotting paper at each other. Every now and again a student would be lifted from the front bench and passed up over the heads of his fellows to the back bench; or, alternatively, a student would be picked up from the back bench and passed rapidly down to the professor's bar. One had just arrived there with his nose bleeding, his collar about his ears and only one shoe when the door opened and the professor shuffled in. He took no notice of the student, who made his way hurriedly to a seat, but bowed to the class with a courtly grace. The class responded by beating the floor with its feet and cheering loudly. There was a silence after this and the professor, supporting himself on his fists, began to read the roll.

" Mr. Adams . . . Mr. Allan . . . Mr. John Allan . . . Mr. Arkieson . . . Mr. Abrahams . . . Mr. Andrew Campbell . . . Mr. Allan Campbell . . . Mr. Alistair Campbell . . . Mr. David Campbell . . . Mr. John Campbell . . . The Campbells are not coming to-day." (*Applause, acknowledged by the professor with bows and smiles.*) " . . . Mr. A. MacDonald . . . Mr. A. J. MacDonald . . . Mr. Alistair MacDonald . . . Mr. Donald MacDonald . . . Mr. Donald F. MacDonald . . . Mr. Donald R. MacDonald . . . Mr. Donald T. MacDonald. . . I don't believe there was ever a massacre of Glen Coe."

The list closed with Mr. Yellowlees, and the first lecture began. It was a very extraordinary affair.

Johnny Cleland had been taught by Goodsir, who had been taught by Knox, who was the patron of Burke and Hare. He used to refer to his late distinguished predecessor, Dr. Alan Thomson, who had been in his grave these forty years, and who had owed at least some of his material to the resurrection men. He had one personal devil with horns and a tail—the late Mr.

Huxley, who had been in his grave for less than ten years, but who had crossed Johnny Cleland's path in the middle of the previous century.

"A certain humble individual of whom you may have heard, his name was John Cleland, had one day many years ago the intimidating privilege of addressing for the first time The Royal Society on certain investigations he had made, this humble individual, on the embryological origins and anatomy of the *gubernaculum testis*. And he was as you know and imagine in a pitiful state of trepidation, or to put it plainly, in a blue funk. His hands were shaking, his knees were knocking together and he did not know whether he was standing on his head or his heels. However, by the mercy of Providence, he struggled to the end of his thesis; and Mr. Richard Owen, who with all his faults was a gentleman, commented very kindly on poor Cleland's work. He was followed by a fellow of the Royal Society to whom that description gentleman does not apply. Mr. Huxley, instead of extending to the young, bashful and diffident member of his profession the courtesy and kindness he had a right to expect, referred to me in his opening sentence as a ' provincial anatomist '!!! Now, Gentlemen, if you don't know already the sort of man Mr. Huxley was, you ought to. He was a ridiculous fellow. An ignorant, aggressive, impudent fellow. . . ."

At this point he would take a fit. Quite often the very name of Mr. Huxley would induce a fit. These fits were very alarming at first. They were a mild variety of the falling sickness. His voice would become incoherent and murmuring. His monstrous head would swing back and then fall forward on his chest; his mouth would twitch and the saliva would run from it; he would reach for a chair, pull it under him and sit down. Sometimes he slid down the wall and sat on the floor. He would gasp for a few moments and shake his woolly mane and recover. He would then apologise and proceed with his lecture. He told us these fits occurred because his *foramen magnum* was too small for the size of his head. The *foramen magnum* is the large hole through which the spinal cord passes out of the cranial vault. It was of the *foramen magnum* that a medical student, reflecting Hamlet-wise, said, " Many a good drink has gone down through that hole."

Be that as it may, Johnny Cleland always took a fit when he mentioned Huxley. Anything else that enraged him was apt to bring on an attack, but this always succeeded. We never knew his true opinion of Huxley, for, when he began, his seizure invariably interrupted him. We gathered that his opinion was not high. We gathered also that he thought little of Evolution and Natural Selection; but, as he always prefaced any remarks he had to make on these subjects by a reference to Huxley, we were left in ignorance as to what he thought.

We were left in ignorance as to a good many other things he wished to impart to us. It is impossible to give in print any idea of his peculiar turn of speech. He lisped a great deal and separated his syllables in such a way that the word Adams, for instance, appeared to contain at least four—" Aa-du-am-aza." Some of his students made a steady reputation as entertainers by imitating him. Added to this he spoke as if he had a large toffee ball in his mouth. If he had not had the habit of illustrating his rhetoric with gestures we should have had little idea of what he was talking about at all; but he would show us how the *sartorius* muscle was used in the game Ring-a-roses by leaping round the floor with his knees bent, clasping the hands of imaginary partners and singing the words of the song. He had also a wonderful impersonation of a lion eating a bone, and differentiated this cleverly from a leopard's method of eating a bone. The bone was seized between the professor's two paws, and the professor mumbled it with furious growls.

I have mentioned fits of rage at other objects than Huxley. Such an object was George Fletcher at an oral examination. Fletcher held, probably correctly, that no gentleman passed his examination in anatomy at the first attempt. While he was waiting for his *viva voce* he read *I Will Repay*, by the Baroness Orczy and resigned himself to his fate. His fate was as follows. Johnny chassé-ed up to him concealing all but a tiny portion of a human bone under the lapel of his morning coat and said,

" Now, Mr. Fletcher, if you were to see this bone coming along the street, how would you accost it? "

FLETCHER: " I beg your pardon, sir? "

JOHNNY: " What bone is it, Mr. Fletcher? "

FLETCHER: " I shouldn't like to dogmatise on the subject, doctor, but I should say it was the ulna."

JOHNNY: " Without committing yourself to dogma in any way, Mr. Fletcher, could you hazard a guess as to which ulna? "

FLETCHER: " I don't want to stake my professional reputation on it, doctor, but I suggest that it is the right ulna."

JOHNNY: " Would it surprise you to know, Mr. Fletcher, that it is the left ulna? "

FLETCHER: " Nothing surprises me in anatomy, doctor."

JOHNNY: " Mr. Fletcher, I have taught medical students in Galway, in Dublin, in London, in Edinburgh and in Glasgow. My experience of them is that one is more lazy, idle and impertinent than another. GET TO HELL OUT OF HERE, SIR! "

104

When I had heard the sound of Johnny's first lecture for an hour I went with two of my seniors down to the anatomy room. It was unlike what I had expected.

The peculiar odour of mortality and disinfectants was not matched by any similar odours during the war and has to-day lost a good many of its characteristics. It reached as far as the quadrangle doorway and became thicker as we descended the dark spiral steps to the lavatory. We went along a short dark passage and through a swing door into a big brightly lighted hall. On twenty tables or so corpses were lying in the attitude of the daily dozen in which the devotee lies on his back and makes pedalling movements in the air. The corpses were naked and bronze coloured. The general effect was rather gay. My head swam a little and I had an impulse of flight. A Japanese coming out of the end room where he had been examined in osteology by Dr. Hutton, the assistant, smacked a corpse on the abdomen with a cheery greeting and passed on. My friends and I crossed the room and reported to the senior demonstrator, a haggard chain-smoker with a black skull cap. He told me I must learn my bones before I would be allowed to dissect, but allotted me an arm in advance. He then dismissed me to Stewart, the attendant ghoul who looked like a corpse himself and wore a deep sea sailor's hat and a long black leather apron. Stewart showed me a locker without a word and told me to put my instruments in it and charged me eighteenpence.

I hurried to the fresh air and coffee in the Union. Another cycle was to roll over my head before I should be free of the anatomy room.

My seniors were very good to me and made me free of their company. To begin with they were old boys from the Glasgow Academy, and I got the impression

from them that, while I might associate with the better
sort of High School boy, I could do myself little good
by mixing with the riffraff and ragtag and bobtail who
had been unfortunate in their early education. I was
content with this for at least a year. Adams, Roemelle
and Brown were contemporaries of my own and medical
students. John Morris Walker and Tom Watt were
also medical students who had played in the fifteen
when I was a mere child. Strathie, who had also been
in the fifteen, was in Arts, but friendly, and there were
many others. I was introduced to a very pleasing
group of medical students who were high-brows and
took their coffee in Hubbard's because it was better
coffee than what they got in the Union. The group
included Albert Patterson, Tam Morrison, Adam
Patrick, R. M. F. Picken and John Kinloch. With
this group and others I talked of this and that and
ranged far out into the infinities. Although at this
stage I did not make many acquaintances I could
always find enough conversation to make it unnecessary
for me to attend my lecture or my dissecting room with
any regularity. In the evenings I sometimes went out
and sometimes stayed at home. I had been promoted
to a room of my own at the top of the house. It had an
open fireplace and a large fire. I used to spread
Cleland and MacKay's *Anatomy* on my knees and go to
sleep.

On other evenings I used to attend the parties that
were common to that time and that city. I went to the
house of one or other of my friends who had sisters at
eight o'clock. The dress was morning dress. I was
shown into the drawing-room and found a number of
people of both sexes sitting round the room. I shook
hands with my hostess and told her how my parents
were. I then sat down as far away from anybody else
as possible. Almost immediately somebody was asked

to sing. This made me happy, no matter what the
song, for I was not compelled to talk. I could talk in
Hubbard's and in the Union, but in a drawing-room
never. The songs varied a good deal in quality and
were seldom perfectly executed; but it was pleasant to
sit among friendly disposed people and listen to them.
Occasionally somebody recited, for we did not despise
recitations in those days. I had at that time invented
two songs and was sometimes forced to sing one or
other of them to my own accompaniment, and to wish
I were dead. If there weren't enough talented people,
games like consequences, clubs or telegrams were
played, and sometimes livelier games like hunting the
slipper or spinning the plate. There was no dancing.
At about ten we adjourned to the dining-room and
were given a sort of buffet supper which included
trifle and lemonade. I found these functions, as I say,
very enjoyable and grew very fond of the people I met
at them, though I seldom exchanged two words with
them.

At home we had our diversions. We had parties
like those I have described for my brothers and me, and
my parents were at home every Monday night to their
friends. I found my parents' parties much more
delightful than my own. They attracted some good
musicians and some pleasant talkers, and it was not
necessary for me to take any part in them whatever,
beyond handing round the tea-cups.

I went a good deal to the play; but I could not abide
plays in which there was no music or dancing, unless
they were funny or by Shakespeare. My judgement
was probably correct. I cannot help thinking that the
straight or problem plays of the period were the most
tedious form of composition that the mind of man has
ever invented. I saw Irving only three times. He was
playing *The Bells* and *Waterloo*, *Coriolanus*, and finally

Becket. We are all born dramatic critics, but I came to no judgement of Irving. I accepted him. He is almost the only public figure I have ever accepted blindly without passing him first through a crude sieve of criticism and ridicule. I suppose this is a tribute to his greatness. He seemed to me to be nothing but Irving and never suggested the character he was intended to represent; but that queer figure was enough for me. He seems to have been enough for all of us—even for Mr. Shaw, though he kicked against the pricks.

I saw Tree's *Hamlet*, but I think at an earlier period. I thought little of it, but was captured by his *Svengali*, though not by his curiously Hebraic *Colonel Newcome*. You see, I had read the book. I saw several musical comedies by the ideal method. The ideal method is to go to the gallery at nine o'clock and leave at ten. This has the added advantage that sometimes the box office is shut and it is not necessary to pay.

Two ladies took me to see Sir Frank Benson in his dressing room. It was the first time I had been behind the scenes, and was to be the last for many a year. Benson talked, I think, about Physical Fitness. He was in the costume of Petruchio. He was not a young man then, but his eye glowed when he talked of swimming in icy rivers, running rapidly from place to place before breakfast, leaping obstacles, climbing trees and rone-pipes and playing a game called hockey. How he enjoyed playing Petruchio, by the way! It was astonishing to see that lean intellectual manhandling his wife and doing acrobatics with the furniture in one of the earliest James Cagney parts ever written. James Cagney was not then born; but when next Rheinhardt gets his clutches on him I hope it will be in *The Shrew*. For Katherine I should like one of these young ladies who earn a living by being tossed from

hand to hand on the music hall stage. I should like to
see the London critics sniffing at that! For some reason
or other they affect to despise *The Shrew*. So do not I.
It is one of the rare Shakespeare comedies in which he
is consistently funny.

I saw also *Peter Pan*. The actress who played the
part was Cissie Loftus. She sang a song by R. L.
Stevenson which has since dropped out of the canon.
It was " All round the House is the Jet Black Night."
It followed on the line " My old bones would rattle."
It was the most delicious thing in the play. I re-
member thinking that at the time, though Peter Pan
had quite captured me. I knew the play by heart.
When Seymour Hicks after many years was cast for
the part of Captain Hook he told me that the part had
been written for him, but that he had never seen the
play since the first night. I offered to take him
through the part word for word without the book, and
I could have done it. But he did not accept my offer.
I had my revenge by not going to see him as Captain
Hook. I have not seen *Peter Pan* for thirty years.

I have an idea now that I was wrong in admiring it.
Boys who never grow up are not agreeable characters
in real life. Barrie should have been better grounded
in the doctrine of Original Sin than to have invented
such a character. He observed truly, but deliberately
obscured the cruelty, irresponsibility and lies which
were the principal features of his matchless boy. It
was unfair to make these qualities attractive by having
the part played by a series of enchanting actresses.
The whole business was a deliberate twisting of morals,
and was much more vicious than any of the timorous
goose-booings in *The Yellow Book*. I liked *The Yellow
Book* too, not, I think, because it was vicious. I
didn't like *Peter Pan* because it was vicious; but I had
a strong taste for the fantastic at that time, and I liked

my fantasy properly done. It was well done in *Peter Pan*, though there are lapses.

I was not such a fool even then as to confuse cleverness with genius. I did not think there was genius in *The Yellow Book*, and the writings of Mr. Wilde made me sick, but I thought I detected genius in J. M. Barrie. Genius is denied him by the commentators as it is to every great literary figure who has died since the war. Perhaps the two Lawrences, D. H. and T. E., are exceptions. They have passed into Valhalla with equivocal sort of pencil marks on them that might be interpreted as testimonials. Barrie, Kipling, Galsworthy, Chesterton, George Moore, Bridges, Thomas Hardy, Conrad, all the notable literary figures in England who were so injudicious as to survive into this pernickety period, have been put firmly in their places as men of talent, perhaps, but of limited intelligence and no distinction. In the beginning of the twentieth century they seemed splendid fellows to me and, whatever genius may be, I thought they had it.

Barrie's genius was a ticklish business. The things for which he has been praised are as little authentic as the things for which he has been blamed. What is called his " stage craft " for instance, is very good, but it is quite within the compass of anybody who takes the trouble to devote himself to theatrical tricks. If you study the use of the window curtain in *Dear Brutus* and find out when and why it is opened and shut you will readily come to understand why professional playwrights admire his adroitness. But that adroitness sprang from the exigencies of the naturalistic play and the box stage. It was a mere manipulation of material, and a good many people could and can do it better. The genius is a person who does something that nobody else can do or even imitate.

Barrie distorted values and played the spiritual nudist in blue limelight [1] with an aplomb that nobody since Sterne has been able to approach in our language; but that was not his title to genius. I think his title to genius exists in this: that he was the only legitimate descendant of the ballad writers. In the midst of a long succession of posturings he would suddenly make a gesture that raised the hair on the scalp. I have never been able to make anybody see this, but that is because few people nowadays have any appreciation of the ballads further than that which accepts them as crude and lively stories. We have a blind spot to their real magic—that drawing aside quickly and as suddenly dropping back of the veil before we have time to see what is beyond. These moments in the ballads and the curious sardonic ecstasy with which their singers relish the knowledge of the things they have to show us if they would, are to be found in Barrie. He only once lets them have anything like full play—in *Farewell Miss Julie Logan*. This was the story that Stevenson was trying to write all his life and couldn't. He hadn't the gift. It is the ballad quality that makes *Mary Rose* so inescapable. You may find *Mary Rose* contemptible or even hateful but it haunts you. It certainly does not haunt you because it is about a ghost or because it is a very inferior and journalistic adaptation of Hogg's *Kilmeny*. It haunts you because of an atmosphere that Barrie seemed to do his best to destroy with his dolly domesticities on connubialities, but the atmosphere

---

[1] The censorship of plays, like all survivals in themselves essentially ridiculous, is kept alive by a curious and complicated system of rules and regulations. Under one of these rules an actress may appear on the stage naked to the waist, or apparently so, under two conditions. The first is that she may not move; the second is that if she does move she must be lit entirely by blue light. The use of amber lighting subjects all concerned to a heavy fine.

was there. He got it in a way in which Hogg would have given his eyes to get it, and Hogg had the ballads in his bones. It comes out into the open, I think, in only one line specifically. When Mary Rose tells her lover that the little old woman, the queer one, pointed out the island to her. Why that line should make the ballad lover catch his breath I do not know. I do not know what it means. I do not know why the man should have dreamed his dreary dream beyond the Isle of Skye. I do not know why a nut-brown sword *ritted* through a young colonel is a more immortal method of dispatch than any other way of killing a young colonel. I do not know why, when Barrie said that the ghost of Mary Stewart wore her ruff high to hide the red mark round her neck, the queen haunted me for months and has not left me yet. I only know that Barrie had the knack with which the strange mixed races of the borders used to frighten each other at night. Everybody else has forgotten it.

If a man has a trick like that, I do not care whether he is a realist or a communist or a psycho-analyst or any other kind of machine-made intellectual or not. I call him a genius. It is a pity that Barrie had not that sublime confidence in his own genius that other great writers have and that he made people dress him in chancellor's robes and give him baronetcies and Orders of Merit to lift his little figure up to what seemed to him a normal stature. He was no Mussolini to be photographed on the upper step or with the camera pointing upwards. He was no Augustan to depend on lords and ladies for countenance; but he did so elevate himself and so depend. Probably the names of the ballad-makers are forgotten from some such reason.

I discovered Barrie for myself. My father had no great opinion of him. He also disliked Meredith and Bernard Shaw, and it was some time before I could bring myself to read their works, because although I pulled in the opposite direction from my father he could still inoculate me with prejudices. I find unsuspected prejudices learnt from him showing their heads to-day. In my period of emancipation I took to Meredith before Shaw. I puzzled him out with a fine sense that I was performing an athletic feat, and thought very well of him till I read his biography. I forget who wrote the biography and it was not very well written, but it told me enough. Meredith was a Literary Man. One ought to be able to read an author's work for its own sake without looking through the lines to the personality behind them. But when I formed an impression of Meredith's personality the false rattle of his words became dead to me and the sawdust streamed from his spectacular dummies.

I don't suppose there was anything particularly repellant about Meredith's character, but it repelled me. I had liked his beautiful face and his flocculent hair and beard; but, as I plodded through his *Life*, the hair and beard fell off, I saw through them the smug set of face and penetrating eyes, the weak, pursed mouth, the forefinger pressing the cheek, the heart of mean fancies and furious jealousies, the Literary Gent.

What a quantity of the *National Dictionary of Biography* is taken up by accounts of how these literary gents lived, moved and had their breakfast! How distressed we are when they fail to set us the sort of example we are entitled to expect from the truly great!

It all hangs on what we mean by great. If we are justified in calling a man who runs a hundred yards in nine and a half seconds a great sprinter, or a man who makes three thousand runs in a year a great cricketer, then there is no necessity that a great cricketer or a great sprinter should be a great man. The hundred yards in nine and a half seconds is a masterpiece; but it is a masterpiece that may be composed by a man with no effective organs higher than his lungs. A literary masterpiece may be composed by the same sort of biological sport. Indeed, other things being equal, it is likely to be so. Most works of imagination, like most works of pure piety, can be explained by the Law of Compensation. When I meet a man with a load of piety I often wonder what hideous counter-weight of vice is balancing that piety at the other end. When I read the product of a powerful and effective imagination I suspect it to be the work of some wizened and frustrated person without the faculty of enjoying the ordinary experiences of life. It is well known that most novels of passion are written by confirmed virgins. Men who have never lifted their hands in anger supply most of the stories featuring raw heads and bloody bones. Works in glorification of thought are often composed by people incapable of more than a simula-crum of that exercise. Systems of government are invented by men who allow their wives to sack the cook.

The monopoly of publicity enjoyed by writing fellows leads them to exalt the importance of other writing fellows. If my theory about writing is true there is little wonder that they are unfit to bear the burden of that importance.

.   .   .   .

Literature in Glasgow University, so far as it con-cerned me, was represented by the *Glasgow University Magazine*. Walter Raleigh was leaving, or had just left, and MacNeile Dixon had not yet won his spurs. The editor of the *Glasgow University Magazine* was called Robert Browning. He was a poet and the author of a hymn entitled " We've had no beer." This poem began,

> We've had no beer and we are very dry,
> We've had no beer.
> Though day is done and ten o'clock is nigh
> We have no beer. . . .

And it ends,

> And with the morn we shall go rolling home
> To that same tavern where we started from.

He was a master of form and I still prefer him to Calverley.

His predecessor, Donald Carswell, whom I also knew well, had been content to follow tradition. Browning altered the format of the magazine and indulged in wide margins, rough paper and gay typography. I attempted to contribute, but without success. Robert Browning was not, like his predecessor, a Glasgow Academy boy.

The only piece of communal excitement I remember in my first year was the reception of George Wyndham, the Lord Rector. We dressed ourselves in fancy dress, lit torches and marched down to the Central Station to receive him. He was lifted into his carriage, the horses were taken out, and we dragged him through the narrow streets. He was an apprehensive but beautiful person with his frosted golden hair parted in the middle and the only neat frock coat I ever saw. We thought he was the last of his particular kind of statesmen, but the type has been revived—the Edens and Duff Coopers of our own day. As I was an intransigent Liberal I did not take the trouble to go and listen to his speech. I am told that it was about primordial protoplasmic globules.

. . . .

In spring I enrolled myself in the classes of botany and physics. The botany class met at eight o'clock in the morning and my certificate of attendance reads,

" I hereby certify that Mr. O. H. Mavor attended the class of Botany with little regularity, and that, in accordance with ordinance, he duly performed the work of the class."

In the corner of the card is written the number twenty-two per cent., indicating the average marks I had reached in the class examination. I spent most of these mornings seated on an iron bench beside the University flag staff, brooding on the River Clyde and thinking great thoughts. My professor was F. O. Bower, a little, stocky, bearded man like a sea captain. When I went in five minutes late and heard his first lecture I could not believe he was a professor at all. Cocky Young and Johnny Cleland had set my standard high. His assistant, Lang, who looked like an apostle, was said to have walked through fields of mimosa for several days without seeing the daylight. There seemed to be a great deal of unconnected detail about these botany lectures, in so far as I was able to take any intelligent interest in them at all. It was almost impossible to be in time.

I am told there were botany excursions. I attended one. As the professor seemed to have the idea of taking us for a walk over a huge great hill, and as I could not think of anything in the excursion to repay so much exhaustion, I lost myself very early and caught a train home. My other class was that of physics. My study of physics began very strangely.

The lecturer was late and we sang and talked noisily. The later he was the more the hubbub grew. When he did come we fell silent suddenly. His face was very white and his eyes shone like lamps. He looked at something far away beyond the backs of our heads and began his lecture.

" I am supposed " (he said) " to direct your attention to the study of physics. I cannot imagine why. Physics deals with the laws governing inanimate matter. . . . But Life's the thing . . . We don't know what that is . . . It would be worth while lecturing to you on that . . . But we don't know, you see. Anything about it . . . Except that it makes the laws of Physics look foolish . . . I don't know why I'm standing here. I don't know who you are. I suppose Life has something to do with it. But I don't know. Nobody knows. . . ."

At this point the factotum, Black, a little, sardonic man who had cleaned the blackboard for Lord Kelvin, came in and took the Lecturer by the elbow and guided him gently through the doorway. He closed the door, but we could still hear the Lecturer in the passage, wondering about Life aloud. We sat for some minutes not knowing what to do or say, and then a little white-haired, bull-necked man came in and told us in a harsh but subdued voice that the Lecturer had taken ill and that we might go.

At the examination in September I was ploughed in Physics and passed in Botany. I proceeded to the study of Zoology and Chemistry, with occasional visits to the dissecting-room as a background.

I do not wish to take you step by step through the whole medical curriculum. Very little of it interested me, and I cannot think that it would interest you. I must, however, tell you about Soda.

Soda was the Professor of Chemistry. He lectured to the combined classes of Science and Medical Students. Others who had nothing particular to do in the morning used to come in and join in the fun. There was an air of reckless gaiety about these chemistry lectures. For one thing we sang all through them. We sang "Bonnie Mary of Argyll," "I wouldn't leave my little wooden hut for you," "I to the hills will lift mine eyes," "We've had no beer," and parodies of popular melodies, introducing the name Soda instead of that of the heroine. Police whistles, mouth organs and rattles were freely used; and the drum parts were played with the feet on the creaking floor. Those who were near enough to the Professor to be heard by him shouted instructions and jocosities at him, demanded fresh conjuring tricks, and warned him to keep his beard out of the Bunsen burner. This beard was a magnificent, patriarchal affair, like that of Aaron. Soda was an old man, but he looked older than it was possible for anybody to be; his back was bent, his head bald, and his skin pale and seamed with a million wrinkles. His voice, when we could hear it for the din, had the cracked tremolo of great age.

Soda was a very learned man, and it was said of him by Freeland Fergus that he knew exhaustively all the chemistry there was up to the Christian era. It was said of him by others who were very informed on the matter that he could have filled with distinction any chair in the University. His students, however, chose to regard him as a butt. Not even his age protected him. He looked too old to be true. He had one unexpected foible. He went to all the University dances, dressed in an evening suit that could easily have been worn by Mr. Michael Angelo Titmarsh. Its waistcoat was decorated with an enormous gold watch chain. From the first waltz to the galop at the end Soda danced like a young one. He was said by the women to be the best dancer of them all. He was a curious man, with his head full of necromancy and forgotten wisdom. We could probably have learned much from him; but in his class it would have been impossible to hear a cart-load of iron girders drop.

At the end of the session Soda did an unexpected thing. He refused to grant class tickets to upwards of fifty of his students and stuck to it, though he must have known that this would make it necessary for them to attend his class again in the following winter. I joined the sad queue which lined up at his door to try to melt his flinty heart. First to go in was Pat Wilson. He was a big fellow with a grizzled moustache. He had come back from playing against England at Dublin and found that he had lost his ticket. He had a black eye, a broken nose and a Colles' fracture of the wrist from pushing the flat of his hand into an English face. He was closeted with Soda for a few minutes and came out with his ticket.

" What did you say to him, Pat? " we asked.

" I tould him I had a wake heart," said Pat.

Robin Brown and I did not get our tickets till six months later. We dreamt away a peaceful summer at the Technical College, pouring things into test-tubes and out of them, and afterwards succeeded in persuading Soda that we had fulfilled the necessities of the ordinance. In the class of Zoology I did better. Graham Kerr had recently become the professor, and his pleasant, gentle voice did not interrupt the writing of blank verse, which had become for me a beguiling substitute for Dab Cricket. In his laboratory I gained a second class certificate, my one University honour. To tell you the truth, I went to pieces after this early success, as so often happens to young men whose heads are turned. I was ploughed in Zoology and again in Physics. In the autumn I was ploughed in Zoology, Physics and Chemistry, and indeed, during the whole of this fourth cycle, my failures heavily outnumbered my successes. The professors and their assistants were kind to me. They took me to their rooms during the vacations and took pains to explain to me the elements of their mysteries; but I met them with an invincible stupidity and failed again. Each six months was a recurrent agony, for I did not take these defeats lightly, and I would gladly have spared my father disappointment. I had a curious kind of palsy of the intellects which made it impossible for me to absorb anything which I was taught, or even to learn these subjects by heart out of books. All that could be said for me was that I did not crib, as did others who were afflicted as I was. One young man burst through his whole medical course and became a doctor by the strategy of wearing a heavy overcoat and tearing a text-book in two and putting a half in each pocket.

When I had worn down my examiners and passed the First Professional I was faced with Anatomy. Johnny Cleland passed, after a very beautiful valedictory address which opened the dead century before our eyes from its nave to its chaps. He was succeeded by Bryce, and still I could not pass. I wrote a poem at the time which went as follows:

> Oh, Dr. Bryce, Oh, Dr. Bryce!
> Your predecessor ploughed me twice.
> Oh, Bryce,
> Let twice
> Suffice!

I had a theory that the whole of Anatomy could be learned in a fortnight. I made no fewer than five sacrifices to this theory, but finally proved it. By that time my fifth cycle had gone.

In my second year I took part in a Rectorial Election. In the Scottish Universities the Rector is an official elected by the undergraduates. He serves for

three years and is President of the University Court
and second high officer of the University below the
Chancellor. In my day the custom was to elect a
politician. In practice the Rector seldom presided at
Court meetings. He appointed an Assessor to represent him on that body. The Assessor was usually a
wealthy Glasgow gentleman who felt it his duty to
subscribe handsomely to the various bankrupt student
societies. The election itself used to be a memorable
affair. The political associations in Glasgow and the
West of Scotland took us very seriously and would
subscribe large sums of money to the funds of the
Conservative and Liberal Clubs. The bulk of this
money was spent in renting and fortifying two large
shops in Gibson Street, a steep thoroughfare leading
up to the University. These shops were liable to
attack by members of the opposing clubs. They
were gutted and furnished with tables, benches and
pianos and were used as meeting houses and committee rooms. The attacks to which they were liable
were of two kinds: they might be burgled in the small
hours of the morning by desperate bands who dis-
figured them with paint and took any records or party
literature they could find and threw it in the Kelvin.
They could be attacked *en masse* by the full forces of
the enemy. The big assaults were usually prearranged.

The defending party crammed as many of its supporters as the shop would hold inside with store of
ammunition. Permitted ammunition was eggs, pease-
meal in paper bags, ochre, soot, and the offal of animals.
A hose-pipe was also used. The plate glass was removed from the windows and stout storm boarding
substituted. Barricades were built inside the shop.
For all this the politicians of Glasgow cheerfully paid.
The interior on such a night was hell before the fight
started and was something worse later when the con-

fined space was full with floating pease-meal and soot
and the odour of sweating bodies. Outside on the
pavement students ranged themselves six or seven
deep to bear the first shock of the attack.

I have said that Gibson Street was a thoroughfare.
On either side of it were shops and blocks of flats, and
down the middle of it tram-lines. It was not a very
effective thoroughfare on the night of the shop fights.
Every three years the Chief Constable let it be known
that shop fights were forbidden and that he would take
steps to deal with them. Every three years the police
kept back the Glasgow crowds and an Inspector blew
his whistle for the fight to begin.

At the blast of the Inspector's whistle a hundred
Tories with locked arms threw themselves at the
Liberal phalanx on the pavement under a heavy barrage
from the opposite side of the street. The first shock
usually failed; the attackers were disengaged, and the
hose was brought into play on both sides. After the
morale of the defenders had been shaken by half an
hour's intensive bombardment a second attack was
made. It was followed by successive waves of fresh
shock troops, and the pavement line invariably broke.
For a time the battle was waged in small groups up and
down Gibson Street. Prisoners were taken to cellars
where a garden hose was played on them and they were
either locked up or released on parole. A siege company with grappling hooks and hatchets—which were
both forbidden under the regulations—began to deal
with the window boards. At this point sorties were
common from the besieged shop, and until they had
broken themselves the issue was in doubt. Then a
grappling hook was fixed, the Tories tailed on a wire
rope, the window boarding gave and fell outwards on
to the pavement, making a ramp up which the storm
troops charged. By this time there was little life in

the defence. One by one they were hurled out into the street and the work of destruction began. Gas brackets were immune, but everything else that could be torn away was taken to the river and flung into its icy waters, the Liberals ruefully looking on. This is a composite picture of several shop fights; the attacking party usually won. The Liberals usually numbered fewer fighters and more intellectuals than the Tories, though the strength of the Highland Brigade, who were Liberals to a man, was as the strength of ten because their hearts were pure.

In the intervals between the holocausts a continuous stream of pamphlets and magazines were issued, cabs dashed to and fro, party leaders were kidnapped, printing offices were besieged, dances and smoking concerts were organised, prominent statesmen, and among them a little black-haired, gesticulating man called Lloyd George, addressed crowded meetings. Classes were not attended. The candidates were Mr. Asquith and the Marquess of Linlithgow.

I drew caricatures for the Asquith literature. No notice was taken of the law of libel, and I weep to think of what I might have done if I had taken advantage of my opportunity; but I was young and genteel, and my caricatures, though intended to give offence, gave none. This was not true of the cartoons of A. D. Thomson, who drew portraits of Hebrew undergraduates with their noses supported on little trollies, with more of horrible and awful that e'en to name would be unlawful. It was not true of the verses of Douglas Muir. They bit like serpents and stung like adders, and in the end Mr. Asquith won by a majority in all four nations.

He did not win without another kind of fight. The doors of the polling place had to be stormed and held, parties of students in waggonettes had to comb the

suburbs and fight running battles with other waggonettes, the Liberal and Conservative Clubs down town
and the leading newspaper offices had to be plastered
with ochre, the Western Infirmary at the foot of the
Gilmorehill had to be busy with sticking plaster and
splints. For a week we all spat blood and could not speak,
and our clothes had to be burnt. It was a fine time.

. . . .

Number Four of my incarnations rolled very slowly
along his allotted groove. As I have told you, his time
was mostly occupied by conversation and sleep. As to
the conversation, what he said to other people was of
little or no importance, and what they said to him I've
forgotten. His even progress through this forest of
words was punctuated by bursts of hysteria. I remember that a proportion of the conversation was skato-
logical. The young bourgeoisie of Glasgow in my
time—or at least those with whom I came in contact
at the University—were mostly puritans. They found
relief from the torments of puberty by talking smut.
Even the religiously inclined talked smut. At school
there was very little of it, and that provided by the two
or three leering and furtive boys who couldn't help it
was not found generally acceptable. At the University we slipped imperceptibly into a gross form of
talk and narrative, beginning with the story of the
man whose wife was in bed with sciatica (" Why
didn't you break the blank blank Italian's neck? ") and
sinking to untold depths. The coarsest men were the
Divinity students, the most expert mud-wrestlers were
the medicals. They had an almost unlimited supply
of material. Their everyday talk was more depraved
than anything I have ever heard since. Their conduct
was more than monastic in its chastity. I think it was
a fashion of the time, though the Scottish Universities

still preserve a reputation for this sort of culture. Vice was not our only topic. We were also philosophers.

The first time I sat Anatomy I wrote on the first page of my examination paper the following words:

" I should be wasting my own time and the time of my examiners if I attempted to answer any of these questions."

In spite of this, I proceeded to my oral examination because I believed rightly in the need for practice in such things. I was locked with others in the Anatomy Museum for four and a half hours in an atmosphere of distress and apprehension, comparable to that in a revolutionary prison. At the end of that time I was led by Stewart through Golgotha the place of the skulls into the Lecture Room. Alec MacPhail, the External Examiner, a friend of mine, was arranging horrid objects on a large table. Johnny loomed up to me with his curious step, which was half skip and half shuffle. He thrust his huge hands into the belly-warmer pockets of his trousers and looked down on me for a moment or two without speaking. Then the old giant began to laugh. He roared and howled and chuckled for a full minute. Then he said,

" Well, Mr. Mavor, I suppose it is no secret to you that you know nothing at all about Anatomy? You'll never be a doctor. Run away and be an artist. But even an artist has to know something about Anatomy. Go away and try to be a credit to your father."

I went away.

My father took me down to Rothesay to a hydropathic when blows like this fell. We were nearer to being friends then than at any other time. He did not reproach me, but tried to understand my point of view. It is doubtful whether there was any point of view to understand. I remember three comments on my conduct.

MY FATHER: He is lying fallow.

MY MOTHER: Nothing but leaves.

DAVID ADAMS: He thinks the world is a marionette show put up for his amusement. All he does is to jerk an odd string every now and again to make some puppet dance more funnily.

I do not know. Probably my father was right, and it was a fallow season. I never walked when I could stand. I never stood when I could sit. I never sat when I could lie down. In my later incarnations I was to have furious bursts of energy at long intervals, but in Number Four these bursts were purely physical and completely unproductive. John Morris Walker was the quarter-mile inter-University champion, and I used to go out to the playing fields and train with him. I played third fifteen rugby every Saturday, and the smell of damp muddy cloth still awakens nostalgia in me. About once a month I went for a terrific march into the country either by myself or with others, and once spent the night on a cold hillside north of Loch Lomond when the tempest had made me lose my way. I also enlarged my circle of acquaintances and once, in the Materia Medica class, made a list of them. I found that I knew upwards of five hundred people.

There was a curious pair of brothers called the Hislops who ran a sort of salon on the top flat of their father's house. With them and their assorted friends I went to Arran and lived for a week in a cottage. They had a genius for selection. There were ten of us, all completely different, with the Hislops as the only link between us. There were prizemen bound for Balliol, divines, athletes, poets, a musician or two and crude medical students. It was there I discovered Shaw, my father's *bête noire*, through *Major Barbara*. Strathie and I read it to each other.

I tried religion. The Christian Union was quite

properly under the control of Glasgow Academy boys. There was an evangelistic tradition in the school that began with Dr. Morrison and was carried on by two great families, the Arthurs and the Sloans. Many of these played for Scotland, went to India and became knights, governed the school. In the third cycle I went from time to time to their Sunday afternoon meetings in the Hillhead Borough Hall. The boys sat to the left of the main aisle and the girls to the right, and there was much shouting and singing and competitions in Scripture knowledge. Arthurs and Sloans led the singing and lectured to us in front of a blackboard on which there were symbolic designs in coloured chalk. Some of these designs were on pieces of black paper superimposed on the designs beneath. We would see a rock in a thirsty land. A bit of desert would be pulled away, and Jacob would be seen sleeping with his head on the rock. A bit of sky would be pulled away and we would see a ladder with tiny angels ascending and descending. A long strip at the top would be removed, and there were the Golden Streets themselves in bright yellow. It was all very interesting.

The drive communicated by these vital Arthurs and Sloans usually carried Glasgow Academy boys through the first two or three years of their college life. After that they either lapsed or took to the more complicated and less picturesque brands of religion expounded by the School of Divinity and its acolytes. For the first two or three years our religion was of the good blue and white Academy blend. Clergymen were grafted into our system gently and with reservations. The stable unit was the Bible Circle. The Bible Circle consisted of a dozen Old Boys under the guidance of some senior Old Boy who intended to become a minister. Their text-book was not the Bible but an extremely tedious little work devoid of any authority or literary grace, in which somebody or other expounded passages of Scripture according to his own watery lights. We were encouraged to express our own opinions, but these were often received with such a hurt gravity by the Study Leader that we learnt to be very careful. When it came to my turn to lead the Bible Circle in prayer I prayed, but did not return to the next meeting, nor indeed to any meeting at any time at all.

Instead, I fell in with the magazine gang. Robert Browning had gone down and been succeeded by Archie Browning, who was a Glasgow Academy boy, but who wore long curly hair and an enormous black hat. He was one of the lost sheep—a gentle Swinburnian. He was succeeded by another lost sheep called Arthur Wallace, a man of the world and the son of the editor of *The Glasgow Herald*. I drew pictures for Archie Browning without provoking any considerable reaction in that great man. Arthur Wallace, on the other hand, began right away to groom me for stardom. I was admitted on Sunday nights to the top flat of his house in Athole Gardens, where the Magazine Committee met to make up the week's issue of the Magazine and to receive the latest instalment of the silly serial from Douglas Muir. Douglas Muir was also a Glasgow Academy boy who had strayed from the fold. He was a divinity student with long black hair, a piercing eye and a heavy pipe. He was all the Marx brothers rolled into one. If anyone told him a funny story he would listen with great seriousness and bide his time till the afternoon. He would then tell the funny story to the teller, word for word in the greatest detail. When, at the end of the story, the teller would say " But that is my story," Douglas Muir would say, " I know, you told it to me." He cultivated a strong Glasgow accent, and was the first amateur of the Scots comedian that I ever met. He became in time a beloved clergyman who referred to his pulpit as " the dickie." Later he took Franciscan vows of poverty, and I do not know where he is now.

The floor was covered with damp galley slips. Archie Black, the sub-editor, was tyrannical and laconic. The rest of us sat round and solemnly tried to be funny, but we were deeply impressed. When his year ran out Arthur Wallace nominated me as his successor, but this was altogether too much Glasgow Academy for the Students Representative Council. They put up MacDougall Hay, who was later to write a novel called *Gillespie* in the school of *The House with the Green Shutters*, and to die, like the author of that book, before he had reached full achievement. The Students Representative Council decided on a compromise, and appointed George Fletcher. J. D. M. Rorke, who was seven feet high and was to write a remarkable book called *Musical Pilgrim's Progress*, and I were appointed his sub-editors.

George Fletcher is still alive, and it is impossible, under the existing laws, to give anything like a full account of his character and attainments. At the time of which I speak he was already a legend in Glasgow University. He was a mature little man, prematurely bald, with a huge blunt face and shaky pince-nez. When I knew him first he wore fancy waistcoats and knickerbockers. When he became Editor of the *G.U.M.* he exchanged these for sadder garments. He was a socialist, an orator, a poet and a wit. His oratory was displayed usually at street corners at one o'clock in the morning after Union suppers. Even at that unpromising time he could draw an immense crowd from nowhere to hear an address on John Stuart Mill. In more select circles his topic was chiefly the spirit of

Calvinism, of which he did not on the whole approve. He had a very brisk way of talking, and walked as if his feet were miniature rocking-horse rockers. Like so many others of his generation he was Rabelais in his public and Cardinal Newman in his private life. One of his historic phrases, " When Ah hear ma dress suit clearing its throat, Ah leave the house," is valueless from a historic point of view, though it seems to me to have merits as a piece of pure native wit.

George was the youngest of a very large Kirkintilloch family. His brothers were elders at the Kirk before he went to school. When George did go to school the teacher asked him whether he was the baby. " No," said George. " I'm the cat."

I am not privileged to write the biography of George. Indeed, I am supposed to be engaged upon my own. I hope, however, that I shall be privileged to use him to enlighten the drabber pages on the history of the next five years. I got to know more than one odd figure who was to grow to importance as the years went on. One of them—a Glasgow Academy boy— was seated in the Union reading room on a heap of periodicals. He was reading the *Illustrated London News*. He wore a black hat and a long black cloak, and had the air of a solitary. I pulled *The Graphic* from under him, and he turned on me with a fierce expression. I said, " Hallo, Elliot." He said, " Hallo." We had not known each other very well at school, and he was on the science side at the University.

I sat down on the couch beside him and began to read *The Graphic*. He went on reading the *Illustrated London News*. He was not then a very sociable man. He read all the novels that were ever published and walked to his home in Lanark for fun. Before the week was out I had him playing for the third fifteen and writing for the *G.U.M.* Before three years were passed he had captured the University. Before twenty years were passed he was in the Cabinet.

. . . .

I began to be impatient. I did not feel that being steadily ploughed in physics, zoology, chemistry, anatomy, physiology and materia medica was getting me any further; so I enrolled in a surgical clinic, and bound up cut fingers in the dispensary. I attended the clinic with some regularity, when I could spare time from the corner of the filthy garret full of brown paper parcels and type. This corner had been cleared for us in Hodges', the printers, to enable us to bring out *G.U.M.* every week. Fletcher, Rorke, Elliot, a lean and hideous man called Sprochles, C. J. Kirk and I ran a little glee party there. We sang at our work sometimes, but more often not at our work. Stewart, Hodges' manager, used to think us very funny, until it was time to put the paper to bed and George's Editorial remained unwritten. He used then to swear; but Fletcher met him at every point and drove him blushing away.

" I wonder," he said to me, " how he can think of such things, and him so young."

Daddy Renton's clinic was in pleasing contrast to all this squalor. The Chief was a little bird-like man, with a white waterfall moustache and an ineffable gentleness of manner. "Here," he would say, "is a poor man, and the question for us is, what are we to do for this poor man? " What he did, I am glad to say, was usually to adopt expectant treatment. In the intervals he demonstrated the anatomy of inguinal hernia to us, with the help of dusters and sheets of cartridge paper. His theatre was a beautiful, restful, white, shining, spotless place, and the seats in it not uncomfortable. The clinic was small. Daddy was not the most popular teacher in the hospital, but he was by far the most humane. I could not have chosen a more pleasing introduction to my kindly trade. I began to be less indifferent to what I was taught, but the real business of life was conducted in Hodges' top flat.

* * * * * * * *

I do not know why I dislike Number Four so much. I have shown him a giggling, jeering, lethargic oaf. He wasn't—he was humble and he had the endearing quality of being able to enjoy things it was decent to enjoy.

Strathie was a good influence on his life. Strathie dug him out of his lethargy and transported him to the Hague. On the ship was a withered Dutchman who smelled of musk and cheroots. He had only one complaint to make of Great Britain. In London, public girls were ridiculously dear.

We "did" Rotterdam, the Hague and Antwerp. We ate Rembrandt and Rubens. I saw what I still think was the greatest picture I have ever seen—the Descent from the Cross in the Antwerp Cathedral. When one is young the sense of repletion is the greatest joy in life. I regret now that exquisite sense that I have eaten so much that I can hardly move. Something like that sensual pleasure I felt in the Dutch and Belgian picture galleries. But Strathie and I were of too fine a metal to be content with that. We discussed First Principles. We exercised ourselves with the Nature of Art.

In a general way I knew that this was Art and that, like music, or religion, or education, it was good for me. But, every now and again we and even the artists who make these objects ask ourselves, What is the use of them? How do they do us good? Or do they do us no good at all and do they come into existence and remain in existence because of some right inherent in themselves?

We are apt to think of every conceivable thing in terms of its " usefulness " to ourselves. The sun is a thing that keeps us warm. A sheep is a thing that gives us wool and mutton. Men and women are things that work for us, tell us what to do or simply keep us company.

But if we did not exist at all, the sun would still shine. Sheep might be proud and fierce wild animals, ranging the mountains in search of a destiny of their own. As to mankind, many of us have been to places where porters are not polite, where there are no cooks or housemaids, where the inhabitants are too busy meditating on their own individual importance to be bothered with us at all.

In short, the theory that the Universe was arranged for our comfort has only a limited application.

It is a dreadful thought that even the policeman on the beat may be there, not so much out of a maternal sort of solicitude for our safety as because he likes wearing a blue uniform, exercising authority, walking up and down, being a policeman.

So the artist may be making these odd objects because he likes doing it, or, perhaps, because he MUST do it. He takes a certain amount of pleasure in receiving our admiration and, perhaps, our money. But, like David's wife, he despises us in his heart.

To put it with more urbanity, these pictures and statues may have come into being for a purpose with which we are not directly concerned.

Nevertheless, we do concern ourselves with them. And according to our custom, we may take the wool off their backs whether they like it or not. We appear to have as much right to do that as the sheep have to exist. If there is no *prima facie* use for these objects, we shall set about making one.

Well, in the first place, they clearly belong, if they belong at all, to one of the higher orders of usefulness. We cannot eat them or use them for clothing or shelter; and, in the present state of the markets, they are, to say the least of it, highly speculative investments. If we are to find a use for them, it must be to enrich some of the less material parts of our nature. How can they do that?

Before I answer that question, I must hold, as 'twere, the mirror up to nature as it is exemplified in this room at this moment. For Shakespeare very clearly sets out that this is one of the functions of the Show Business (in which part of my life is heavily engaged).

Few of us have never said—to those who love us well enough not to be irritated by platitudes—" This is the Age of Speed." Things, we say, are going too fast. There is no time for a man to sit down and invite his soul.

In spite of this we are rather proud of our Age of Speed, as we call it. As we wrongly call it, for neither of these two things we are always saying is true. It is not an Age of Speed at all. We are not going too fast, we are going too slowly. And there is more time than ever there was to sit down and think.

That is why we misuse our time so prodigally.

We talk of speed! We, who are composed of millions of cells, functioning, dying and being born again at such speed that, if they were men and women, the world would be depopulated and filled again within a year. Adam and Eve were made of the same sort of busy cells. And the cells of Adam and Eve were themselves composed of little objects moving at a speed that would make our fastest aeroplanes look like flying tortoises.

Speed! When our entire recorded history from Abraham down is an insignificant fraction of the time we have been eating and sleeping and loving and fighting on this earth.

Speed! We are like the needless Alexandrine, " which, like a wounded snake, drags its slow length along."

And while we are on the subject of Man's relation to the Universe—a fascinating subject—let me remind you that in some millions of years the earth will be a frozen lump—a bit of molten toffee—a cloud of white hot dust—our prophets are not quite sure which, but it will be something unpleasant. If we do not do something about it we shall all be dead then and that will be a pity.

For we have in us, each of us, the elements of immortality. This is not a mystical assertion but a good, sound rock-bottom physical fact.

Now, we do not mind dying ourselves, as individuals, but we have the strongest possible objection to perishing from the earth and becoming nothing, all of us, forever.

You must now allow me to digress for a moment. Believe me, I have been sticking closely to the point so far.

If you are up in modern psychology—and who is not?—you will know all about Wish-fulfilment. It is a curious thing about modern psychology that keeps on using words in the opposite sense to their plain meaning. The Unconscious, for instance, is a kind of consciousness; and the words Wish-fulfilment mean that wishes are not, in fact, fulfilled. But they are, if we wish hard enough. We were told, long before the invention of explosives, that we could remove mountains and cast them into the sea by making up our minds about it.

Well, we have seen mountains removed. It's a matter of touching a button. But, whether we realise it or not, our wishes are fixed on something less childish than altering scenery. We know we can jump like a flea across the Atlantic and speak with dull people in Australia—even see their stupid faces while we are talking to them. But what we really want is to find a way to perpetuate the living human race after the Universe has finished with its home, the Earth. Sun, Moon and Stars can do what they like. If they evict us from our home we shall find somewhere else, some other way of living. Our wish is for Immortality. No less.

And it is pleasant to think that we, of all created things, have been given the means to make this possible. An instrument called the Mind.

You have been waiting patiently to hear the use of these objects of art which surround you. Here it is.

Before we have our wish, at least two things are necessary. We must be a good deal stronger and cleverer and more wide awake than we are at present. And we must be cheered and guided by intimations of that Immortality that we seek.

To fulfil the first requirement, we must learn to see and to hear; for the eyes and the ears are the best servants of the mind.

The painter teaches us to see. He teaches us to look at things we have never noticed. The play of light on a bird's wing. The pattern of interlacing branches.

If we cannot see these everyday things, how can we hope to recognise the subtle gate, the narrow, strait gate of Paradise when our eyes fall on it?

The form and colour of the outward world is significant. We must learn that before we can come on the truths of which they are significant—the truths that will save us alive.

Painting and sculpture, then, teach. Are they also intimations of Immortality, and in what sense are they so?

In the terrible onward surge of life we look around for something of which we may say, "This is permanent." Even the illusion of permanence comforts and reminds us. We look out of the window at the street and, in the very act, the street we looked at is gone. In every instant of time it is changing.

The painter takes his palette and brush and, in a little while, he shows us a moment; fixed; safe; guaranteed to last our time. We look at this picture and know that he has won for us a local success against the forces that destroy.

If man can win once he can win again. A comforting, uplifting thought and, no doubt, not without an element of truth in it.

CHAPTER V

The Fifth Five

THE FIFTH CYCLE IS of some interest to me, because in it
I woke, sneezed, blinked at my environment and
began clumsily to move it about. I swung suddenly
from the negative to the positive pole.

I had been four years at Glasgow University and
should, if I had been a decent, hard-working citizen,
have had my final in sight and been preparing to earn
my living. As it was I had huge arrears of examinations to pass and more formidable examinations in
front of me. I was not to emerge from this drain-
pipe till the fifth cycle was complete.

In the meantime I found the place congenial. The
Glasgow University man had already displaced the
Glasgow Academy boy as the noblest fruit of the
human race. His main characteristic was infinite
variety. He could adapt himself to anything—even to
crime. The St. Andrews University undergraduate
was obviously a student. He wore a red gown, had
wide-open innocent eyes and thought it necessary to

commit Latin tags to memory and to quote them.
The Aberdeen student was a rough tyke who conscientiously and self-consciously lived his life to the
full. He had a moral and physical digestion like a
horse. The Edinburgh student was, is, and always will
be impossible. The inhabitants of Edinburgh are for
ever calling their beautiful city the modern Athens or
the Northern Oxford or the Scottish Wigan or something that it isn't or, at least, has no business to be.
The Edinburgh students of my day, with many notable
exceptions, were solemn, beefy-faced young idiots who
talked disgusting Englified jargon, and looked forward to jobs under the Government. They had not
begun to practice hospitality as it was understood in the
other three Universities. They were like Stevenson's
preacher, gesturing and cold. They are perhaps
responsible for my firm conviction that Edinburgh is
the stupidest town in the world. This cannot be true,
because Edinburgh contains over a quarter of a million
solid Scots, but the citizens themselves are to blame for
a prejudice I shall carry in my bones till I die.

The Glasgow student, on the other hand, was a
delightful fellow. He was a man of the world in the
best sense of that description. He was lively, violent,
unprejudiced, friendly, noisy, sympathetic, moderate
even in riot, interested, disinterested, intelligent,
balanced, unaffected, chaste, adaptable, knowledge-
able, humorous, companionable, wrapt like a mantle in
commonsense yet radiating poetry, downright, upright,
a considerer of the lilies, a philosopher. The places in
which he spent his working and loafing day were
without grace or inspiration in their architecture and
furnishings, but he illuminated them with his presence.
A medical student who had followed that calling for
fifteen years once told me that although Glasgow
University was very enjoyable one could not savour it

to the full till one had been there for at least twelve years. He may have been right. After four years it was good enough for me.

I have mentioned one Chronic. The Chronic, or oldest inhabitant, was a feature of the place. These old gentlemen matriculated year after year, attended no classes, sat no examinations. Nobody interfered with them. They gave body to the vintage. They gambled and drank quietly and were full of a kind of wisdom. Many of them had served in the South African War; but it had not stamped their characters as the later war was to do with its sheep. They seldom talked about it. It was an interlude in the even progress of their studies.

One of them, it is true, went to the South African War and did not return. Though his name appeared in no casualty list he was believed to be dead. Nothing had been heard of him for two years.

One Sabbath evening a dozen of the Chronics were seated at the end of the Union billiard room under a dim gas bracket, playing a game of chance. Games of chance were forbidden in the Union if they were played for money and cards were prohibited. The Chronics had an arrangement for gathering their cards and counters into the tablecloth and replacing them with bibles, text-books of physiology, dominoes or other innocuous objects on the sound of the alarm.

On this particular evening the swing door at the far end of the billiard room swung open and a pale face outlined itself in the darkness. The Chronics clutched the four corners of the table-cloth and turned their heads simultaneously towards the dark vista. A figure approached them. A keen-sighted Chronic said, " It's Boloney," and they turned again to the game. Their lost comrade took his seat among them, and they dealt him a hand. No further word was spoken.

Two brothers sat in their lodgings in Gibson Street.

The elder brother said, " Willie, I want to speak to you seriously." Willie said, " Yes, John," for he respected his elder brother. John said, " Willie, you well know that our father has a hard struggle to keep us at college. He has played the game by us and we ought to play the game by him. Now, you are far too much with those toughs in the common-room. They are not the right company for you, Willie. They'll only get you into trouble. Now look at me. Our father allows us five shillings a week for pocket money. You don't see me gambling with my allowance. This is Friday. I've saved half a crown, and I'll have seven and six next week to start with."

Willie told me what his reply was. It was very dramatic. " I never said a word. I put my hand in my inside pocket and took out . . . TEN QUID! "

One who did not properly belong to the Chronic Circle but who was in the direct succession was a wee man whom I shall call Zaccheus. The story of the adventures of Zaccheus would fill a book, but I shall give you a specimen day. Zaccheus was invited by a friend to refresh himself with the cold airs of the Ayrshire coast. It was either late autumn or early spring, and the only entertainment offered by the resort was a travelling show. To this Zaccheus and his friend went, after fortifying himself at an inn. Being quiet men they settled themselves down to a peaceful game in which one billiard ball is played against another billiard ball with the object of knocking pennies balanced on the second billiard ball outside a circle marked on the table. Zaccheus and his friend were practised hands and began very well indeed. First Zaccheus made fourpence; then his friend made two-pence. Then Zaccheus made fivepence. Then his friend made . . . But the proprietor of the booth had had enough. He swept the winning or losing pennies off the table, and said, " Hard luck, sir! Now stand aside and let somebody else have a chance."

Zaccheus and his friend were quiet men. Zaccheus' friend protested against the cheat quietly and effectively by putting two of the billiard balls in his pockets.

He did not do this unobserved. The proprietor called for his assistant. " Here's a guy's going to make trouble. Tak' aff your jersey, Alec."

The assistant, a powerful youth of middle height, began to struggle from his outgrown jersey. For a moment his profile was outlined in the wool, and at this profile Zaccheus struck with all his force. He was rewarded by a spreading stain of red. Whatever it is that showmen call when they wish to rally their forces —I believe it is " Hey Rube " or some such thing— the showman called. In a moment Zaccheus' friend was on the ground being expertly kicked. Zaccheus himself seems to have escaped notice. He was a wee man.

The Ayrshire farmer may have some barbarous traits, but he does not like to see a fellow creature lying on the ground being kicked by people in jerseys. A number of rosy-faced rustics with hands like hams joined issue with the show people. Zaccheus took his semi-conscious friend by the coat-collar and dragged him along the muddy road to the gate of the field. At the gate the two village constables were blowing their whistles like mad. Zaccheus turned to look at the scene which he had just left, and found that the billiards booth had disappeared, that huge clouds of steam were issuing from the merry-go-round and that its horses were being used as weapons. He got his friend to his feet and hurried him back to the inn as night was falling. They had a hurried wash and brush up and then thought it well to be on the move, lest any of the combatants should visit the inn. They moved,

however, to another inn and sojourned there for a little.
Zaccheus' friend felt better and Zaccheus himself was
in fine trim. They decided to go to the house of Zaccheus'
friend for supper. It was only about eight o'clock, but
the night was as black as a boot. On the sea-front
there was a bedroom window. They knew it was a
bedroom window because the shadow of a round mirror
was shown on the blind. Zaccheus decided that it was
a night on which to make love. He raised the sash
and began to climb in by the window. A man in a
nightshirt sprang out of bed. He seized Zaccheus by
the scruff of the neck with his left hand and lifted up a
hair brush with his right. He beat Zaccheus about the
face with the hair brush, until Zaccheus' friend pulled
him out of the window by his ankles.

In the mirror advertising Bass's beer in the nearest
inn, the face of Zaccheus looked like that of a patient
with haemorrhagic measles. It was decided that the
sisters of Zaccheus' friend would be horrified by the
spectacle, so Zaccheus and his friend took a train which
happened to be leaving for Glasgow. They got to
Glasgow at about ten, and decided to visit the Princess
Pantomime on the south side of the river. This was,
and is, a very popular pantomime, and its principal
boys and girls are more beloved by the proletariat than
Hitler is by the Nazis. The house was full, but the
stage box was empty. Zaccheus' friend had just
drawn his bursary and there was enough money left
to buy it. They bought the stage box and went in and
sat in it to see the last half-hour or so of the performance.

In more respects than one Zaccheus was smarting
from his defeat. And he was still vaguely in love. He
wanted to ask Miss Daisy Dormer to marry him and got
on to the stage to do so. Zaccheus, after a brisk
struggle with the stage hands, was thrown out by the

143

stage door, after hitting every step on the way down. He would have been better not to struggle. His delaying action gave the gallery time to get down to the stage door to meet him. When Zaccheus picked himself to his feet he could see nothing before him but a sea of angry faces lit by the gas lamp in the lane and the prospect of sudden death. Zaccheus did not fear death. He took off his coat and waistcoat and threw them into the gutter. He then began to hit the faces he could reach. Through the fog of battle came the reminiscent sound of a police whistle. Zaccheus was lifted up under the arm-pits and borne with his feet off the ground into the Gorbals. The mob followed with many an eldritch shriek and hollow. The two policemen hurled Zaccheus into a moving tramcar and turned to deal with the gallery boys. Zaccheus knew no more. He came to himself at Simpson's corner in Renfield Street. Glasgow, for a Saturday night, seemed strangely calm.

. . . .

I have begun this chapter, as Shakespeare began the plays of *Romeo and Juliet* and *Macbeth* with battle and the sound of blows, thumb-bitings and bloody sergeants. It will not be all like that. It will not be like that at all.

. . . .

As I say, round about my twentieth birthday I woke up and became something different. I was a tallish, skinny youth, and if it had not been for my bulbous head I could have passed through an alderman's thumb-ring. As my allowance of sixty pounds a year was supposed to cover books, clothing and other necessities, and as I was mildly extravagant, I developed a slight eccentricity in dress, thus making a vice of necessity. I wore a battered bowler hat with a hole in the crown. I wore a red neck-tie, a jacket the colour of tomato soup, a waistcoat from another suit and a pair of magenta trousers striped with mauve which had belonged to my grandfather. My socks were blue with horizontal black stripes, and my shoes were brown brogues. As if this were not enough I also wore a monocle. I am happy to say that this *ensemble* was effective and I became very highly respected about the University growing, at one time, to the dimensions of a myth. Instead of listening to conversation, I began to monopolise it. Additions to the University Union included a quiet little room for the secretary in a far corner of the building. In this room I sat with my feet on the mantelpiece day in and day out and arbitrated on the elegances while a succession of secretaries tore their hair over their accounts. With a number of colleagues I invented several traditional habits for Glasgow University students. Many of these still persist and are solemnly traced back to the fifteenth century by the more historically minded of the undergraduates.

Among these traditions was the College Song, whose peculiar history I shall now relate. It is still sung as a special compliment to great scientists, film stars and educationalists whom the University delights to honour.

At Lochranza in Arran there were gathered together Alfred Wareing, George Fletcher, Arthur Wallace, Walter Elliot and myself. We were living in a tent by the side of a burn. We followed George Fletcher's definition of camping, which is that one surrounds oneself with every conceivable discomfort and then drinks bottled beer to forget them. Apart from one bright day when I swam out to a yacht in the fairway and was nearly drowned by the undertow on the way back, it rained steadily all week. Among other things,

Arthur Wallace told us of a colleague of his on *The Manchester Guardian* who had just come back from a Welsh Eisteddfod. He had heard sung there an extraordinary song which, so far as Arthur could remember, went as follows:

> Salasava, salasava.
> Cora Bella, Cora Bella,
> Ching, ching, ching, O.
> Lloyd George Ygorra
> Lloyd George Ygorra.
> Ygorra, Ygorra, Ygorra
> YGORRA!

Neither he nor his friend knew what it was about, but there was a vague idea that Ygorra meant " He is a great man."

Now, it happened that, through a set of circumstances I shall explain later, Mr. Lloyd George was a candidate for the Lord Rectorship of Glasgow and I was one of his supporters. His opponents were Lord Curzon and Mr. Keir Hardie. Elliot, I think, fought for Curzon and voted for Keir Hardie, but he had no objection to assisting in the candidature of Mr. Lloyd George. He and I foisted the song on the Liberal Club, explaining that it was Welsh for

> Hail to the Saviour of his People!
> He is a man of war and at the same time of peace.
> He is the Protector of the Poor.
> Lloyd George is a very great man, indeed.

The song was duly sung throughout the election. Lloyd George was defeated, but the song did not die. About this time the Officers' Training Corps was instituted by Mr. Haldane, and Ygorra came in handy as a marching song. The next Rectorial Election it was sung by both parties indifferently. In 1914 the War broke out and nearly every Highland student in

Glasgow enlisted in Lochiel's Camerons. One day, in the winter of 1914, I was standing on Laffan's Plain, near Aldershot, with the Ninth and Fourteenth Divisions of Kitchener's Army. I was with the Fourteenth. The melting snow was over my boot tops and I, with twenty thousand other men, was soaked to the skin. The sleet was falling steadily. We had been there for three hours, waiting for Lord Kitchener and M. Millerand. What with the sleet and the steamy fog it was impossible to see anybody but the battalion in front. But we kept, in our misery, a vague impression that the plain was full of soldiers. The seeping sleet fell, silently blanketing all sounds but occasional grunts of distress and invocations to the Redeemer from the suffering troops. Suddenly, from miles away, on the right, I heard Ygorra. The Camerons were singing it to keep themselves warm.

By the time of the battle of Loos our Highland recruits from Glasgow had all been killed or translated to commissions; but Lochiel's Camerons went over the top dribbling footballs and singing a song that puzzled their officers very much. I am told a piper played the accompaniment. Their Chaplain wrote to the papers about it after the War, and the song he had managed, by listening carefully, to transcribe in some sort of mangled version, was Arthur Wallace's Ygorra.

Another tradition is Daft Friday. This Saturnalia has been traced back to the time when Glasgow students lived on oatmeal and eked out the last of the poke with rioting. In point of fact, I invented Daft Friday. On the last day of term I was sitting in my chair in the secretary's room overcome with tedium and clergyman's sore throat; and this was odd, because it was not yet ten o'clock in the morning. I began to roar and bawl for some sort of entertainment. When the president of the Union asked me politely what sort of entertainment I would like, I said I would like a concert. So the president and I and his satellites and my satellites went down to the committee room on the ground floor and dragged a piano into it. A pianist began to play and we all began to sing. Hard working men on their way to their lectures and exhausted men coming back from their lectures stopped at the open door, drifted in and began to sing too. After about half an hour the committee room was so full that they had to remove the piano into the debating hall. At about five in the afternoon a foraging party brought in a cluster of stars from the city pantomimes, and the concert which had been proceeding without intermission since ten o'clock that morning gathered new vigour. At about ten o'clock at night the Union manager provided us with ham and eggs and Daft Friday went on till Saturday. Nobody with any tincture of humanity in him attended a class that day.

· · · · · · · ·

I began the fifth cycle with a Rectorial Election. These elections were prepared many months ahead. Money had to be gathered for shop fighting and cabs, and the minor matter of the candidates had to be considered. We of the Liberal Club had chosen as our champion Sir Henry Campbell-Bannerman. It was of Sir Henry that R. B. Cunninghame-Graham said,

"He has all the qualifications for a great Liberal Prime Minister. He wears spats and he has a beautiful set of false teeth."

Towards the end of April 1908 the president of the Liberal Club spoke to me in a great state of agitation. He was an Englishman called Marsh and was destined for the Church. He was a very eloquent little man with a curly moustache. He said he had dreamt he was talking to Campbell-Bannerman and that the

Prime Minister had suddenly disappeared. Marsh had gone to a room upstairs and found the candidate lying on the hearth rug with his head in the fire. Marsh asked him what he was doing there and was told that it was part of the treatment. Marsh told this story to his landlady, and his landlady said that Sir Henry would be dead within the week. The next day Sir Henry *was* dead, and we had no candidate.

Marsh was desolated. Apart from the fact that he had been very fond of the great man, it was late in the day to get another candidate. The winter session was finished and more than half of the electorate had gone down for the summer. The election was in October. There seemed to be nothing for it but to withdraw from the contest and allow Lord Curzon a walk-over, for we were not in those days sufficiently Marx-minded to give Keir Hardie the ghost of a chance.

I wanted a fight. My father's patience might give out or I might get through my examinations and never see another Rectorial. I found a magnificent full page picture of John Morley in a weekly paper. His long nose and head, his screwed-up eyes and his tolerant mouth made a great appeal to me. I took the picture to Marsh and said, " Go at once to London and ask Morley to stand." Marsh lit up quickly to enthusiasms. He caught the night train, and I did not see him for two days. He saw Morley, who said that ambition had died in him. He saw Asquith, who suggested Lloyd George. He saw Lloyd George, who captivated him immediately and accepted nomination. He came back full of fight and very pleased with his candidate. I told him his candidate was awful and that we hadn't a chance. We in Glasgow were not very excited about Lloyd George. He had just become Chancellor of the Exchequer and nobody could understand why. He did not seem to us a weighty person.

Though we did not lay great stress on scholarship and gentility among ourselves we liked a savour of them in our Lord Rector, and Lloyd George did not appear to us to reach pass marks in these qualities. Nor did we like Welsh Nonconformists. Our feelings on these matters were well expressed by Johnny Mowat at an annual general meeting of the Liberal Club.

" Well, I got Mary Armour in for vice-president and they can take their buns and their bibles to hell."

We thought he could very well have stayed at the Board of Trade and that it was weak of Asquith to kowtow to the Welsh Nonconformists. We thought that his boots were too big for him and that he would presently fade out and be heard of no more. But he was all we could get, and with heavy hearts we set to work to make the best of him.

The Liberal Club was poor in fighting strength, but it had an unlimited supply of fluent publicists. I became the Dr. Goebbels of the outfit and, with Elliot and Sprochles, conducted a daily newspaper with head-lines and all. We left the politics to Marsh and printed wads about Free Trade and Local Option without even bothering to correct the proofs. Our duty was to denigrate the enemy and to make a hero of Mr. Lloyd George. In both we were successful. Lord Curzon and his undergraduate supporters were left without a rag of character to their backs. The baser arts of propaganda were prosecuted quite regardless of expense and reached proportions that had never been dreamt of before. In Hodges' top flat the poison pen was working overtime. The opposition made dismal attempts to rival our output and to hold on with numbed fingers to their dignity; but they were not in the hunt. Hodges' top flat wrote the heads off them.

One night they appealed to the arbitrament of force. As Sprochles and I went out for a coffee in the

afternoon we saw an earnest young man in a deer-
stalker hat passing us with a strenuous air of unconcern.
When we came back the same young man was walking
briskly down the street, this time in a cap. He was a
spy. Our lair had been discovered.

We had been composing, I think, a song book.
We had forgotten about the song book till that morning, and Elliot and I composed thirty party songs
between breakfast and tea-time. They were not, on
the whole, very inspiriting. One of them contained
the lines,

> Yo, ho, Yo ho, the Tory crew
> Are corpses stiff and stark.
> Their dead cold eyes glare upwards as
> They lie there in the dark.[1]

We finished the song book and rang up Marsh.
The printer's devil had brought us news of lurking
figures in every close-mouth. Marsh told us that a
hundred able-bodied Tories in full fighting kit had
just left their rooms for an unknown destination. He
hoped that the song book was ready, as there was just
time to rush it out in a swift motor car. The song book
was not ready. The daily paper was. It was carried
out wrapped about the bodies of three or four in-
offensive-looking employees of Hodges' and by the
manager, Stewart, with a Gladstone bag. They took
it to the Queen Street station and loaded it in a cab,
while the spies were following severally Elliot,
Sprochles and me through winding streets and up dark
alleys. The Tory storm troopers had not yet arrived.

When we shook off our pursuers we went back to
North Frederick Street, where Hodges' offices were,

[1] Later I stood on the platform beside James Wood at a meeting
addressed by Thomas Shaw, the Lord Advocate. The song was
mournfully sung by those who knew it. James Wood said : " That's
a good song."

and found the street heavily blockaded by storm troopers. We asked them what they were doing there and they jeered at us. We borrowed cigarettes from them and went to join Marsh. We found him in one of his woebegone states. It was Friday. The Liberal fighting men had the week-end habit. He could only muster a bare dozen. It was hopeless to try to fight the song book through. We decided to watch developments and send out the Fiery Cross in the morning.

Hodges' were working overtime on the song book. We learned by telephone that they were finished about midnight. The employees as they left the building were systematically searched by the blockaders. A crowd had gathered. Braziers were lit. They were prepared to fight it out along these lines if it took all night.

It was very cold and wet, and we, who were watching the watchers, looked for somewhere to take shelter. We found in Argyle Street an hotel (called the Ritz or the Savoy or the Waldorf-Astoria or some such name) which still showed a light burning. We mounted a rickety stair and went into the lounge. We thought it was the lounge because the letters L-O-U- remained of a sign above the door. They may have meant something else. The lounge was not over-decorated. It had a big table in the middle of it and badly wounded leather settees round it, two cracked windows opening in a dead wall and a few decrepit chairs. The floor was covered with linoleum. The place was brightly lit with unshaded mantles. Two boys of about seventeen or eighteen got up when we came in, pulled their caps over their eyes and leant against the wall. We asked them if there were any chance of anything to drink. They said no. We said, " Coffee or anything? " They said no and spat simultaneously on the linoleum. We then drew in to the table and began to discuss the

siege and what we should do about it. We had agreed
to get a lorry to rush into the covered way, when two
more hotel guests appeared. One was a tall, clean-
shaven albino in a covert coat and cap. He wore a
clean white collar and his little pink eyes were set close
together. The other was an old gentleman like Mark
Twain in a black sombrero and a black frock coat.
The tall man looked at us and we looked at him. Then
he began to speak to us with great eloquence in an
Australian accent.

He said,

" I don't know what you gentlemen are doing here.
I do not enquire. I am a gentleman and you are a
gentleman and we know our own business best. I
have no wish to intrude in your councils. But there is
one thing it is my duty as a gentleman to ask. And I
ask you, as gentlemen, to reply. Do I owe you any
money? "

We said he didn't owe us any money. He said,

" Very well, then. That is very satisfactory. I
don't owe you any money, you don't owe me any
money. We can each have our own thoughts and mind
our own businesses and not ask any bloody questions."

He turned fiercely to one of the boys leaning against
the wall and put a formidable rasp into his voice.

" And what, may I ask, are you looking at? Who
the hell do you think you are? I'm talking to these
gentlemen. They know their own business. I know
mine. They are gentlemen, but what are you, you
bloody rat? Do I owe you any money? "

The boy mumbled something we could not catch.
The albino went on.

" And take that look off your face. What do you
know about gentlemen or the feelings of a gentleman?
If you think you're going to bloody well insult me
you're bloody well mistaken. I'll take you by the

throat, you bastard. I'll take you by the throat and throw you out of the bloody window into the bloody street. You and your mate, any fifty bloody dozen of you. You think I wouldn't, hey? "

He began to gnash his teeth and to pull off his covert coat. Mark Twain took him by the arm and said in a very gentle, cultivated voice,

" Be calm. He is nothing to you. You demean yourself."

The albino sent the old man staggering a couple of yards with a punch on the chest. We were rather frightened, for he was a desperate-looking dog, but we prepared for action and helped the old man to his feet.

At this point the door of the lounge opened and a strange figure appeared in the doorway. It was a little man very like J. M. Barrie. His nightshirt was tucked into his trousers and he had bare feet. Across his chest were folded two enormous muscular arms with the blue veins standing out on them. He stood still and did not speak. The albino put on his coat.

" All right, Mr. Cook," said the albino. " I'd no intention of creating any disturbance. This man insulted me and I lost my temper. These gentlemen will bear witness that I don't owe them any money. I am very sorry. I think I will go for a little walk."

Mr. Cook said nothing. He moved aside to let the albino and his tutor go out. Then he looked at us and back at the boys. The boys shook their heads. Mr. Cook disappeared.

We went up in the grey dawn to North Frederick Street. The place was alive with Tories, so we went home to bed. Sprochles and Walter and I agreed that it was up to the fighting convener to get the song books out, and decided to take no further interest for we were very tired. I believe that a heavy covered van rushed the song books out and that the police protected it and

dispersed the Tories, of whom they were becoming a
little weary. This was a black mark against the Liberals and took a lot of living down. They were accused
of calling for police protection, but, in fact, Messrs.
Hodge had hired the car and dispatched the song books
before the fighting convener was out of his bed. The
girls in the office were frightened to come in. The
police had acted on their own initiative.

In the upshot, after the usual *mêlée* round the great
South Door, Lord Curzon was elected by a majority
of twelve. We all settled down to normal routine.
Three thousand of us to study medicine, science and
the humanities, Sprochles, Walter and I to edit the
G.U.M.

About this time Alfred Wareing arrived in the city.
He was a sleek person with an innocent baby face and
a most ingratiating manner, and he proposed to start
a Repertory Theatre in Glasgow. Miss Horniman's
company had already been there. We were given *The
Silver Box* and *Cupid and the Styx*. Among the
players were Miss Sybil Thorndike, Mr. Lewis
Casson, Mr. Basil Dean and Mr. Iden Payne. My
theatre correspondent was a little patronising but
appreciative. Mr. Wareing promised us something
better than Miss Horniman's company and was as
good as his word. He opened with *You Never Can
Tell* at the beginning of April 1909. It fought bravely
on till 1914, when Wareing took ill and the War
broke out and the Glasgow Repertory Theatre died.
The business men of Glasgow have not yet recovered
from the horrifying sensation of losing a few hundred
pounds on an artistic venture, and we have never had
another, although the last year closed with a small
profit. The University gave it more support than it
usually accords to cultural organisations in its city.
Phillimore, MacNeile Dixon and Cathcart were on the

board, and the students went when they could afford
it. When they couldn't, Wareing gave them free seats.
At least our support compared favourably with that of
the rest of the town. One night the only people in the
auditorium were four schoolmistresses in the front row
of the pit. Wareing came before the curtain and
invited them forward to the stalls, and they had a full
performance to themselves, as if they had been middle
European princesses. Those who stayed away missed
a wonderfully collected set of plays, beautifully acted,
for Wareing had a *flair* for plays and actors. Indeed,
I sometimes think that the short period when the
English Repertory Theatre was in flower came very
near to being a golden age. We shall probably have to
wait a hundred years for another.

. . . .

A week or so after my twenty-first birthday I went
to a Conference at Aberdeen. In each of the Scottish
Universities there is a body constituted by law called
the Students' Representative Council. It is the undergraduates' parliament. To the average student it is as
important as the real parliament is to the average man
—perhaps less important, for it has few opportunities
for persecuting him. To the member it presents some
advantages. He is entitled to walk in certain pro-
cessions. He is entitled to express his opinion of the
Senate in set speeches. He may be elected a delegate
to an inter-University conference. If he is President
he may wear a very beautiful gown with gold braid on
it. The Editor of the *Glasgow University Magazine* is,
ex officio, a member of the Council and a delegate to the
Conference. I went up to Aberdeen on a cold January
day with Galbraith, James Hendry, Archibald and
Mathams. I found when I arrived that I had forgotten
to pack my dress shoes. I had, indeed, a pair of patent

leather slippers which I wore on indoor occasions, but to get from place to place I had to blush in evening clothes and brown boots. In any other city this would have been a source of embarrassment almost unbearable, but in Aberdeen air embarrassment does not flourish.

We met the St. Andrews and Edinburgh delegates in a hotel, changed, and were escorted to the Union in the Marischal College. The Marischal College is like an enormous bride'scake. I am told that the University hope to sell it to the Corporation. I wish them luck. We sat down to supper in an immense, cold room through which a snell wind blew. By the fish course we had put on our mufflers, but our teeth still chattered. Our glasses were steadily filled by the firm hands of granite-faced waiters and a little after midnight I was sitting in a chair in a corridor along which a hurricane howled, trying to tie my brown boot laces. Dense waves of blackness were descending on my spirit and I called, through bitter tears, for James Hendry to tie my boot laces for me. This that noble-spirited man did and assisted me back to my hotel.

It was a bad start to a most enjoyable occasion. It is true that sessions of the Conference were held at which we decided that honours degrees should be made more difficult; that Scottish Universities ought really to teach Celtic Literature; that Lectureships in Art should be instituted; that all four Universities should teach diseases of children in the same way; that all women students should be segregated in separate colleges of their own. There followed, I think, a dance, but I put on my brown boots and went with Hendry and Galbraith to see *Rob Roy*. After that we rejoined the other delegates and danced with the police in the snow and with the statuary in the hotel. There

were other two sessions and then the Conference dinner.
After the Conference dinner there was an Aftermath
during which we sat in the firelight and said in turn
what we thought of the other members of the Conference. On the following morning we attended the
service in King's College Chapel. My head was filled
with one expanding, splitting, bursting agony and the
foolish old missionary who preached the sermon talked
to us for an hour in a loud, booming voice on the
technique of converting the heathen. King's College
Chapel is no doubt very beautiful. I am told that
Aberdeen is a seaport town, and I hope on some future
visit to Aberdeen to behold the ocean. I have been
there ten times and have not seen it yet. There has
always been too much to do.

I find it very difficult to recall any of the things I
thought about during these years and my writings of
the period do not help me. To-day I cannot find out
what my juniors are thinking. I should put this down
to my own insensitiveness and natural prejudice against
the young if this thick, frosted plate-glass window did
not obscure my own past mind. I seemed to do something that passed for thinking, for I was for ever
talking and the subject, I gather, was generally Life.
I promulgated laws on this subject, but I cannot
remember what they were. My father told me that
when he was my age his mind was a seething cauldron
of doubts, difficulties and ideas. I replied quite
honestly that so had mine been, but that I had already
made up my mind. He said, " About what? " I said
" About everything." I was not trying to be funny.
What my conclusions were I cannot tell you, for I
have forgotten them.

I suspect all autobiographers of making up out of
their own contemporary heads the thoughts and
emotions of their nonage. The only evidence I will

accept from them is that of letters written at the time
and this evidence I shall scan very closely indeed. The
average boy writes letters either to please, to irritate,
to fulfil a duty or to impress. He seldom uses them to
express his mind. None of my letters of the fifth phase
survive. At least I hope they don't. Many years ago
I read some of them and went hot and cold all over, so
full of lumpish affectation were they. I am persuaded
that I was a better man than these sheets revealed.

It has been said that letter-writing is a lost art. It is
more than that: it is a lost practice. Those who find
relief in the continuous exercise of talk need never
learn to write letters, and a modern letter of the modern
town-dweller is a makeshift method of communication.
Sometimes it has not even been discovered that it is a
method of communication at all. When I committed
the impertinence of censoring letters during the war
I found that fully sixty per cent. of the correspondents
used simple formulae or even copied passages out of
newspapers. They had not realised that letter-writing
was a kind of speech. It is possible that one of the
elements in the circuit on the left side of the brain has
already become atrophied in part of the human species.
I, for one, have seen more cases of apoplexy in which
speech is knocked out and writing preserved than I
would have been led to expect by the older text-books.
Be that as it may,[1] I seldom receive or even see what is
called " a good letter " nowadays.

My printed works during this period are a poor
guide to my line of thought. I was more occupied
with style than with content (hard as it may be for the
reader of this book to believe that) and the style was
not the man. I find a commonplace cynicism, a

[1] " Be that as it may "—what a divinely useful phrase! It directs
the traffic like a good policeman.

critical attitude towards my neighbours, a real enjoyment of my situation in life and a strong preference for sound over sense. My verse was all direct or indirect parody, and so, I am afraid, was my prose. I drew pictures in half a dozen unassimilated styles. It is true that Strathie once told me that there was a Message in my Editorial and that I tried thereafter to convey a message. I cannot say to-day that my messages were very vital. I had some idea of a polity within our little state and kept driving at that week after week. I seem to have figured it as some sort of raffish yet puritanical epicureanism. You can readily understand that such a system is very difficult to reconstruct after a lapse of time.

What I do recall is that my spirits rose and sank like remittent fever. My temperature was either very high or very low, and these changes were periodic. The fastigia of this unfitful fever usually coincided with what George Fletcher called High Emprise.

One High Emprise was undertaken in the winter when some of us went to Arran and made our way from Brodick to Corrie and from Corrie to Lochranza, first in a rainstorm and then in a blizzard. There were eight of us, and in Corrie Inn we slept four to a room with the wind rattling the window sashes and Galbraith groaning in his sleep.

" Take in the soul! Take in the soul! "

We invented a creature called the Chorp. I find, on reference, the following words which remind me somehow of Walter Pater:

" Stan Leigh wanted to help on the *Glasgow Herald* with a lyrical ode beginning ' Gibber, gibber, little corpse! ' That was because I told him (to cheer him) that when doors are left half ajar any corpse that may be in the room sits up in bed and chatters noiselessly with rolling eyes. Thus it was that we came upon the baffling realisation of the word Chorp. . . . The Chorp does not laugh. It weeps often. It is a two-foot long, pathetic animal, a little like a big lizard, but more like an earth-worm. It lives among the wreck and the dulse and Dead Men's Fingers and sea anemones; and in the night, or the grey dawn, or the tender purple twilight, it creeps up over the shingle on its soft, stubby, chaetae and climbs in at windows for companionship. If it comes in at the door there is something wrong. It is a fey, for it nearly always dies on reaching the inside of a house and then it disappears gradually, leaving no trace but two tears on the carpet. The Chorp is all soul and is for ever in the depth of a gentle sorrow that fills his blind brown eyes with tears and robs it, in the end, of a rather joyless little life. . . ."

At breakfast next morning we talked almost exclusively about the Chorp. A tall man called David Adams stretched his legs among the tea-cups and ham and eggs and told us what he thought. R. M. Grant made ecstatic, tentative gestures with his subtle white hands. Strathie tried to get the Chorp on a sound biological-philosophical basis. Roy Archibald said it was all bloody nonsense. By this time it was snowing heavily outside and we struggled over to Lochranza with the snow two feet deep on the roads, David Adams carrying a travelling rug on a pole in front of us and telling us from time to time that it was the Banner of Lorne. In Lochranza we drank toddy and read Browning aloud. On the following morning we took a rather smelly ship called the *Kintyre* and returned to the Broomielaw of Glasgow. So much for that.

It had been very pleasant, and in the following year we tried to recapture its joys; but the party had dwindled to three; the weather was foul without being exciting, and beyond the kissing of the cold lips of the bronze Duke of Hamilton at Brodick and a furious row with the landlord at Corrie there is little worth recording. Happiness, in my experience, resents being hunted.

Another platitude is that a small radius in space may contain a world of experience. I had influenza one spring and had just got out of bed when Walter Elliot and John Boyd came to my house suggesting that we should walk over the Campsie Hills to Fintry and spend the night at a cottage occupied by some Bolsheviks in that village. To this I consented and we took train to Lennoxtown. In the murk of the Glasgow streets we had not realised that the countryside was still enveloped in snow and, at Lennoxtown, we were told that the snow plough had been held up by drifts and that Fintry was cut off from civilisation. The distance was only about seven miles, and John Boyd said that he knew it like the back of his hand. As for fourteen-foot drifts, we could go round them. We had pies and hot drinks in Lennoxtown and started off at about half-past seven at night, making good going along the tracks of the snow plough. At eight o'clock it began to snow heavily, and before nine we were completely lost. While John was casting about to recover his sense of direction, Walter and I dug with our sticks and found we were standing on top of a rough stone wall. John announced that he had gathered the lie of the land through the falling snow and we followed him, floundering up to our waists. In time we came to a little burn and sat down for a moment to drink and to decide what to do next. We decided to walk down the burn, which must sooner or later reach the River Endrick and a practicable road. John, who was very light and wiry, led off. Walter followed. At a lengthening interval I followed him. My influenza was telling on me and I was all out. I recalled that I had been told that a death in the snow was the pleasantest

form of death and decided that I would never reach the
Endrick. At this point I fell into a drift up to my neck
and was fully persuaded that the moment had come.
The mild shock of the fall, however, stimulated me and
I shouted. It was a feeble, croaking sound, and I
made up my mind that it was hardly worth repeating.
I felt comfortable and contented in my drift, and it
seemed a shame to make the other two men retrace so
many laborious steps only to find a corpse. On the
other hand, I thought, it would be a pity if they reached
the Endrick and felt that they ought to come back all
that way, particularly as only my head was visible, as it
too was rapidly becoming covered by the falling snow,
and I should no doubt be very difficult to find. I
raised another contemptible croak—this time so nearly
inaudible that it made me laugh. It was answered
from the other side of the burn. A shepherd had come
out of his cottage door to have a look at the night
before turning in, and he heard me. He shouted to
me and I replied. He appeared dimly on the other
side of the burn and jumped across.

"Good God Almighty!" he said. "What are you
doing there?"

"Nothing," I said.

"It looks like you'll be doing nothing for a long
time," he said, "if we can't get ye out of that."

He helped me out. I could not stand up and sat
down by the side of the burn, while he called back
John and Walter. John had plugged on for nearly a
mile, Walter for less than that. The burn, it appeared,
emptied not into the Endrick, but into the Forth.
Walter and John had a twenty-five mile walk before
them before they would have seen a house. He put
us on the road at the spot where it had been cleared
from Fintry and Walter and John oxtered me down to
the Bolsheviks' den. The Bolsheviks had all gone to

bed, but we soon had them out of that and they sat by the fireside and talked about Karl Marx while we slept. The next time I surveyed death so closely and dispassionately was when I attempted to swim the Tigris by moonlight, but fortunately thought better of it before I got very far.

I was fond of walking, but I preferred roads to moors and hills. This fact is pertinent to the theme of this book. If I was driven off the road by choice or by necessity I was usually involved in some sort of misfortune. I remember a miserable night on the hills above Loch Lomond, because the floods had made me miss a bridge in the twilight. I fell over precipices, was half-drowned in torrents and finally made myself a bield of rotten trees and slept on a howling hillside with no supper but a porridge of disintegrated water biscuit, mashed cheese, wet match-heads and Murray's Belfast smoking mixture. Next morning the bath in the inn was tepid, they had no dry clothes to offer me and the first train was at four o'clock in the afternoon.

Mark Twain began one of his novels by condensing all the Weather prevailing throughout the action into the first chapter. He thought it necessary that his public should know that he could do weather very well, but he had no intention of holding up his story with long descriptions of thunder storms. I am not very good at scenery, and scenery is an essential part of a walking tour. I think it would be better to spare you any account of my tours of the Western Highlands. On one of these, however, David Adams and I entered a tiny public house with our eyes still swimming in golds and greens and peacock blues; and we heard there much talk of Mr. Lloyd George and his schemes for socialising the land. A little man nursing a pint of beer in a corner was anxious to play his part, but the technicalities were above his head. At length one of the debaters returned from outside and the little man saw his chance.

" You're a dishonest drinker," he said.

" What for because? " said the other man.

The sweet monotony of movement and thought, the air and the variety of sight, the warming completeness of the fatigue at the end of the day held something as near satisfaction as it was possible for me to reach. I think that the forced monotony is an important element in happiness. I cannot understand the pity young authors have for the clerk who adds his figures, catches his train, digs in his garden, listens to the wireless, goes to sleep, wakes up and goes through the same day again. By such activities the human spirit is more likely to be freed than by those in which it is watching every step and expecting lions at every crossing. Be that as it may. . . .

In 1909 I joined the Officers' Training Corps. There, too, the present medley of routine and adventure made a great appeal to me. I finished with the O.T.C. in camp in Ilkley, where the adventure seems almost to have swallowed the routine. I heard my last *reveille* from the railway station where I was sitting talking to the night porters in the lamp-room. It was an interesting camp. Before a couple of years had gone many of those who attended it had been killed in battle. I was lingering superfluous on the stage of Glasgow University. Most of my friends were doctors long ago. I felt a pleasing detachment from the camp and extra-camp sports. It was the biggest camp I had ever attended. Except Oxford and Cambridge all the Universities in Great Britain were represented, and our Commandant was a Brigadier who wore the Victoria Cross. His name was Gough.

One night the English contingents dressed themselves in pyjamas and, led by a penny-whistle and biscuit-tin band, marched on Ilkley to paint it red. A Scots concert had been organised in the town that night, and I was singing a song. When the news of the invasion came I said

"Scotland protects the town,"

and the concert broke up. I went to the main square where there was a huge cluster of lights. Round this I found a group of half a dozen St. Andrews cadets in uniform. Round the rest of the square were some seven or eight hundred pyjamaed Sassenach cadets. They were making a great noise. As I arrived, their "General" turned to them and called for three hearty boos for the Scotsmen. I went to him and asked him what was the matter with him. He said that the St. Andrews cadets had prevented his army from turning out the lights in the cluster. I asked him why, and he said that they had told him that Scotland was protecting the town. The St. Andrews cadets corroborated this. They said that the word had gone round that the town was under Scottish protection and that these lights would be turned out over their dead bodies. The victory of prestige over force was complete. The Saxon army gave three more hearty boos and marched off about their occasions after we had forbidden them to light a bonfire in the town.

While the Scots had been otherwise engaged they had succeeded in painting the White Wells with a decorative arrangement of stripes, but this was practically all the damage they succeeded in doing. When they broke up into raiding companies these were followed by Scots in twos and threes and, whenever they attempted mischief, they were sternly told to desist and obeyed. The most dramatic moment, perhaps, came when they lined up to attack a pub from which a cadet had been wrongously and grievously thrown earlier in the week. They found the cadet—

an Aberdonian—standing on the steps of the pub with four of his bulky friends and threatening massacre in a loud voice to the first man who laid a finger on the building.

My impression is that these things are true. If this account meets the eye of one of my comrades of the English contingent, and if his impression is that they are lies, I shall not quarrel with him about it. I shall apologise and withdraw; but I shall keep my beliefs.

One late night I was returning to a camp at Gailes at peace with myself and the world. Two drunken Glasgow Highlanders were reeling in front of me. One was a piper in full dress with medals. I was wondering whether to join them for company on the road back when we passed a little group of houses at the end of a village from which came the screams of a woman in pain and affright. I said,

" Hello, Highlanders! It looks as though there's a row here."

They said, " Oh, a row? " straightened up, and became the complete British soldiers. I marched with them towards the cottages at the double and we found a crowd gathered round a little dimly lighted alleyway. The screams had died to a sustained whimpering. My army and I pushed our way through the crowd and entered the alleyway. By the light of an unshaded gas jet I saw one of the most enormous men I have ever seen. He had an Irish-looking face and tousled fair hair. His shirt was open to the waist and he was in a gesture of defiance. The glimmer of the light on the piper's medals caught his attention. He said,

" Clear out with you, the whole pack of you! Or if you want a fight, come on, man to man, and I'll plaster the causeway with the lot of you. . . . You there, you think because you've got a blank kilt and a row of blank tin medals that you can play the blank tin man over me.

I was in the army myself and I ate twenty of the likes of you for chuck before lights out."

The piper said,

" Now, now, mate, man to man's all very well, but man to woman's no' the clean potato."

At this point, to my astonishment, the large man began to cry. He asked the piper if he was a married man himself and the piper said he was. He then elaborated a story of mounting woes and distresses, of intolerable insults nobly borne, of slattern habits over-looked, of neglect and unfaithfulness forgiven, of a last straw that broke the camel's back. He had come in, it appeared, not drink taken but just cheery, taken off his boots and asked for a cup of tea. His lady had not only refused this reasonable request but had thrown his boots out of the window. He had corrected her. He would correct her no more. He had no wish to make trouble or to pick any quarrel with a decent man; but as for these nosey monkeys, his neighbours, they had better snap out of it quick. He then shook hands with the Glasgow Highlanders and with me, and we bade each other good-night. For some reason or other I did not accompany the Highlanders, but sat on a wall and laughed for a good half-hour.

At Folkestone I reached one of my highest points of pure sensual happiness. All through a blazing hot morning we had fought a rearguard action against the King's Royal Rifles and I made camp with a few minutes to spare to catch a train to London, because one of our men had sprained his ankle and I had brought him in. The Medical Officer rewarded me with two pints of beer and remarked how they hissed as they went down. He then lent me his dinner jacket in a heavy suit-case and I trotted off to the station. I had an appointment to dine with my father at his club. We foregathered, had some talk and I changed. The other guest was one Sir William Byles, the M.P. for Salford, at that time and on that date a rather morose and depressed little man with a white beard. Heat, exhaustion, and having had no lunch except two pints of beer made me sulky. Sir William was a teetotaler, and when my father asked me if I would have a ginger beer I took immediate offence and refused to drink anything at all. The consequence was that when I caught the train to Folkestone with a few seconds to spare I was as desiccated as a Bombay duck. The compartment was packed with people, mostly carrying home fish in grass baskets. It was two or three miles from Folkestone to our camp at Shorncliffe and I dragged in the Medical Officer's suit-case sometime after midnight. I was more dead than alive. It was sheer animal instinct that led me towards the guard tent. Five guards out of six had a fair supply of beer to comfort them through the long watches. I was unlucky. John Reith was sergeant of the guard and he had a sense of duty, discipline and the fitness of things which has since led him to very high places indeed. He told me he did not want to arrest me, but that I must go instantly to my tent as the adjutant was in the lines. He told me it was very foolish of me to get so drunk as this, and that if the adjutant saw me I would get into very serious trouble. The bitter cynicism of his suspicion was almost too much for me. I looked up at the sultry stars and back again at my superior officer, said what was in my mind to say about him, shambled wearily towards my tent and fell like a log on my paillasse. I reached a hand for my water-bottle that I might moisten my parched lips. My hand closed not on the water-bottle but on the icy neck of a china-stoppered bottle of lager beer. I thought that this was death, that I was glad I had been good, or, at least, must have been better than I thought I was being.

There was no other explanation than that this was Heaven. Cool, bubbling, vivifying, astringent, the lager went down like Lodore. I stretched out my hand again. Another bottle was put into it.

Fortunately or unfortunately there was a simple physical explanation for this miracle. For miracle it was to find good liquor in our penurious tent after midnight. A friendly German who had been with us the year before had been appointed chemist to a brewery and had not forgotten his thirsty friends in his days of plenty.

That camp finished with the departure of the beloved Hook. Hook was our adjutant. He was called Hook because he had lost an arm in the South African War. He was a long, lean captain in the Highland Light Infantry, and we longed for a war that he might lead us. All of us felt an adoration for Hook greater than any I saw or heard of from men to an officer in the real war. The nearest I heard to it was the story of Colonel Green, who commanded a battalion of the Rifle Brigade. He was strolling along a badly shelled road when a sentry, cowering in a ditch, was heard to say to his mate,

" There's our adjective colonel. He don't give a noun for them nouns."

Hook marched us from Shorncliffe to Folkestone for the last time to put us on the train. After we had passed the guard he gave us the order " March at ease." What we did next was entirely unpremeditated and unarranged. Not a single man moved from the slope or opened his mouth to speak. We marched at attention to the station. It was a curious gesture. I have never seen anything quite like it in my life.

Its nearest relation as an odd bit of mass psychology was the Coliseum Riot. A music hall entertainer and magician had got himself into trouble with the police by printing the letters M.D. after his name in some of his advertisements. He said in court that the letters did not mean Doctor of Medicine, but Merry Devil, and waved the matter aside with a light laugh. He was punished by a small fine. But we, who could not become M.D.'s without at least seven years of hard work, did not so easily forgive him. When he came to Glasgow to give his entertainment a handful of medical students in the gallery hissed and booed him. The magician came down to the footlights and delivered himself very aptly on the subject of the medical profession in general and of medical students in particular. He wound up by quoting the poet Burns to the effect that,

" They gang in stirks and come oot asses."

He then proceeded with his entertainment, which consisted in passing enormous quantities of electricity through himself and his assistant and in healing half a dozen of the incurably lame by hypnotism or animal magnetism. I have no recollection that he pretended to be anything more than a showman, and what followed seems to me to have been beyond his desserts.

On a certain Thursday morning a Jewish medical student wrote on the back of an envelope " Meet at the first house of the Coliseum to-night." Not more than fifty men can have seen the notice, and the Jewish student was quite an obscure person. But by half-past six that evening the Coliseum music hall was packed with students. Their pockets were bulging with missiles and grim determination was written on their faces. The atmosphere was electric enough to provide the magician with free current for the rest of his life. The turns preceding his were galloped through at top speed and greeted with thunderous cheers. The fatal number went up. There was a dead silence. After a pause the curtain rose on a sort of woodland glade in which a prominent feature was the Cage of Death, an alarming structure of polished metal connected with miles of flex. There was no magician. The orchestra struck a few chords, and a lady in blue appeared tentatively from the wings, followed by the doctor himself. The mob had somehow been unprepared for a mixed target. They shouted to the magician to take the woman off. There was a short, irresolute interval. And then an ungallant potato hit La Belle Electra on the knee. Down came the fireproof curtain and the audience surged forward to the orchestra, shouting, yelling and swearing. My own experience of what happened next is a little limited. A drunken lad in my neighbourhood produced a revolver, announcing that it was loaded and that he was going to shoot the buzzard. I reached over, took the revolver from him and kicked it below the seats. I then tripped him up and sat on his head. When I looked over the seat-back I saw the stage occupied by five students, who were giving an impromptu music hall turn of little merit. They were capering, singing and waving sticks. They were joined by a more determined figure, a broad, prognathous man called Alexander Garvie. He took the stick from the nearest student and thrust it through the fireproof curtain. Most of us were very much astonished, for we had believed the fireproof curtains to be made of wrought iron; but Garvie pulled the stick upwards and downwards till he had made a six-foot rent in the curtain and through this rent he boldly entered.

I had got my murderer into a chastened mood and now held him on a plush seat with his arm twisted behind his back. The students were now charging down the corridors and over the backs of the seats, making for the rent in the curtain. The circles and the gallery were standing up shouting for the magician at the tops of their voices.

After he had passed the rent, disarmed a stage hand with a broom, Garvie saw an unco sight. On the stage were two hundred policemen. I have checked the figures and know them to be accurate. He had never seen so many policemen before. He was seized and thrown through the rent his own hands had made.

We saw Garvie perform a back somersault, hit the stage and fall over into the orchestra. He was there seized by the throat by a plain clothes man and removed rapidly from view. Then through the hole in the curtain poured the police, with batons drawn and battle in their eyes. Except for that one potato, our ammunition was intact, and we let them have it. They came bravely one by one, and on each was registered at least a dozen hits. Peasemeal bombs, bags of maize, eggs, potatoes, tomatoes, herring, soot, thickened the air, and policeman after policeman leapt from the stage over the orchestra railing and into the eel-pit. They were blinded and angry and they laid about them with their batons. The mob hit back with ash sticks and knuckles, but were being driven back slowly to the entries, and it looked highly probable that somebody would be killed when Williamson, an ex-President of the Union rushed up to the police lieutenant and seized him by the lapels, shrieking at him.

" Call your men off or I hold you responsible for anything that happens."

The word responsible penetrated the angry lieutenant's consciousness, and he blew a shrill blast on his whistle. Everything became astonishingly quiet. The policemen stopped bludgeoning, and the students stopped fighting and swearing. Williamson, the lieutenant and the President of the S.R.C. made their way to the stage. Williamson shouted in his little, thin voice that he would make the magician apologise and that then we must all go home quietly; and the party then disappeared through the rent and shortly the fireproof curtain rose. In the meantime there had been a good deal of skilful and unostentatious shouldering of students out into the street. The platform party consisted of the three before mentioned and the magician. The last-named appeared to say something, a tomato hit Williamson on the chest, the platform party began to argue with one another, the fireproof curtain fell, a few shots were fired, but the police "had the matter well in hand." We went out into the open. There we heard that some of our number had been taken to the southern police station. Such was our state of unbridled ὕβρις that we immediately went there in large numbers and demanded their release. A bland sergeant assured us that he had nobody inside and we were firmly pushed out of the lane. The rest of the evening was spent in visiting the premises of the unlicensed portion of Glasgow's quacks. Beyond the breaking of a few windows and a few scuffles with police cordons, nothing noteworthy happened. On Monday five students appeared in the police court on various charges arising out of the incident. A bewildered bailie sat on the bench; the prosecuting counsel was a police officer in uniform; for the defence there appeared two magnificent King's Counsel, one of them a sheriff, and two or three distinguished juniors. This array of wigs and gowns had a striking effect upon the bailie and the police witnesses. A few leading liars were put up to testify to the impeccable behaviour of the five martyrs. One was fined a pound, another was admonished, and the other three left the court without a stain on their characters. It has been claimed in recent years that other seats of learning have priority in the torture of the poor magician. Our demonstration was the first and most tremendous.

The faculty that distinguishes the human being from the brute and the artist from the human being is the faculty of selection. In so far as I have this faculty I find it very difficult to apply to the fifth five years. They were a rousing time. They were full of entertaining people and incidents exalting and pathetic. This whole book could be written about them; but whether they would interest you as much as they interested me is another thing. I must go warily in my account of the virtues of my favourite child. Quite unconsciously I have given him the air of a thick-eared tough and it would take another forty pages to modify this impression by telling you of his beautiful virtues. I must hurry over, therefore, the occasion when three mass meetings of the students demanded the resignation of their Rector, Lord Curzon of Kedleston. He had postponed his inauguration ceremony at the last moment in a very off-hand telegram, and we were not accustomed to be treated in this fashion by mere ex-Viceroys. The Students' Representative Council circumvented the issue by calling a plebiscite, and the backwoodsmen forgave Lord Curzon by a large majority. But it was all very amusing while it lasted. Some of us had met that very distinguished man before at the house of his Assessor. He did not seem to us to bear out in his person the cruel pedigree, Family Butler out of Queen of Sheba. He seemed to us a singularly amiable and patient person.

Johnny Mowat, who was later to describe Lord Curzon as " Chanticleer," who conscientiously believed that the sun would not rise till he had crowed it up, had occasion to rebuke him at the party of which I am speaking. A semi-circle of presidents and secretaries was disposed in front of Lord Curzon's chair, on the arm of which Williamson was sitting. Johnny Mowat and I were wandering about the rest of the room discussing great matters. As we passed the apex of the semi-circle we heard the Rector say,

" I suppose dull moments in my speech will be enlivened with bursts of song? "

Johnny Mowat's flying elbows opened a space between the secretary of the Temperance Society and the president of the Bible Students' Union. His large, pale face and fiery, red-rimmed eyes confronted the statesman and, in his somewhat metallic *tenorio robusto* voice, he observed,

" You'll have to see that there are no dull moments in your speech."

Lord Curzon bridled. He said, " Ah! Shall I hand it to you to revise before I deliver it? "

" No," said Johnny. " I've no time. I'm working for my final. But Mr. Williamson will be very glad to do it for you."

I do not know whether this story seems to you funny. It may appear to you simple rudeness. Rudeness was undoubtedly part of John Mowat's character at that time. But it was rudeness directed principally at the great and famous. Affectation was no part of John Mowat's character, and he had a ready boot for those he considered affected, whatever admirable excuse they might have for their pretensions. His method of addressing the great was, " Hi, Mr. Belloc! Shut up! Listen . . ." and at a very pompous public dinner he insisted on shaking hands with the chairman on the grounds that he was the ugliest little devil he had ever seen.

The Mowat Legend is a large one and very honour-- able to its hero. I should like to tell of how, when a panel patient called him up in the middle of the night

176

on some trivial pretext, he gave him back his fourpence
by throwing it from the bedroom window on to the
pavement. I should like to tell of the whining old lady
into whose lap he threw an armful of tulips torn from a
garden plot, exhorting her to put these on her grave.
I should like to tell of how he was rescued by a divinity
student, who was nevertheless a b——y Christian
(" inasmuch as ye do it unto the least of these my
brethren, ye do it unto Me. The least! And I was
through my third! "). I must refrain and intrude no
longer into the privacy of one who is now the most
unimaginably respectable of medical practitioners. I
should like, however, to quote one of the poems that
flashed from time to time through his excited brain.
It is about K. G. MacLeod, the greatest Scottish three-
quarter of all time.

> When all around him forwards crowd,
> And speedy halves break through,
> Though doubts his comrades' minds may cloud,
> He Kenneth what to do.

One sometimes had the illusion that Johnny Mowat
was the only man in the universe or the University at
that time, but there were others. I find that I wrote of
Walter Elliot when he was presiding at his first Union
House Dinner (Mr. Birrell being Lord Rector and all
the nobility and gentry of Glasgow being present):
" . . . The President of the Union, a large, lumpish,
salmon-coloured, ill-dressed figure, obviously from
the country, but, then, again, hardly healthy enough
looking for that, alternating a certain joviality with
glum silences reminiscent of some of the more distressing creations of Mr. Thomas Hardy; wearing a
dress suit cut by sheep shears, a crumpled shirt and
hands like soiled bunches of bananas; and, alas, what
boots!

" Do you recall how Mr. Birrell stood up for twenty
minutes and exercised a pretty if somewhat stereotyped
wit at our expense and then sat down wearing what
would, on a less noble and distinguished countenance,
have been a smirk? And do you remember how that
amorphous young man, the President of the Union,
wobbled to his feet, hands in pockets, every brace
button showing, veiled sensual eyes exploring the
cornice, and how, in a loud, fluent and unpleasant
voice he showed a much prettier wit than Mr. Birrell's,
a wider variety of general information than Principal
MacAlister and an impudence defying all comparisons?
He spoke for forty-five minutes. It was his first
public speech and it was too short. . . .

" If you would like to know some of his characteristics, I will tell you that he is an eloquent but clear-
minded person. . . . He is acutely interested in most
liberal subjects, and if a subject arises now and again
in which he is not interested, why, he just goes to
sleep. When he is awakened, he shakes his ears a
little, like gentle Gargantua, and goes on talking."

There was Zeek, the atheist, who wrote nearly all
the stuff in the *Glasgow University Magazine* that
makes me laugh nowadays, and went to America and
watched forest fires, sold real estate and edited a
Salvation Army magazine. He writes to me regularly
every twenty years. There was James Aubrey Fair
Boyd, who came from America—from the Golden Gate
of California. Aubrey had only one arm. He was the
still unravished bride of quietness. He considered,
deeply, the lilies of the field. He wrote beautiful
English. He went to Toulouse to learn the French
language; left his lodgings at dead of night because
he couldn't pay the rent; bought some bread with
English postage stamps; slept under a boat on the
sea-shore; was arrested; was taken back to his land-

lord who received him with open arms and immediately got him pupils to whom he taught Californian English; drove with a negro chauffeur to Paris; met at the Gare du Nord American friends with whom he had some sort of vague appointment in the Fall; was installed by them in a corset factory; left the corset factory and came back to Glasgow, where he led a peaceful existence, exercising charm and little else. Nobody I ever met was carried more gracefully down the river of life than Aubrey. There was David Adams, a long, gangling, sensitive man with a beautiful face. When he was dying and was too ill to write a letter he sent me a scribble of a swordsman with a long nose. I knew that he meant that he was Cyrano de Bergerac fighting his last duel. There was Robin Brown, with whom I did dissections for an extra-mural lecturer in Anatomy in a mouldy dump above a book-shop. At intervals he would put down his scalpel and forceps and walk to the window, which opened on a sunny avenue. From the window he would intone the words:

"Never since the glorious days of Mr. Gladstone have I seen before me such a large and enthusiastic gathering as I see before me to-night. Gentlemen, the things that are seen are temporal. The things that are unseen are eternal. Yet when the things that are seen come into conflict with the things that are unseen I have sufficient faith in the good sense and spirituality of my fellow countrymen to believe from the bottom of my heart in a happy issue."

He once wrote a letter to *The Spectator* simply for the sake of introducing a phrase that had come to him in a dream. The phrase was: what boots it for Mr. Balfour to cry peace when there is no peace? There was Sprochles, who began life as a brilliant mathematician, continued it as a *dilettante*, and who, according to George Fletcher, added an air of shabby gentility to the party. There was Macartney, who composed and sang oratorios I still think brilliant. There was Charlie Kirk, who put the heart of Clydeside into verse. There was Bill Brewer, Dan Stewart, Peter Gurney, Peter Davey, Dan'l Whiddon, Harry Hawk, old uncle Tom Cobbley and all. I'm overloading my cast. If happiness is to be measured in the number of one's friends, I must have been happy indeed.

I hunted with several packs, but latterly became absorbed principally into the powerful body known as the Union Clique. I organised this clique into a society called the Independent Leisure Party. It held Chapters at regular intervals in the Union Board-room, under the Presidency of a sad-eyed divine. The business at these Chapters consisted solely in considering and rejecting with contumely candidates for membership. The contumely was provided by Macartney, and very distressing contumely it was. I was returned to an elder group of associates by an attack of scarlet fever. The Hubbard Highbrows, of whom I have spoken, were now physicians at a Corporation fever hospital, under the superintendency of one John Brownlee.

John Brownlee was an adept in the art of living. He was a widower and, as he always dined with his resident physicians, he chose them with great care. Every dinner in the Residents' mess at Ruchill was a dinner party. The conversation was good, the food was good and the wines were good. It was the only civilised residents' mess I have ever visited.

One night there was an earthquake and Brownlee came into my ward at one o'clock in the morning to ask me which way the electric lights had swung. I was reading Morley's *Life of Cobden*, and Brownlee said,

" I can't stand John Morley. He writes in common time."

He said Free Trade was a heresy and he would like to see it destroyed. He said that Protection would inevitably destroy all the heavy industries and the large corporations, and that, after a period of famine and revolution, we would become what God intended us to be—a nation of small craftsmen. He said he was very ill and that cigarette smoke and the eating of new bread had induced a fibrillation of his ligament of Treitz. This ligament, as every schoolboy knows, is in fact the suspensory muscle of duodenum. In it, muscle fibres interlace the connective tissue, and when these begin to tremble—according to Brownlee— there is no mistaking the symptoms. He could usually cure it by playing the piano accompaniment of the *Erl King*; but he was too busy to-night watching a culture he was growing in the laboratory and answering telephone messages from damned town councillors.

He left me and I lay and listened to the wind, to the moaning of a mastoid child in the next ward and to the thump of the feet of a night nurse whom I disliked. My left ear was throbbing vaguely and was presently to become the seat of an acute *otitis media*. I began to hate the night nurse. She was a hard little Highland pedant. She scolded me and gave me orders and hurt me whenever she touched me. She was very con- scientious and she never kept still all night. One night a ceaseless activity made her nose bleed so badly that she had to be taken off duty, and she was replaced by a young nurse who knocked over everything she touched, forgot my medicines and temperatures, whistled while she worked like the Seven Dwarfs, but had a pleasant personality and a fine fund of gossip. I should have got better very quickly if my middle ear had given no trouble, and presently a little bold surgeon came and

thrust a bistoury into it without an anaesthetic. It was
very painful. Indeed, the whole business was very
painful. I used to eat my pillow and groan. The
curious thing was that whereas the good old nurse
made me ill when I wasn't, the incompetent young one
could cure me by just coming into the ward. For the
rest the Hubbard Highbrows played picquet with me
and introduced me to A. E. Housman.

. . . .

As the five years wore on I began to take an interest
in medicine. Two causes contributed to this. One
was George Middleton and the other was my period of
residence at the Maternity Hospital. There were
three teaching hospitals in Glasgow—the Western,
where the University students went, the Victoria,
where we used to go on Saturday mornings to hear a
hurricane of diagnoses and wise saws from a Welsh
surgeon called R. H. Parry, and the Royal Infirmary,
which occupied a hinterland into which few of us
penetrated. Its students at that time were women,
Indians, Chinamen and students of the extra-mural
colleges who were taking a diploma instead of a degree.
My teachers at the Western Infirmary had been
extremely kind to me. Every now and again they
would dislodge me from the back seats of the huge
lecture theatre, wake me out of a doze and try to in-
struct me in the elements of medicine and surgery.
I felt ashamed of putting them to too much trouble
and at impeding the progress of students more ardent
than I, so I did not attend very regularly. I got some
spiritual delight from watching the great Sir William
Macewen. Ralph Stockman's satire I found invigor-
ating when it was not directed at me. William
MacLennan had a pleasing and buoyant personality;
but none of them succeeded in teaching me anything

at all. I had heard that the Royal Infirmary was a place where one could roam free and not bother about class tickets, and so I went with two or three others to explore. From the moment I found Middleton I did not miss an attendance. I wondered why nobody had told me that medicine was so interesting. Old George was the hairiest man I ever saw, except for his bald head. Hair luxuriated from every other square inch of his face and overhung his steel spectacles. He wore a little black alpaca jacket and carried an old wooden stethoscope. He talked in a high-pitched, testy old man's voice and kept strictly to the point. He had been an assistant to old G.,[1] and had inherited his brilliance as a diagnostician. I remember him sitting down at a bedside to interview a new patient. He asked the man three or four questions that seemed to have little bearing on the subject, and listened carefully to his answers. He then turned to Elliot and me and said that this would be an interesting case for us to investigate over the week-end. He had only seen the patient for the first time and he never made spot diagnoses; but he thought we would find that the patient had a tumour about the size of a hazel-nut on the floor of the fourth ventricle of his brain, and that the nature of the tumour was a gumma. On the way out of the ward he said we would easily find out in the post-mortem room in a fortnight's time. The man died in a fortnight, and a tumour of the size and situation he described was found. I asked him how it was done and he said,

" When you've seen a good many cases you get to recognise them."

At the end of the term he invited me to become his resident, but I had to refuse because I had not yet

[1] Sir William Tennent Gairdner, the god of all Glasgow practitioners of his generation.

passed anatomy. I went back to the Western and to
the clinic of the professor of Medicine, feeling that I
could see the boots off the professor and his entire
army of swots. The professor of Medicine was
Samson Gemmell. There are no entertaining anecdotes about George Middleton; but there are a
thousand about Samson Gemmell. Middleton was a
physician *pur sang*; Sammy Gemmell was a sophisticated rhetorician, intoxicated with the exuberance of
his own verbosity. I have learned from him some of
this verbosity, and used some of his more picturesque
periods in one or two of my plays.

I assimilated Sammy Gemmell's style very quickly
and wrote my reports in it—" This phenomenon, taken
in conjunction with certain other clinical findings,
leads me insensibly to the conclusion that the murmur
is aortic in, origin." He liked my reports. He did
not ask us to be Ruskins but it cheered him to detect
a little Addisonian grace.

One day he seated himself by the side of an Irish
navvy who was recovering from pneumonia. My
report read that he had been beholding a football
contest at Ibrox Park on an inclement afternoon and
that, in the full rigour of the game, he was violently
seized by a sharp, stabbing pain in his right hypo-
chondrium. This was followed by a rigor, and after
an indeterminate interval of time, by vomiting. Samson read these phrases with some appreciation and
then turned to the navvy.

" And when, sir," he said, " did these symptomatic
manifestations begin to make themselves apparent? "

" Yes, sir," said the navvy politely.

" Ach, himmel," said Sammy. " He cannot understand a question stated in the simplest imaginable
terms. There's your modern education for you!
There's your compulsory free school-board education

for you! And this individual is going to march confidently into the polling booth after me and cancel my vote. Your modern democracy, sir, is Judas Iscariot voting against Jesus Christ. That is soh."

At the upper end of the ward there was a man sick of the dropsy. Samson led us past him shaking his head sadly.

" There he is," said Samson, " look at him where he lies. He is going out with the tide. He was not one to indulge himself in an occasional orgy of wantonness with his fellow alcoholics. Day in day out, week in week out, year in year out, he soaked his tissues in the noxious fluid. He laid upon his kidneys, gentlemen, an embargo impossible to be borne. Daily he trucidated his emunctories, till an ineluctable nemesis overtook him. And there he lies, anasarcous to a degree. I have assaulted him with diuretics, I have crucified him with hot packs, and his daily output is going steadily downwards. Am I Moses that I should bring forth water from a rock? "

There was richness indeed in the Medical Faculty in those days, and I could fill this book with them if I had not promised myself to expound to you one way of living and the one individual who lived in that way. In time these great men pushed, heaved and pulled me through my examinations, and I preserved a certain blandness through this torturing process. I descended from my cloud cuckoo-land once or twice in the way of business. At one part of the curriculum it was necessary to conduct ten confinements in the poorer quarters of the city; and during this exercise I came into contact with what, I suppose, was real life.

Before I became officially a student midwife myself I spent an evening with Fletcher and Sutherland in the flea-bitten lodgings where the young Doctor Slops was segregated. These lodgings were moved later on into a building under the eye of the Maternity Hospital—a building in which my mother spent her childhood when the neighbourhood was respectable. I slept in my mother's nursery. The Maternity Hospital is situated on the top of a diseased hill along whose ridge runs the Rotten Row. The only houses on that hill with any amenities are a row of aged public houses; but terraces of some distinction and dignity look out through black and broken glass on the littered and sour-smelling streets. The hill has a sordid charm, and it was on it that I felt for the first time that singular sensation, *nostalgie pour la boue*. It is not a common sensation among young bourgeois Scots, and I was astonished and interested to find it in myself.

The telephone bell rang. Fletcher knocked the thick black out of his pipe. Sutherland reached down the black bag and we started out into the muddy streets. In the hospital waiting-room we found a woman wearing a shawl over her head and we walked with her to a back alley off the Gallowgate, where our patient lay.

She lived in a very clean, whitewashed, single room on the ground floor, and her five children were asleep in orange boxes which had been painted green and neatly arranged round the damp walls. The kitchen range was black-leaded and shining. There were one or two brass ornaments, also shining, on the mantelpiece and the inevitable china dogs. There was no carpet, but the floor was well scrubbed. The built-in bed and one chair were the only furniture. The patient was thirty years old, but looked sixty; she had a clean and sorrowful face. Her husband was in prison, serving a six month sentence.

There was nothing very odd about all this; but standing in the middle of the room was a well-dressed woman of about forty, with red hair and bright green eyes. She had a well-cut, cream-coloured face with very little expression on it. But there was an intensity behind the eyes that made the face memorable. She wore a black dress with patent leather shoes like a shop assistant. She was a shop assistant.

We asked her if she was a relative of the patient and she said no, she had not seen her till that evening. One of her girls had told her that a neighbour was in trouble and, as there was nothing much doing up at the shelter, she had come down and tidied the place up a bit and got things ready. There wasn't much to get ready, she said. She said she hoped we'd brought plenty of stuff with us. She said that if we were new at this game we ought to be careful; that the woman had done her best but the room was very verminous, and perhaps Sutherland wouldn't mind pouring a little ether down the back of her neck when she had got a basin of hot water ready. We asked her if she was a nurse and she said no, but that people had told her she was rather a natural nurse. And so she was.

This woman and two or three others worked all day in a fashionable haberdasher's shop. Her hours were long and sometimes she felt a little tired; but a day spent in pandering to the wants of selfish idle rich women did not seem to her well spent. She and her friends saved a little money and rented a little room on a street floor. In this they installed a stove, some seats and a coffee urn. The coffee was for the Glasgow prostitutes (the most miserable of all members of that profession), because, she said, they get frightfully tired walking about these pavements all night.

.   .   .   .

Two companion pictures occur to that of the lady of the Gallowgate. Matthew White and I were called up to the waiting room with our little black bag and

found an extremely dirty little fat man adding to the
indigenous odours of the place a powerful aroma of
strong waters. He apologised for troubling us at this
early hour of the morning and led us downhill through
the deserted streets to a filthy back land, entertaining
us on the way with reflections on politics and sport.
When we got to his house he ushered us in with great
politeness. He said,

" I'm sorry to say you'll not find many ameenities
here. I've been kind of busy, one way and another,
but I'll get a bit fire lighted and you can make yourselves comfortable."

It would not be correct to say that the room was
indescribable; but I must be excused from describing
it. It will be enough to say that among the many
objects and substances on the floor cabbage leaves
were the only one which were clearly recognisable.
Floor, walls and ceiling were coated with a black
slime which did not disguise their state of disrepair.
The woman lay on a ruptured grey mattress in a corner
of the room. She joined in her husband's apologies
for the amenities, but in a faint echo. He had obviously the more powerful and dominant personality.

" A working man," he said, " has not much time on
his hands for tidying up, but I'll light a fire for ye."

The second picture is clean out of the place and
period, but it keeps obtruding. The scene is a Conservative Club at half-past eleven at night, during the
landslide election of 1931. The room is full of fat,
rosy men smoking Coronas and nearly mad with delight. At the far end of the room a weary looking man
is announcing streams of election results. A name
preceded by the not ill-earned title of Right Honourable is read out with the news that another distinguished
public servant has been flung into the gutter. The
clink of glasses and the babel of talk is overwhelmed

by a loud, yelling animal roar. The country has been made safe for democracy.

Do not be alarmed: I always vote Tory. I visualise the muddy river on which I am being carried to be lost in the cleansing ocean, as froth, flotsam, stream and silt. I have great confidence in the stream. It has borne and will bear me up.

Among the silt into which Matthew White and I dived and delved was a house near the Municipal Buildings and back to back with a fire station. It had been a noble house in its time but was now farmed out. There was no light on the rotten staircase, and we had to pick our way over and among drunken men lying among their gastric contents. The passage was not too difficult, for it was a broad and well-designed staircase. The corridor at the end of which our patient lived also contained its hazards and was not supplied with light. Among the rags and filth of the little Irish home the patient and her mother were having a first-class row. The Virgin and the Saints were being invoked to the accompaniment of words from a rather less exalted vocabulary. The baby was just about to be born. I had to conduct the confinement by myself. I was protected by a cold in the head from the atmosphere in the room, but Matthew White had to retire to the street and be ill. Before the *accouchement* I am sorry to say we had to lift our hands to a woman not in the way of kindness. We threw the grandmother downstairs and didn't see her again. It was a fine, healthy boy. The young howdie waits with a good deal of trepidation for the baby's first comment on the world into which it is born. This little purple Celt gave tongue grandly, I remember.

In the morning I looked out of the disreputable window and saw the firemen's wives cleaning up before breakfast on the verandahs of their tidy little flats.

The sun was shining—not, indeed, into the room where I stood, but the mother was very pleased with her child and with us. She thought her husband would be very pleased too when he got back from his three days' scatter.

Cleanliness and honour and filth and dishonour were pretty evenly mixed in the " district." Among other things I found that the caste system, which provides such engaging little comedies among the well to do, was held here with a desperate passion. The respectable poor saw their children walking on rotten planks. At any moment they might fall into the cesspool and be drowned. The badge of rank was cleanliness, and cleanliness was preserved in bug-infested houses with one tap in a kitchen sink as its only instrument. The children went out to school like new pins, and there was a patch of clean air in the foetid fog.

. . . .

As for me, I began to pass examinations and to write plays. I had to clear the decks for my sixth cycle. I wrote *The Son who was considerate of his Father's Prejudices*, *No Wedding Cake for Her*, *The Duke who could sometimes hardly keep from Smiling*, *Ethics Among Thieves*, *The Baron who would not be convinced that His Way of Living was anything out of the Ordinary*. These plays were performed to loud applause at various undergraduate functions. The manuscripts have been lost, as has also the manuscript for a commissioned play I wrote for the Glasgow Repertory Theatre. It was a satire on Edinburgh, but Wareing conveniently took ill and it was never produced. I spent a pleasant fortnight of Wareing's convalescence in Lord Howard de Walden's island in Loch Moidart. We drank claret and ate lobsters and cut down nettles while Wareing told me legends of the

singular world in which he had passed his life—a
world I was to explore many years later.

. . . .

The activities of our little group of half-baked men
of letters went on, and new recruits to the group were
added, among them Arthur Lang who was killed in the
War and wrote the following verses to his moustache.

> . . .In twain the harvest field is cleft,
> Making two gardens of delight;
> Some hairs there are upon the left,
> The rest upon the right.

> The former are more clearly seen;
> Their names are five sweet symphonies—
> Cecily, Gertrude, Magdalen,
> Margaret and Rosalys. . . .

Our patron and friend was John Swinnerton Phillimore, the Professor of Greek. Once he came down to
Walter Elliot's flat in a dressing gown at half-past
twelve in the morning, bringing with him a bottle, a
black pipe and a deal of encouragement. In that
morning we collected a book of verse and published it.
A much better book of verse was collected in 1927;
but we began it. Phillimore wrote the preface to the
first book and contributed four poems to the second.
His friends Mr. Belloc and Mr. Chesterton often
came to see him and, when they did, came over to the
Union and spoke to us. I do not believe in Schools,
Influences and Derivations. Matters like that may be
safely left to the professors. But it is interesting to
note that the young poets of Gilmorehill rapidly took
on something like mastery in their medium from the
moment Phillimore began to take a hand. The sentimentality was squeezed out of their work, and their
verses stood up like rows of neat little crisp, dry sponges.
One was not in the row—Charles Kirk. He was a poet
of the people and stood by himself.

The evening of the fifth cycle was a happy time. I began to appreciate the truth of what my chronic friend had said when he hinted that Scottish University life could only be enjoyed after a long apprenticeship; but my father's Christ-like patience was wearing thin and, in any event, the five-year cycle had to come to an end.

    .   .   .   .

" And high time too," said Mrs. Aphra Behn, who was eating an orange and spitting the pips into the orchestra pit. Her arm was round the waist of Dodie Smith who seemed to resent the attention without knowing exactly how to disengage herself courteously.

" Rat me," said Mrs. Aphra Behn, " what kind of a praying jack is this? A chronicle of youth, marry come up, without a petticoat tail in it. Was your College a College of gelded bullocks? Was there never a merry drab in the town to cheer you with her pretty ways? "

" Ma'am," I said, " I have explained that matter fully. We were well conducted youths who venerated your sex."

" At a distance? "

" At a respectful distance—at least so far as I was concerned. But, lest you should think I had not pondered the matter deeply, I shall satisfy you in the next chapter, if you have the patience to wait so long."

" You propose a disquisition on Woman? "

" Madam," I said, " I do."

CHAPTER VI

The Sixth Five

There was a jingling of jewelry, a rustling of silk and a flutter of feathers as the Restoration Dramatists filed into the Stalls, clack-clacking on their high heels. Mrs. Behn threw herself over the footlights into Rochester's arms, Dodie Smith scuttled into the wings, the A.S.M. shouted orders to the electrician and I advanced downstage with a series of modest coughs.

I felt in retrospect my retrospect warmed by the Secretary's Room fire and I did not feel in the least nervous. I would tell, I thought, these fellows where they got off.

A spot from the Dress Circle dazzled me a little and there were occasional shouts of " Speak up " from the dim figure of Mr. Lonsdale seated at the back of the pit surrounded by the Neo-Carlovians. It is true that I am a great mutterer and mumbler, but usually when I am not convinced that what I have to say is worth hearing. I tightened my diaphragm and let out a prodigious bellow.

" Can you hear that? " I roared.

" Yes," piped the Neo-Carlovians.

" Very well, then, give a little order please," I said arrogantly and proceeded to deliver the following rhapsody on Woman.

A LECTURE ON WOMEN

By James Bridie

It is said of women that they are uncertain, coy and hard to please. But this is in their hours of ease and, with this qualification, the same is true of men. Indeed, it is foolish to generalise about women. There are several hundreds of millions of them, all different. They may be sisters under their skins, but when we have said that we have said nothing.

We are the more foolish to generalise about women because few of us are able to take a nice, scientific, objective view of the creatures. If we select a specimen for intensive study we quickly find ourselves oscillating between extremes of love and hate, irritation and rapture, very clouding and embarrassing to the judgement. We cannot study botany properly if a yellow primrose is something more than a yellow primrose to us. And the same is true of the science of zoology and the amphioxus ; of geology and the old red sandstone ; of physics and those interesting pith balls which dance when we approximate to them a glass rod which has previously been rubbed with catskin.

On the other hand, if we desisted from every enterprise because it happened to be foolish, we should have a dull life indeed. Nay, more, we should be false to our natures ; for, if there is one generalisation about males which is truer than most generalisations, it is this : That males are fools who delight in their folly more than in the most excellent wisdom. It is for this reason or anti-reason that we indulge so frequently in generalisations about women. It is for this reason that I purpose to generalise about women now.

Some generalisations, even if they are made about women, are true. At least, they are what are called facts. The first of these facts is that women are, in many respects, differently constituted from men in a physical sense. The second is, that, in many important respects, they tend to behave differently.

Let us consider their constitution. When they are babies, they are as big as boys. Between the ages of nine and fourteen they are actually bigger. To this we must make an exception. Liverpool girls of twelve are smaller than boys of the same age. After fourteen they become smaller and lighter than boys. They stop growing altogether much earlier than boys do. At maturity women of the same race and social class are much smaller than men of the same race and class.

They are different in other respects. If you find two skulls and take them to an anatomist, he will tell you, offhand and with a light laugh, which is that of a man and which is that of a woman ; this after all traces of lipstick, eyebrows and permanent waving have been removed by boiling. And talking of boiling, it may be well to quote here an observation of Plutarch. It is from his *Table Talk*. Plutarch had sometimes singular ideas as to the proper subjects for table talk. He says :

" Experience at funerals shows us that the bodies of women are hotter than those of men, for they whose business is to burn bodies always add one woman to every ten men, for this aids to burn them, since the flesh of woman is so fat that it burns like a torch."

A slight preliminary investigation at seventeen different crematoria throughout the country tends to confirm this observation ; and this in spite of the deprivations and starvations to which the sex subjects itself to-day and of which I shall presently speak.

195

There are other differences. One of the first principles of Anatomy, as I was taught it in the early part of this century, was that the trunk in man and in woman is pyramidal ; but, whereas in man the pyramid is an inverted pyramid, in woman it stands upon its bottom. Perhaps there has recently been some reason to doubt this axiom. Both sexes, in these days, seem to have become either cylindrical or pearshaped and these two forms to be quite capriciously distributed between the sexes.

In negroes and in anthropoid apes, the index finger is much shorter than the ring finger. In negresses and in anthropoid apesses, the index finger is often longer. Out of 600 Europeans of both sexes, 500 have longer ring fingers and 100 longer index fingers. Of this 100, 33.33% are males, and no fewer than 66·66% are females. This hyperdevelopment of the admonitory finger places the female somewhat higher on the evolutionary scale than the male. But what she gains upon the shies she loses on the roundabouts. Her thumb is too short. This is also true of her great toe. To put the matter simply, if evolution suddenly turned and went backwards, the ladies would be first up the tree.

Keeping in mind the notorious preferences of the Tired Business Man in his theatrical entertainments, we must regretfully admit that the lower limb is uglier in the female than in the male. It is lumpish and unsymmetrical and cycling turns it an irregular salmon pink. So unusual is it for a female to be supported by two sightly structures that large sums of money are paid to their possessors for the purposes of exhibition. The average woman is forced to cover her legs with beautiful fabrics and to tilt them into an appearance of grace with high leathern props below the heel. The only other alternatives are to hide them altogether, as our grandmothers did, or to present a nauseating spectacle.

This defect, among others, prevents a woman from being able to run as fast as a man. On the other hand, she can dive, swim and play golf, skate and dance as well as you or I. She cannot, as a rule, grow whiskers ; and thus loses what is, perhaps, the most valuable period for reflection in the life of a human being—the period of the daily shave. We shall consider the effect of this later on.

Their jaws are smaller and their teeth are larger than those of men and, perhaps, with these instances I may close this part of the catalogue. I have sufficiently proved, I hope, the thesis that the two sexes present profound physical differences. I do not wish to appear to labour the point unduly, but you will see its importance as I develop my argument. If I meet, in a dark alleyway, a living thing weighing two or three tons, covered with a tough and crinkled integument, armed with a trunk and two formidable tusks, I do not pause to consider that we are both God's creatures. Not at first. I am impressed first of all by the difference between us. I try to find a way of approach (or the reverse) which, I realise, must be somewhat different from that I should have used if I had chanced to meet a bald, obese and amiable Scotsman in spectacles and a tweed suit. I may be wrong. I may learn later that it is a nice elephant. But I think that I am right to appreciate the difference between us and to be careful.

We have decided that the physical frame differs in the two sexes. We have deprecated a materialistic conclusion from this observed fact. It now falls to us to consider the more recondite differences that occur in Behaviour.

The first act of both sexes, when they have awakened from that little death which is called sleep and have performed ablutionary and other necessary actions, is to clothe themselves. With man, this is a matter-of-fact business. He slips one garment over his head, steps into a little pair of trousers which button from left to right, pulls on a pair of short stockings or socks. The next garment is a bizarre thing called a shirt which has been shaped by hundreds of years of tradition. To this he fastens a collar by means of little studs and, under the collar, arranges a tie—his one pathetic concession to the principles of aesthetics. He then steps into two columns of thick untearable tweed and prevents them from falling down by two elastic bands fixed over his shoulders. A warm, sleeveless garment fastened by six buttons follows and above this he arranges his jacket. The three last-named garments contain at least ten pockets between them. The result of the whole process is—I forgot his shoes. They are thick and often comfortable—the result, I say, of this process is that he is warm, inconspicuous, protected from casual bruises and extremes of heat and cold. He can carry on his person most of the necessaries of life and some things that are not necessary and yet have his hands free for combat or caress. To brush his hair and put, in one of his pockets, a square of linen cloth for the absorption of rheumy exudates from his nasal passages, is the work of a moment. He is ready to face the world and what may happen in it with some confidence.

Nothing could be more reasonable. From the strict, utilitarian point of view of one so clothed, nothing could be more unreasonable than the woman's attempt to solve the same problems of protection, usefulness and decency. I do not wish to weary you by particularising but there are one or two salient points about woman's costume that must be mentioned.

In the first place it is difficult to put on. It consists partly of elastic and partly of fabrics that are very easily torn. A proportion of them have to be pulled over the head and this means the rearrangement of a relatively large and elaborately arranged quantity of hair every time that it is necessary to change ; and, as we shall see, a woman changes her clothes as often as she can in any given day. Those garments which are fastened by buttons are fastened from right to left instead of from left to right. This must be most confusing and, indeed, seems a lunatic way of doing things altogether.

At times, especially in the evening, she uses buttons purely for ornament. The actual fastening is done by hooks and eyes. Sometimes there are no eyes, only hooks ; and the woman has to grope for a tenuous and invisible loop of thread which may, furthermore, be carried away by any sudden and unguarded gesture. To give you a concise conspectus of the whole business, she dressed, as a Scotsman jokes, with difficulty, and when she is dressed has certainly not fulfilled the requisite ends at which the process is normally directed.

I have defined those ends as protection, usefulness and decency. Even when she is fully clad the woman is an unprotected female. Apart from the elastic tissue that constricts her torso she might as well be wearing nothing at all above the waist, and, to return for a moment to anatomy, it is above the waist that the lungs, the liver and the kidneys are situated. These structures are left vulnerable to the chill air and to chance buffets. At times even the delicate bronchial tree is left unprotected except by skin, bone, muscle and the exiguous contents of the anterior mediastinum.

I do not intend this summary as an attack on the female reasoning faculty. My object is far otherwise. I am simply concerned with variations in habit from the standard habit of the male. Whatever we may think of the rational basis of female costume, we must admit that it shows courage in its wearer. Pneumonia, cholecystitis with its concomitant hepatitis, acute glomerular nephritis are, in turn, braved—to say nothing of tracheitis and rheumatic fever. The average woman faces death with every journey to the pillar box. Small wonder that she takes as much time in preparation for a journey of three or four hundred yards as a Polar explorer would take to equip his expedition. These matters demand thought and even prayer.

And yet she does not die—or very seldom. She is not, of course, immortal, but her expectation of life is greater than that of the male by several years. Dr. F. E. A. Crew of Edinburgh tells us that it is much safer to be a female than to be a male ; and this in the piping times of peace.

We thus readily dismiss her costume as a protective instrument. Is it useful, we must now ask, and is it decent? To this it may be answered that if it is useful it is not decent and if it is decent it is not useful ; for the only practical aspect of woman's costume is the aesthetic aspect. Its object is to draw admiration to its wearer. It has no other object, if we except that of the creation of envy in other women. But these objects are the same ; for envy is jealousy and jealousy is the intolerable thought that any man whatever may take delight in gazing on any woman but one. The admiration the costume is designed to draw is, exclusively, the admiration of males—a great and deserved compliment to the superior aesthetic sense of the male.

I have heard this denied, this superior or more acute sensibility of the male. It is denied through crass ignorance or unscrupulous dialectics. Every schoolgirl knows that a male can smell prussic acid in a solution of 1 in 112,000 and that a female cannot detect it in a solution as strong as 1 in 20,000. This is true of Kansas, of Turin, of Paris and of the whole world.

Who ever heard of a great woman cook? Or wine taster? Or carpet manufacturer? Or sculptor or painter or composer, for that matter? From every laboratory in the two hemispheres comes the message that men are sensitive, temperamental, flinching, tender, sympathetic, psychic, tremulous, receptive, beauty-besotted beings ; hazily listening for the music of the spheres, dreaming in the contemplation of misty sunsets ; afraid of pain ; afraid of reality in every form. And that women are the real tough babies . . . the india-rubber monkeys.

If they are less sensitive than men, they are notoriously more courageous. It is true that when they are attacked by burglars and bag-snatchers they scream. But you try screaming if you are really frightened. It is almost impossible. And the screaming is often accompanied by an heroic attack on someone twice their size and very often armed. It is true that in happier times they often made an appeal to the protective instinct of their men by flutterings and gaspings at the approach of some trivial or imagined danger. But this appeal was deliberate. Like many of their most admired antics in association with males, it was calculated play-acting. It has passed out of use.

Nothing is more characteristic of the sex than this discarding of worn-out methods. Any competent woman can alter her manners, her appearance, her religious convictions, her whole personality at a few hours' notice if necessity arises or fashion dictates. How different are we! We struggle in the rearward of the fashion, clumsily striving to adapt our stiff and stereotyped selves to that personified swiftness called woman.

I can say nothing of their souls, except that they are different from ours and that they do not, in all probability, go to Heaven. I say this because women are incapable of altruism as we understand it. In stage plays no heroic or unselfish act by a male used to be thought valid unless it was performed on behalf of some pure and desirable woman. This was because stage plays always have been written for women. They destroy by their indifference any play which does not conform to their peculiar, and perhaps temporary, ethic. The truth is, on the other hand, that no act performed in a state of erotic frenzy is an heroic act. If the Albert Medal were presented only for the rescue of handsome and healthy young women, it would very seldom be awarded. Few handsome and healthy young women require rescue. The refusal of the Moving Pictures to realise that fact is the sole reason for their popularity.

You will see now why I was careful not to emphasise the physical differences between men and women. It was because that was not my strongest card. The endocrinologists go so far as to say that there is essentially very little difference indeed between the chemico-physical structure of the two sexes. Endocrinologists are, with the exception of metabolists, the silliest of all men of science, but they present a very strong case. Well, they can keep their glands of internal secretion. We cautious and yet universal observers can do without them, at anyrate for the purposes of our argument. We have plenty of differences to go on with.

I think it was in a story by a Frenchman that a young man fell in love with a waxen doll in a haberdasher's window. It was a life-size doll with a charming and sympathetic smile. I am wrong. It was in a play by Lord Dunsany. Gentlemen, we are all in that young man's case. Between us and half human creation, stands a plateglass window and we cannot pass. I remember an incident in South Russia. It happened at a party. I was sitting beside an Armenian widow and I was talking to her in that fluent French that some men acquire when they have been drinking vodka. I was by far the most intelligent man in the room and she was an extremely well-educated woman. I had just spent a couple of years with the rough soldiery in the Mesopotamian desert. I was thirty-one years old. I was witty, eloquent and well-informed and I was in magnificent condition. I was Pope, Horace Walpole, Charles Lamb, Voltaire, Sydney Smith, Burke, Pepys, the Ettrick Shepherd and Dr. Johnson, all rolled into one. What a genius I had then! We talked and talked. She swore 'twas strange, 'twas passing strange. 'Twas pitiful, 'twas wondrous pitiful. We developed a delicious argument on the music of Brahms and I rolled full tilt into a sonorous period, a Hungarian rhapsody in words. I was pleased with it, with myself and with my partner till I looked at her eyes which were large, brown and melting. They were not looking at me. They were following the movements of a large, stupid, curly-headed subaltern who was dancing with a Russian Jewess. And yet I could have sworn she was interested in what I was saying. She had all the right answers.

It is not that we don't understand women. Everybody but a born fool understands women thoroughly. The trouble is that, moving through our lives with the same speech and a roughly similar shape, they should yet be as remote from us and our way of thinking as the planet Venus itself. When I was a very young child, I remember the thrill of horror I felt when I realised that a dog was alive in very much the same sense as I was alive. It was its eyes and the way they looked at a person. And yet it was covered with thick hair and walked on four legs. Even yet it frightens me. I would rather touch a dead man than a dead dog. It is probably the same feeling that makes us all, except microcephalic voluptuaries with greasy hair, afraid of women. There is nothing to be afraid of really. They are seldom cruel unless they are startled and they are admirable companions. But they are too like us and yet too different. It is seldom possible to have more than the illusion of comfort in their presence. It is only a very rare type of man who does not look a posturing idiot when he is talking to a woman not his sister.

Perhaps it is this that has given rise to that extra-ordinary and satisfying institution, the CLUB. I know that the CLUB is often regarded as a funk-hole into which a man retires when he has been worsted in a battle of wits with his wife. But there are bachelors' CLUBS and I know of many pillars of many CLUBS who are happily married men—that is, men married to women who realise the importance a man attaches to what he calls his self-respect and is really his vanity. No. My explanation is the correct one. A CLUB is a place of refuge from a haunting and unreasoning dread.

May I once more draw on my own experience? I was once Secretary of a Dining Club organised in connection with a very venerable institution. It was a good CLUB. I used to select the High Table on the following principle. The President was always a round, red-faced man with a shining bald head and a grey moustache. If two of the Members had white beards, they were placed on either side of the Chairman. Red faces and bald heads were chosen for the remaining places and they were graded down to the most delicate shades of mauve and pink on the flanks. The old boys used to shout insults at each other all through the dinner and nobody was allowed to make an after-dinner speech who was not an acknowledged expert in that difficult art. But anyone was allowed to sing a song. I remember one antique practitioner removing his false teeth and placing them on the grand piano preparatory to sing-

ing, " My Bonnie is over the Ocean." They all drank
burgundy and port and many of them followed these
wines with bumpers of whisky, bless their hearts. Each
stuck an annual big cigar between his rubicund chops,
joined in the chorus and enjoyed himself thoroughly.
The laughter was apoplectic. Lovely times.

One year the Committee met and a brisk young
belly-slitting surgeon made a certain proposal. He
said that under the constitution of the CLUB all House
Physicians and House Surgeons, past and present,
were entitled to Membership. He pointed out that,
particularly during the War years, many of these
officials had been ladies. He moved that, in the
opinion of the Committee, these ladies were entitled
to Membership of the CLUB. I made an effort to get
round the Constitution ; but I was only a young lad
then. Respect for the Constitution carried the day
and, at the next meeting of the Committee, a strapping
young virgin, elected according to Rule by her fellow
Residents at that time in the Hospital, took her seat.

It was terrible. There were seven people on the
Committee. Four of them were over seventy. The
dashing young surgeon was fifty-six. I was a child of
thirty-three. You can imagine the course affairs took.
The lady doctor was twenty-three. She had been
President of a dozen Societies and knew exactly how
business should be conducted. She was fearless in
speaking her mind. She was plump, prettily dressed
and of the rich, opulently coloured type that goes with a
resonant contralto voice. The Surgeon felt himself her
sponsor. The ancients sat smirking and ogling feebly.
I recall one of her first lines of attack. She asked us,
individually, beginning with the eldest, whether women
were indeed welcome to the CLUB. Apparently they
were. When my turn came I blushed and wriggled
uncomfortably and said that, as Secretary, I had no

opinion and that, besides, that wasn't the point. The point was that we had decided they had a RIGHT to be there. The lady doctor looked at me with some contempt and proceeded to the next business, which was the proposal of a President. She proposed a slim and suave gynaecologist, a man of great personal charm but of the most hideous prolixity in his capacity of orator. Nobody dared to rebuke the minx for her impertinence. I said, " No," after waiting for my elders to speak. She turned to me and said, " Oh? Do you hate him? " I said, " No. But he's rather a bad speaker, isn't he? " She said, " Nonsense. He is a most cultured and cultivated man. He gave us a beautiful address at the Women's Medico-Chirurgical Society only last week. I am his house surgeon, so I think I probably know him better than you do. Of course, I know he has enemies. And, oh, perhaps I shouldn't be speaking in this way at all. But you were all so nice, I thought ... " It would have been too dreadful to hurt her feelings. We elected the man.

In two years the only bald heads to be seen were those of meek little middle-aged ophthalmologists or mild and prematurely aged medical tutors. Dry ginger ale was largely drunk and we had to listen to Lay Governors of the Hospital solemnly plugging statistics through the gloom ; and numbers of women sat in rows wondering what part they were supposed to play in this dismal rite. The old boys died and went to Heaven. And so it is to-day, I have no doubt. It is ten years since I attended one of those dinners.

I have been careful to attribute to women no sort of faults or deviations from perfection ; but I must deprecate their habit of forcing their way into the few scattered strongholds of the male. There are hundreds of occasions on which they can entertain themselves and torment their natural enemies. It has been said of old time that " they wimmen spile the Ball," but that is not true. They decorate and glorify the Ball. But in a CLUB they are a pest.

One would think that they would leave Man alone to pursue one of the few pleasures in which there was no danger that he would excite their jealousy by the loose and roving motions of his desires. But no. They aspire to be *bonne camarade* in everything, in these days. They wear trousers ; and very dreadful they look in them, with their short legs and prominent seats. They starve themselves into bony skeletons, the nearer to approximate their appearance to that of their deities. They smoke themselves tremulous and drink themselves stupid, that they may share to the full the raptures of the male. It is very sad. It is like an Angel strapping his wings with elastoplast to make himself fit to associate with an income tax collector.

This perverse behaviour may arise from the emasculation of an entire generation of males ; or it may be a survival of that Nineteenth Century Congress of Witches' Sabbaths called the Woman's Movement. I incline to the latter view. It was during that Congress that " Woman " first became a collective noun. We had heard before that " Man, Man, Man was for the Woman made," and many cynical poets had begun their intolerable jingles with the words, " O Woman." But they always meant one, particular woman.

As a noun singular, woman is a success. She far surpasses man in wit, cunning, gentleness, strength of character, loyalty, generosity, courage, variety, courtesy, energy, endurance and all the qualities civilised people admire in each other. As a collective noun, she is a noisy nuisance and a nerveless failure. If she were not so absurdly ineffective she would be beyond bearing.

She secured the franchise by means that would make

the I.R.A. blush ; and all she has done with it is to make the sillier side of politics even sillier. The Mothers, the Preservers, the Perpetuators of the species have demanded the right to speak in the councils of the Nation and have wasted the time of those councils with small talk. She insisted on entering the field of organised labour and is content with the wages of a coolie. In the two professions in which she is supreme, Nursing and the Stage, she shows the same helpless near-sightedness. The Nurse accepts the remuneration of an untrained under-housemaid *and* the status and disabilities of that occupation. This is after she has undergone a course of training imposed on her by foolish old doctors who insist on her ruining her health and grey matter by committing to memory masses of irrelevant rubbish. The training takes four terrible years. She has never raised a finger to help herself or to right her wrongs and still less have the women Governors of the Hospitals.

Actresses work under still more appalling conditions. They have only to consult the Factories Act to have 90% of their workshops, the West End and Provincial theatres closed and their owners heavily fined. They submit to the most degraded kind of insult from men their parents would not have allowed in the house. When they are out of work, which is most of the time, they are expected to cringe to Agents, work for nothing in Sunday night shows and eat nothing so that they may keep themselves dressed in smart clothes. When they are in work, they make idiotic contracts, slave for weeks without any pay, hang about for hours waiting to play a few minutes of a boring and stupid part, take miserable salaries which are shamelessly cut in the middle of a run. All this because they are members of a collective body of women and such bodies are mean-spirited and incompetent to a degree.

All this goes to show that we should touch not the cats but the glove whether they come in spies or in battalions. Few women are intolerable as individuals and many are magnificent. It may be true that, as Zarathustra said, man at his worst is only wicked, but woman is base. " When she is good," the poem says, " she is very, very good ; and when she is bad she is horrid." But she is seldom uninteresting. It is when she bands herself together with her sisters to institute some monstrous regimen or other that she becomes a menace and a pain in the neck. And a Women's Society is worse than a Women's Club. And a Women's Movement is worse than a Women's Society. And when they advance bodily as a Sex, the hemispheres reel and the Firmament groans. The slim, graceful, dignified figure " I " becomes a disgusting string of figures. We are into arithmetic before we know where we are. And the answer is always wrong.

. . . .

There was some scattered applause and the Audience withdrew. The lights went out, all but a little pilot light at my typewriter. Great shadows filled the theatre. I shivered a little as I sat down once more to my melancholy task. I should have rejoiced if my typewriter had copied Marcello's brush and refused to perform its office—and plunked out sonnets and serenades. But it was a conscientious instrument. It gravely stuck to the squalid job in hand and spaced out slowly . . .

The Sixth Five.

. . . .

My twenty-fifth birthday found me still an undergraduate, but the sands were running out. My friends

had gone down and *dans le vieux parc solitaire et glacè*
I haunted the present and evoked the past. I wrote
for the G. U. M. under unfamiliar names, sneered at
my juniors and flew into a passion when I was contra-
dicted, which was seldom. The G. U. M. was edited
by a grotesque little man with long curly black hair.
His name was Robert Page Arnot, and of him I wrote,

> Robert Page Arnot
> Was a person to feather and tar. Not
> So much because
> Of what he did as of what he was.

He was an unmilitant incompetent in those days,
and wrote the most brilliant nonsense I have ever read.
He is now, I think, Principal of the Marx College,
whatever that may be.

In 1913 I became a doctor. I joined the staff of
the Royal Infirmary as House Physician to W. R.
Jack. Jack was a tall, cultivated man with light red
hair. He looked a little like a flamingo. He was the
last apostle in the line of Gairdner, a scholar, a gentleman and an admirable physician.

The Royal Infirmary is still a romantic place, but
it is not unlike any other large hospital to-day. When
I was a student and scrubbed Middleton's wards, the
old Adam building was still standing. It faced the
Cathedral and was a beautiful complement to it. It
now dwarfs the Cathedral, making the lovely old
house look mean without adding any compensating
dignity of its own. When I entered the hospital as a
doctor about a quarter of the old building still stood,
and two-thirds of the new one had been built. The
old and musty and the fresh and gaudy were jumbled
together, and there were scaffoldings and tubs of
mortar and a continual hammering all day, except on
Sundays, when a Salvation Army band played in the

Cathedral Square. The tradition of the old hospital was not kept alive by its buildings alone. At least two of the ward sisters had bullied their now venerable chiefs when they were students ; and there was one very aged porter who had touched his hat to the great Lister. The matron had begun her nursing career in the hospital ; she was Jane Melrose. She had the aspect of a bull-dog, the voice of a Grenadier sergeant and a heart of gold. The Lister ward was used as a cloak-room for women students. It has since been destroyed by the hospital governors in a grand defiance of a public opinion that worked itself into a fury against them. Architecturally it was quite possible to preserve the Lister Block. It would have made an admirable museum and brought visitors, revenue and honour to the hospital. But the Governors made their gesture as a matter of principle, and nothing can inhibit such a gesture when a body of Scotsmen are determined to make it. What the principle was I am not quite sure. I suspect, from the evidence of several reports from the annual general meetings, that it would have been derogatory to the dignity of the Governors of a great hospital to recognise the work of a mere surgeon. The members of the unpaid staff of the hospital might be encouraged to put some value on their own work and, worse still, " forget their place." It is only fair to say that a beautiful medallion bearing the name of Lister has been erected in the hospital and is there for the curious to see.

Other remnants of tradition were to be found in my day. The first act of a resident in taking up duty was to have the senior resident's master key copied in a local ironmonger's. With this key I opened the little, low, dark, worm-eaten door and found an enormous heap of ward journals deep in dust and festooned with cobwebs. In one of these I read that Michael

Murphy [1] was admitted to the hospital on the day of the battle of Waterloo suffering from lues. His head and body were a mass of indolent ulcers and the bridge of his nose and his soft palate had disappeared. He was given twenty-five grains of calomel and nine grains of opium every day for three months, and was discharged well, fit and hearty to follow his occupation as a fish-hawker.

The literary repository of tradition, apart from these journals, was the senior resident's book. In this book the senior kept a record of all that happened during his term of office ; and nobody but his successor was allowed to see it. I imagine the book was about eighty years old, and during the War, when the resident posts were held almost entirely by women, the book was lost or destroyed.

The tradition of the sealed book was a good one and I shall try to keep it so far as my year at the Royal Infirmary is concerned, though there is much interesting, amusing, romantic and repulsive that could be told. A young man taking up his first job as a house physician or surgeon gets into a strange state. For one thing, he takes the endemic disease. This is called HOUSEMAN'S HEAD, and, indeed, he becomes *entêté* in more than one sense. He is responsible for sixty patients in bed, many of them dangerously ill. He is the judge whether innumerable others will be admitted to the hospital or not. He is putting many years' theory into practice. He finds that this is easy and thinks himself a wonderful fellow. He takes little account of the thousand and one unobtrusive aids with which the hospital supplies him and he gets many a sore shock when he goes out later into general practice. While he is a houseman, however, it is all

[1] Michael Murphy was not his real name. Ward journals are confidential documents.

jam and gingerbread, and he has a man of great
experience at the other end of the telephone if he is
puzzled. Added to this he is in the peculiar position
of being an important male official in a sort of nunnery.
If he is a half-baked and conceited young fool, as in
ninety-nine cases out of a hundred he is, the kind and
devoted women who surround him flatter his vanity
till his head is full of east wind and he seldom attains
even semi-consciousness. He walks in a coma vigil,
with his feet well off the ground.

His chief, it is true, sometimes jerks him down by
the hind leg. But Jack was not that sort of chief.
Jack used to smoke very stout, heavenly and expensive
Turkish cigarettes. One day he left them behind and
was offered and accepted a Gold Flake from his resident to smoke with his mid-day coffee. On the following day he had filled one half of his cigarette case with
Gold Flake cigarettes, so that he might offer to his
resident the brand he no doubt preferred.

A specimen day in the life of a pre-war resident was
this. He was awakened by a probationer banging at
his door in an agitated soprano calling out that the
chief had passed the front gate. He tore off his
pyjamas, flung himself into the bath, half dried himself, pulled on a shirt, trousers and socks, put on his
white jacket, brushed his hair and met his chief at the
top of the stair with an alert and respectful smile. If it
was the time when students were being taught, he
made a show of listening to the first few bars of the
lecture and then retired to the ward kitchen for a
breakfast of scrambled eggs. He then picked up
sufficient information about the patients from the
sisters or the charge nurses, visited those who were
most seriously ill and was primed for the ward visit.
After the ward visit he took coffee with his chief and
saw him off the premises. From half-past twelve till

half-past two he examined patients, wrote reports, carried out treatment and had lunch. From three till six he slept or amused himself at a novelty called the cinema. If he dined in mess he was allowed one bottle of beer. There was a fine if he did not dine in mess. If there were sufficient numbers in mess, songs were sung or polo was played. Polo was played in the pathology department. The residents sat in cane-bottomed chairs and propelled themselves along the slippery waxed floor with their feet. As a whole series of doors were locked to keep them out of the pathology department the authorities were greatly perplexed as to why the floor looked like an ice rink on the following morning. Round about midnight he attended to work that was in arrears and at about half-past one paid his night visit. On my first night visit a man sat up in bed, wide awake, and said to me, in a quiet conversational voice :

" Doctor, what is all this about? You don't suppose I can get any sleep while the clock is making faces at me? And who took away the side of the ward and set the roof on fire? You'll attend to it, won't you? I want to sleep."

But the ward was usually quiet at the night visit, a long dim vista of white and scarlet lit only by the night nurse's red shaded reading lamp. The resident took his microscope into the ward and sat doing blood counts and talking to the nurse in whispers. Half an hour in the test room with chemicals followed, then the resident felt hungry. He strolled round the hospital with his master key till he found a ward kitchen that was making supper. There he had bacon and eggs and tea. At intervals he had to bolt for the linen cupboard when the night sister came round unexpectedly. But there was a system of secret telegraphy in the hospital that followed that devoted woman on her rounds. Nothing could happen at the remotest spot in the hospital that was not immediately reported half a mile away. The resident poured his troubles into sympathetic ears and went to bed before the probationers came on duty at four o'clock in the morning, soothed and comforted, half cabbage, half king. On receiving days he worked from midnight to midnight, and on symposium nights he rioted exclusively in male society.

·   ·   ·   ·   ·   ·   ·   ·

In the first year of my sixth era, I was shaken out of my complacency by a remarkable series of events. My father had discovered an electric gearing for ships that could push them back and forwards in their own length, if a few buttons were manipulated on the bridge. He built a little launch with diesel engines and called it the *Electric Arc*. It was a success. He spent day after day on the Clyde demonstrating it. He then floated a very small company to exploit this invention. This company built a cargo ship at Swan Hunter's on the Tyne, engined it with oil engines and sent it to Spain with a cargo. The gearing worked perfectly, but the engines broke down. The cargo was perishable. The small capital of the company was soon exhausted and the patent was sold to the United States Navy for an absurdly small figure. The British Navy at that time had, I understand, no intention of putting oil engines into their capital ships. At anyrate, my father's invention did not particularly interest them.

My father was not a financier, and the loss of every penny he possessed would not have upset him much. He would have weathered the disappointment quite easily if it had not been for another element. A by-product of his work on the electric gear was his discovery that the dynamics of the ship's propeller had never been worked out. With the help of R. F. Muirhead, a Smith's Prizeman who taught mathematics and physics in Glasgow, he set himself to learn higher mathematics. He worked till four o'clock every morning—the time at which I in hospital had finished my scrambled eggs—for months on end. He perfected a theory of the propeller which is now in the archives of the Institution of Engineers and Shipbuilders and ruined his health. His doctor sent him to Algiers.

At a quarter-past nine one morning in December I was meeting my chief at the top of the staircase when my brother and my uncle arrived. They had had a cable from my mother in Algiers saying simply " Come at once." My brother had a bag packed and had intended to catch the ten o'clock train to London. But I took his bag and went instead. I caught the night boat at Dover and the morning express at Paris and found myself a little dazed in Marseilles. At Marseilles I changed from my hospital rags into a suit of my brother's and learned from a letter in the pocket that my father had taken seriously ill. I came to the conclusion that he was dead and wandered about Marseilles till the small hours. In the morning I found an Italian ship and sailed across the Mediterranean. My cabin companion was an amiable little Frenchman. I did not want to talk to him but he wanted to tell me bathroom stories and continued to do so for the rest of the day. I remember vividly his toilet on the following morning. He had slept in everything except his collar and his outer covering. In the morning he put the plug in the bathroom basin and poured in about a teacup-ful of eau-de-Cologne from an enormous bottle. He then took a handful of what engineers call oily waste and rubbed his face and head with the eau-de-Cologne. He then put on his last night's collar, which was tall and spiky, brushed his hair and was ready for the road.

Perhaps it was because I was unhappy that I found Algiers hateful and mean and the harbour nothing to write home about. I drove up miles of winding streets to the *pension* that was my father's address, and found a kind American who told me that he had heard that my father was a little better, that he was in a nursing home half a mile away, and that he would walk down there with me after dinner. The sun went down suddenly and left the air with a clammy chill that bit to the bone. I found my mother at the nursing home. She had had no sleep for several nights. My father had suddenly taken a toxic delirium. For a day or two he had been violent, but he had now settled down. He was quite rational but would not stop talking day and night. He looked desperately ill. He said he was glad to see me, but complained that I had not come more quickly. He damned the doctors, the nurses and the nursing home up hill and down dale, and said that if my mother had not been there he would have died. We got him home. His mind raced all the time, and I do not think he slept for an hour during the whole journey. If our attention to what he was saying wavered for a single instant he became passionately angry and quoted long passages from *King Lear*. He could not be persuaded to eat. He ordered enormous quantities of food and sent them away again. He ate nothing till he ordered three dozen of oysters at the Euston Hotel and ate them all. He insisted on lunching in the pullman from Dover, but he ate nothing there. He was very gay and behaved like a revelling man. Earlier in the journey I had spent two hours trying to persuade him to take an injection of morphia. I swore, as I thought, too quietly for him to hear. He said,

" This ship was built on the Clyde, and I will tell

you how I know that she was built on the Clyde. The plates still vibrate from the blows of the riveters' hammers. They still hold an undercurrent of the Govan riveters' oaths. How dare you swear at me! "

We took him to my uncle's house and subjected him to a consulting physician, a general practitioner, an alienist and a pathologist. He looked at the pathologist and said,

" You have an eye like a mountain goat. I would rather be your friend than your enemy "—and, indeed, the pathologist was the only doctor he would allow to make a second visit. The pathologist cured him of his delirium in three days, but he was a very exhausted man. He died of pernicious anaemia in 1915, at the early age of fifty-six.

In the Spring of 1914 I moved from the medical wards to a composite office called at that time Casualty House Surgeon. I was at the disposal of the Skin and Ear, Throat and Nose Departments, and was responsible for the organisation of the Gate. The Gate was the most romantic of the occupations. In a white pinafore and rubber gloves I strolled with lordly grace through an endless variety of scenes. I was the link between the hospital and the outer world, and a lively outer world it was.

The neighbourhood of the Royal Infirmary was largely controlled by street gangs. Our protectors in my time were the Chelsea Boys, and we could go in and out at any hour of the day or night under their watchful eye. The gangs of those days fought with cross-cut saw, broken bottle necks, cobblers' knives, knuckle dusters and iron shod boots. The day of the little gigolo with patent leather shoes, flannel trousers and a couple of razors in his waistcoat pockets had not yet arrived. The common injuries were scalp wounds, abrasions about the ribs and often a curious little series of stabs in their shoulders and upper arms made by the cobblers' knives. There seemed, too, to be a greater premium of individual daring than on concerted action. One friend of mine attacked a policeman in the middle of a brightly lighted street, butted him under the chin and took his watch from him. He had promised his lady-love a policeman's watch.

One day the Garngad boys, becoming critical of the treatment of one of their comrades in the hospital, invaded a ward, threw down the screens, pulled off the bed-covers and put the nurses in a state of terror. The whole affair took less than five minutes, and they escaped before the police came. That night they drifted one by one into the Gate, thoroughly stamped with the trade marks of the Chelsea Boys. We bore them no ill feeling and stitched them up tidily.

Round about that period I fell in love, and, feeling the desire for solitude, used to walk in the small hours out to Bishopbriggs in the country. One night, as I was passing the cemetery, I met a man taking off his collar. I asked him why he was taking off his collar, and he told me that he was going to sleep in the cemetery. I asked him why he was going to sleep in the cemetery, and he told me that he was living with his auntie who was a woman of strict temperance principles. He had had six bottles of beer, and was anxious not to upset her. Beer engenders courtesy and consideration as surely as tea engenders hatred, malice and all uncharitableness. The night was pleasantly warm. I wished this gentle person pleasant dreams and passed on my way. I met a policeman with a clay pipe in his mouth and his hands in his pockets, striding along with his long coat-tails flapping behind him. We walked for a little way together and talked about love. He told me he found love very upsetting. Lots of hooligans who would have been much the

better of a good crack on the head followed by a fortnight in the cells had got away with it because he
happened to be in love. Hé couldn't speak for other
people, but this he could say—that it made policemen
soft. He then bade me good-night, putting his pipe
in his pocket. The sergeant, he said, objected to pipe
smoking on duty, and he was not in love.

Shortly after these pleasant incidents I noticed a
John Bull poster that said " To Hell with Servia! "
and in a day or two even *The Glasgow Herald* was
announcing the thickening of war clouds. On the
third of August I went down to the O.T.C. headquarters and collected application forms for the
Special Reserve. On the fourth of August Great
Britain declared war.

Up at the barracks a worried looking R.A.M.C.
major turned me over to two flustered civilian doctors,
and they measured me and passed me physically fit.
In those days my measurements were exactly the same
as Georges Carpentier's, except that my wrists were
not so thick. When I could not see the test letters
they let me read them with my glasses on after consulting their little book. Something made me take the
precaution of committing the letters to memory. It
was just as well, for I was sent for the next day, and the
major made me read the card without my glasses.
I recited my piece to him correctly, down to the fifth
line, and he begged my pardon for troubling me.
Next time I met him was in the middle of Persia.

There followed a time of waiting. I was very
impatient to be off. A number of my colleagues in the
Glasgow Hospitals had joined the Navy, and Robert
Brown had already fallen into the sea, as a result of a
torpedo off the north of Ireland. I was afraid that
the war would be over before I got to it. I was not
otherwise particularly afraid. There must have been

something wrong with my imagination. The defect was to be put right.

I filled in the time by acting as a locum tenens in Springburn. I had hastily resigned from the Royal Infirmary, not because there was a war expected but because there was an impending vacancy at Ruchill Fever Hospital, and I wanted to work with Brownlee. All I remember about the locum tenens is that I attended a confinement at which I waited for fourteen hours for a second twin which was not and never had been there. I am wrong. There was another memorable incident. At another confinement I was distressed by a difficult complication and called for help from a neighbouring practitioner. After a long and anxious wait at the bedside I invoked an old gentleman in a seedy mackintosh and pyjamas. He washed his hands at the kitchen jawbox and delivered the infant within five minutes of his arrival. I felt very much ashamed but he said he was very pleased to be of any service. He said he had carried through two thousand confinements, and that he was never surprised to find an obstruction pass away suddenly of itself.

My uniform was ready just in time for me to go in it down to Aldershot, and there I found myself one of thirty or forty doctors who had been chosen to train field ambulances for Kitchener's army. We slept in tents on Tweseldown Racecourse and later in huts down in the valley as our numbers reached and passed three figures. We ran through damp grass in the early morning, and were instructed in an imbecile exercise called stretcher drill before breakfast. For the rest of the day we drilled our troops who were in civilian clothes, much damaged by the housing conditions arranged by the War Office for patriots at the beginning of the war but of every variety. We had a sergeant-instructor of about ninety whose name was Harris. When we said good-bye to him at a smoking concert he told us of the changes that had come over the army in his experience. He said,

"Now it's ' Come along, chum, and lend me a hand!' In the old days the sergeant used to put his face close to mine and say to me ' You tin-eyed worm!'"

It was at Tweseldown Camp I reached my highest achievement as an athlete. I played for the Officers' team at Rugby. There were three internationals in the quarter line, two blues at half, and three international forwards. Leslie Philip's batman asked his master if I were an international.

There was a Scots colony at Tweseldown who despised all the others heartily. Its Feuhrer was a little man called Douglas Reid King. He had a very husky voice, a monocle and an aspect of intense ferocity. He wore the monocle because he couldn't see without it. He couldn't see very well with it ; but he was dreadfully afraid to wear spectacles, in case his departure to the front should be delayed.

Our field ambulance was the first to be brought up to war strength and the first to receive uniforms and equipment. There were rumours in October that we might go at any moment. King had determined that we should not, if possible, take married officers with us. A number of these were billeted in Crookham, and King used to visit their wives and tell them horrifying stories of the slaughter among medical officers at the front. At last a staff officer on a motor cycle arrived through the pouring rain a little after midnight. There was a light in my hut and he hammered at my door. Twenty-four hours later we were curled round the legs of a saloon table on the way to Havre, soaked to the skin and trying to get to

sleep. Four hours after that I saw through the port-
hole the scarlet trousers of a French sentry.

. . . .

I was sleeping in the school house at Vlamertinghe.
I had ridden in to it on a large horse called Ikey, from a
fancied resemblance to a great financier. It had been
a bright, sunny day and all that could be seen of a war
was an aeroplane flying high and surrounded by dabs
of cotton wool. The houses were a little battered and
the *pavé* was disturbed in places. We cleaned out the
school house and established a dressing station and
went to sleep. I was awakened by an unpleasant
tearing sound. It was partly screech and partly whistle,
and the main impression it made on my half awakened
mind was that whatever caused the sound was angry at
me and wanted to get me. It was followed by a loud
bang that shook the floor and rattled the little windows.
These sounds and their climaxes followed each other
with great rapidity and I sat up in my sleeping-bag in
some consternation. The door opened and Sergeant
Gatehouse, a schoolmaster in civil life, put his intelligent face round the door. He said in the army voice
he had been at some pains to cultivate during the eight
months' training at Tweseldown,
   " I have to report, sir, that this dressing station is
being consistently shelled."
   " In that case," I said, " I'd better get up."
   I found my little advance party in greatcoats and
balaclava helmets standing in the roadway in the raw
misty May dawn. They were looking at the church a
few hundred yards down the road. Against the church
steeple and in the graveyard round it light shells were
bursting in salvos of four. We stood and coughed and
smoked cigarettes and inhaled the throat-catching rime
for about twenty minutes, and then they stopped.

223

In *Journey's End*, you will remember, Osborne's favourite reading was *Alice in Wonderland*. This is a true touch. I discovered on that morning a curious thing about *Alice in Wonderland*. A year or two ago a refugee doctor was going round my wards with me. He said that he had been reading *Alice in Wonderland* and that clearly Lewis Carroll was a schizophrenic dement. I said I didn't think so. I thought he was a prophet.

It seemed to me on that May morning that he had prophesied the Great War.

" ' Tell us a story! ' said the March Hare.

' Yes, please do! ' pleaded Alice.

' And be quick about it,' added the Hatter, ' or you'll be asleep again before it's done.'

' Once upon a time there were three little sisters,' the Dormouse began in a great hurry ; ' and their names were Elsie, Lacie and Tillie ; and they lived at the bottom of a well— '

' What did they live on? ' asked Alice, who always took a great interest in questions of eating and drinking.

' They lived on treacle,' said the Dormouse, after thinking a minute or two.

' They couldn't have done that, you know,' Alice gently remarked ; ' they'd have been ill.'

' So they were,' said the Dormouse ; ' *very ill.*'

Alice tried a little to fancy to herself what such an extraordinary way of living would be like, but it puzzled her too much, so she went on : ' But why did they live at the bottom of a well? '

' Take some more tea,' the March Hare said to Alice, very earnestly."

As I stood there chewing my cigarette on that May dawn I thought to myself " I don't know. I'm not sure. But it looks to me as if this business might quite easily become intolerable."

It did. I encountered frog footmen, white rabbits, Mad Hatters, Dormice, caterpillars, Dodos, and Cheshire cats, to say nothing of Gryphons and Mock-turtles. Above us gimbled the slithy toves, through their anti-aircraft wabe; borogroves bobbed mimsily along the horizon; frumious bandersnatches brought our hearts to our mouths; the jubjub bird passed over-head like a brewer's dray driving along the roofs of Long Acre and left a hole twenty feet deep where it landed; the jabberwock whiffled continually through woods that became more and more tulgey as the weeks went on. The meaning of it all was as elusive as the egg on the shelf of the sheep-shop. We drifted from Ypres to Arras, from Arras to the Somme and back to Arras again. Before the battle of Arras I turned bright orange and was sent home. A rat-like person with a blue band round his hat sent me to Manchester to spite me. I arrived at Manchester in the dark and a girl threw two red roses into my ambulance.

I got well very quickly. Manchester was very cold and foggy and full of people in soft hats whistling "The Passing of Salome." I had one very pleasant dinner with Wallace, Fletcher and Herbert Sidebotham and was returned to my native place with a pulse rate of a hundred and fifty or so but otherwise well. My father was dead, my younger brother Eric had had his thigh shot in two at Gallipoli and my brother Jack, the only soldier of the three of us, was tied by an extraordinary series of accidents to a Royal Engineers training camp. My mother and I stayed with my uncle at Mauchline and then I returned to Sick Light Duty.

Sick Light Duty meant living in the United Services Club and daily taking a taxi up the hill to Edinburgh Castle. In Edinburgh Castle a number of young men yawned, slept, played bridge, read novels or sat on inexacting medical boards. Work for the day finished about five and I returned to the club to dine with Robin Brown, whose ships were anchored at Queensferry. At intervals I was Orderly M.O. and remained in the Castle for the night. There was a night ward visit to do, but no kitchen supper. The whole affair was much more dignified than real life. I lay on my bed and heard the east wind howl round the ramparts.

This pleasant routine was broken by a transfer to Fort George, a sullen dismal place on the Moray Firth. I was attached to the Seaforth's depot and messed with two most charming and characteristic old colonels and a discontented adjutant. Drafts of the H.L.I. were also housed in the Fort, but the Greeks had no dealings with these Samaritans. Among the Samaritans was Esme Percy in a very natty pair of tartan trousers. I had the pleasure of seeing him imitate Fred Emney and speak the Harfleur speech at a smoking concert.

Most of the time I was bored. I sank into a lethargy from which I was roused by the two day visit of a travelling medical board, presided over by an ignorant bully. I wrote a frenzied letter to the D.A.D.M.S. of my division, asking him to arrange for my return to my old field ambulance. The field ambulance was not a highly regarded unit in the British army, but I was satisfied with mine. I had known the men since they were recruits and seen them level up and level down. They were courageous, honourable, devoted fellows, and I had never seen them tired, or unwilling or unskilful or afraid. Shepherd wrote back that the A.D.M.S. would wire for me the moment I landed at Boulogne and that there was a reasonable chance of me being made a temporary Lieutenant-Colonel. As this was one of the cushiest jobs in the war and carried with it an almost automatic D.S.O. I was very pleased. My delight was short lived. A note from another official friend told me that I was booked to sail for

Mesopotamia on the following week. And to Mesopotamia I went.

If you have not read a work called *Some Talk of Alexander*, or if you are unable to obtain a copy of it, it is your own fault. I was at the pains to write that book in 1926, and you failed to buy it in sufficient numbers to recoup the publisher for his enterprise. It tells of my experiences in India, Mesopotamia, Persia, Transcaucasia and Constantinople, and I am certainly not going to the trouble of repeating myself. I finished my sixth cycle eighty miles north of Baghdad and a hundred miles south of the Turks with a riotous party. The war had petered out so far as I was concerned. I have calculated my average day's work in Mesopotamia and find that it amounts to two minutes. The climate was healthy, the company, which was largely composed of Glasgow doctors, was agreeable. I waited with interest to see what the next five years would bring forth. The news from the Western Front made it seem unlikely that we should ever get home.

. . . .

" *I find your War petty and frivolous," said Marlowe.*
" *I cannot help that, you bombastic old blatherskite," I replied. " I wish you had seen all the guns of Ypres opening fire on the morning when the Bosche first put over blazing treacle when I was wandering about Sanctuary Wood. That would have given you something to bang your big drum about. For me, I play the penny whistle and, at times, the oboe. King and I were once talking about that— I mean about how impossible it was to describe this War in rousing words. We were very comfortable. We were sitting by the fireside in an Arras music master's house. The front windows of our room opened on the pleasant Quai de Caserne, the back on a tangled garden and a glass-roofed*

porch. We were having our bedtime toddy and the Germans were shelling a 75 battery along the street. All of a sudden a shell hit our house and down came the glass porch. King crouched under the windowsill and I sat down in an arched doorway, while the air became full of flashes and bangs and clatterings. We then bethought ourselves of our faithful batmen who slept upstairs and were rushing to their aid when they knocked us backward downstairs. They were wrapped in blankets. We adjourned to the cellar, but it was full of water and the shelling soon stopped.

My room on the first floor was full of moonlight and I walked on two inches of finely powdered dust. The blanket window screen had been blown in and the nosecap had gone through my bed at the point where my umbilicus would have been if I hadn't persuaded King to have one more toddy. But that wasn't War . . . I remember . . ."

Aramis, Porthos and Athos dined in the house of Athos twenty years after. Because they did not know each other very well, Mrs. Athos, Mrs. Porthos and Mrs. Aramis went to the drawing-room after the fearless old fashion instead of staying to drink port wine and smoke cigarettes with their husbands.

Aramis, Athos and Porthos were silent for a little, began to talk all at once and then begged each other's pardon.

" You were saying? " said Athos.

" No, no, you go on," said Aramis.

" It was nothing," said Porthos.

" Please, Aramis," said Athos.

" No, Porthos was speaking," said Aramis.

" Go on, Porthos," said Athos.

" I was just thinking," said Porthos, " that twenty years ago to-day I was sitting in the Hotel de Paris at St. Pol eating truffles and drinking Louis Roederer 1906 at eight francs the bottle. I should have got it for less if I hadn't been on the Staff. That was an inn, Aramis, where they could roast a chicken. I had come from the blasted Salient—Cassel, you know. Talk about hardship! My groom was my cook. I found he could do macaroni and cheese. Very well, I said. You cook. So he cooked macaroni and cheese, day in day out, week in week out . . . My God! And bully rissoles. And do you remember that vang rouge? Though you could make salad dressing with vang rouge and melted butter, you know.

"It was after a month of such horror as I dare not describe to you fellows that St. Catherine of Sienna, or some such blessed Saint, materialised. The local padre told me of her. She was living in sin with some gendarme in the neighbourhood. The padre said she could cook. Cook! . . . Oh, luncheon! Little bits of this and that like a fairy dance for *hors d'oeuvres*. Fat olives, most benignant. The soup looked like Primavera's dress and dreamt its way down as yachts do in a light wind. Then there were artichokes, green and melting and sentimental. Then a round of beef. Damned Canterbury, gentlemen, moulded and trans-formed by some ultra-sculptural cantrip, and swimming in dark mahogany sauce . . . I beg your pardon, Athos, you gave us a very nice dinner to-night, but your cook is only a woman. And some Barsac, all golden. The drink you cannot take across the water. And I only paid her fifteen francs a week. And then the General came. Well, Porthos, how are you? Sir, will you wait for dinner? I have a cook.

"Ah! forgive me, friends, there was an Ercildoune dreaming on me, and I knew not what I did. The General stole her. More, he sent me, like the Hittite in the Bible, to the thickest of the fight. To St. Pol. . . . Ah, well! They could roast a chicken there!"

"The first cocktail I invented during the war,"

said Athos, his fine face deeply lined with thought,
" was in the Chateau Barly, on the Western Front.
It was called a Tangerine Sling. It was a cocktail
rather of necessity than of choice. The only two
drinks left to us in the mess after the Christmas dinner
were St. Julien and Rum. There were also some
tangerine oranges and raisins. Into one glass I put a
tablespoonful of rum, into another two tablespoonfuls
of claret. I put two crushed raisins into the rum and
squeezed the juice of a single lith of the orange into
the claret. With a spoon I then squeezed and buffeted
the peel of the orange in the claret glass. I then threw
the peel and the two raisins into the fire, mixed and
shook the two beverages, placed a second tangerine
lith in the mixture, and put it on a frosty window-sill
to cool. After ten minutes I shook it again and finally
drank it. It imparted a pleasant and enlivening sensation to the fingers and toes, and made me wish to
join the Flying Corps. The last cocktail I invented
was after the armistice in Tiflis. Long drinks were
the vogue, as at that time the weather was warm. The
drink was called the Pink Devil. It contained gin,
orange bitters, Angostura bitters, lime juice, liqueur
whisky, cherry brandy, cognac, burgundy, sherry and
vodka. I would tell you the proportions and how to
mix it, but I really think we ought to join the ladies."

" When I was in Amiens I took the French General's
mistress to dinner one night," said Aramis. " The
French General complained to G.H.Q. in the following
terms . . . "

" Another time, perhaps, old boy," said Athos, " but
the ladies will be impatient."

CHAPTER VII

The Seventh Five

YOU MUST NOT BE angry with me. It may appear to you that I have thrown away my big scene ; that I have given you Hamlet without the Mousetrap. I have my reasons.

I was talking the other night to an old gentleman who has just published one of the very few classics of the Great War. It is called *The War the Infantry Knew*. He told me that he was persuaded that it was wrong to write about the war in retrospect. Anything of value must be written on the spot, when the impressions are fresh. Anybody recalling the war must confabulate and embroider and, not to put too fine a point on it, tell lies. I agree with him from the bottom of my heart. My own remembrance of the war powerfully censors the abominations and shows up vividly the happy moments that were seen in relief against the darkness. As an instance, I am not passionately receptive of lovely sights and sounds. My world is too full of people for me to engage myself very closely with the landscape in the background. But scenes and places on the Western Front shine out for me as clearly and delightfully as if they had been painted by Italian Primitives. I was wandering round the line at Arras all by myself, for my companion had had to go back. There was a strafe going on, and I know that I was terrified out of my judgement. For some reason or other, as I remind myself, I was more frightened even than usual, and I had to swear at myself continuously to keep myself at a walking pace. I know that this was so by a long series of relayed reminders, but I cannot recreate my feeling. What I do remember, with a great and happy intensity, is a little ruined garden full of white roses, a swan swimming unconcernedly in a shell-hole and a skylark singing overhead. The skylark was singing in the very short intervals between the crash of the crumps, but I cannot hear the crumps.

It follows, then, that I could tell you nothing but lies about the war. There was one contemporary phrase that must have reflected my feelings. It was to the effect that the war was a cross between a wet Saturday and a pit accident.

It is only fair to tell you, however, from a purely objective point of view how my hero behaved during the war and what obvious effects it had upon his character and personality. He did, on the whole, very well, allowing for the fact that he had cold feet and a hot stomach whenever he came within ten miles of the Germans. Fortunately for him he had a cushy war, for he was a physical funk and had continually to struggle with the impulses that led him to encourage his little brother to approach the goat. He salvaged his self-respect by remaining in areas which, if they were seldom more dangerous than Piccadilly Circus in a rush hour, were at least comprised in any loose definition of The Front. That is to say, he obeyed orders and attempted no wangles. He served with two battalions and a battery of artillery when he was sent to them, and showed himself an efficient, if not particularly enterprising, commander of advanced dressing stations. He was sustained partly by superstition and partly by professional pride. His regular colleagues were brave men but bad doctors, and few of the others had had the ennobling experience of being house surgeons. When a blinded, wounded officer said to him once,

"Who is that? My God, you have got gentle hands! You know your job all right,"
his tank was filled with enough vanity to keep him running through the war and for a long time after it.

I have said that he had a cushy war. His division spent more than nine months in the Ypres Salient in 1915–6: but more than half of that time was spent in looking after trench fever and scabies at a reasonable distance from the line, within reach of such entertainment as Poperinghe had to offer. He spent six months in Arras, but at that time Arras was a quiet sector with little town boys catching hot bullets at the ends of the communication trenches and excellent if slightly battered billets. He stayed on the Somme for four months but was anchored firmly in a Corps Dressing Station, near which shells seldom fell. He made serious efforts to join his comrades in the line, but these came to nothing, for the Corps Dressing Station was an innovation and the darling of the local Director of Medical Services. When he returned to the Arras neighbourhood it was quieter than ever, and three successive attacks of trench fever kept him from any close contact with the enemy. He left his unit in an ambulance in the great February frost in 1917, fully

233

persuaded that the men were sorry to see him go. In the following years of the war he went on an admirable conducted tour of the East, where he did not see a shot fired in anger. He formed the impression that the ideal method of foreign travel is to go accompanied by a brigade of bayonets. This at least ensures civility from officials, and is so unapproachably delightful a way of getting about that he has not been abroad since.

•   •   •   •   •   •   •   •

I did not get back from South Russia until October, 1919, the Armistice overtook me in Kasvin, in north Persia. When I announced it to a ward full of malarious British soldiers the only comment was " Is that so, sir? "

The General made an occasion of it by having a reception for the Governor at Headquarters. We had no band with us, and the local Persian band was not very good. We found out afterwards that it had been trying to play " God Save the King " all evening. My Aberdonian dispenser made some fireworks, and the General and his guests went out on the balcony to watch them. The fireworks guttered and fizzled in a highly symbolic way, but were otherwise unsatisfactory.

We had nine months in Baku, where I had the pleasure of being a somebody for the second and last time in my life ; and, towards the end of 1919, we went home. It was a dismal journey. We went by Constantinople and Taranto with sundry halts, one of them in France. The Captains and the Kings had departed. Posted on the notice-board of the mess in which we spent the night was an order enjoining officers not to spit on the floor and adjuring them to be in at nine-thirty-five at night. The bright spot was at

Faenza, where a delightful old Colonel in canvas leggings met us at the train and told us not to bother about our men. He would look after them. His adjutant took them away and gave them hot showers, a square meal and a football match. We were given baths, an excellent lunch accompanied by the town band playing " Traviata," and an easy in a charming little mess hut, furnished by the Colonel's wealthy friends. I wish I could remember the Colonel's name. He was the only rest camp commander I ever met who had a tincture of gentility in him, and his visitor's book was scrawled all over with lyrical gratitude and blotted with tears. We entrained from our ship, and I, with a detachment of extremely drunk Scottish Riflemen, was carried to Scotland and decanted into a squalid village of Nissen huts. There I was given my freedom and told by implication to go to hell.

It may seem to you that this period of five years was not so clearly cut from its predecessor as the others. Nevertheless, I did cast a skin at the end of 1917 and come out in a new one. I had established myself confidently as a physician, or was beginning to do so. In 1918 I dealt very well with the influenza epidemic as it affected north Persia and the brigade which was holding the Hamadan—Enzeli road. For another thing I began at that point to desire to earn my living in an ordinary, civilized manner.

In the autumn of 1919 I bought a practice in the Langside district of Glasgow and joined the staff of the Victoria Infirmary as a junior assistant physician. My mother, my brother Eric and I took up housekeeping in a little semi-villa with a garden in Langside Avenue. I began for the first time to do an honest day's work. In one way I regretted that I had left my protracted youth behind me. In another way I was glad. In 1918 I had grown up. Many books have been written about

the life of a general practitioner. This life is commonly
conveyed by a string of anecdotes much in the manner
of the earlier part of this book. I cannot imagine how
these anecdotes come to be written. A doctor is on
such terms with his patients that any hint of the
histories in which he is taking an active part is an
abominable breach of confidence. I find that the
patients in these anecdotes usually belong to the poorer
classes. I suppose that the assumption is that they are
unlikely to read a half-guinea book or to be acquainted
with the laws of professional etiquette or of libel.
These laws apart, if a doctor who has attended me or
my family in a professional capacity permits himself
to describe our diseases or to report our quaint sayings
in a public print I shall get a stick and give him a good
beating. I shall report him to the General Medical
Council and take him to the Court of Session. He can
call me Mr. Smith if he likes and alter my measles to
influenza, but if he tells the story well I shall recognise
myself and my neighbours will recognise me. He may
put me into the *Lancet* if he likes, under a number ;
but he must not write down my troubles for money
and for the entertainment of the vulgar and the in-
quisitive.

I find myself tied down, then, to what must be little
more than a series of general reflections. If this is
disappointing to those who like to hear the wise, witty
old family doctor descanting on the funny, bizarre or
courageous qualities of his patients, I cannot help it.
They will have to go with the others who would have
liked me to fill my war chapter with corpses and latrines.
They can join the multitude who will not like this book.
And what care I?

I found myself, then, working for my living and not
liking it particularly. It was not that my earlier training had made me incapable of work or that I didn't

like work in its proper place. I could and still can call out furious bursts of sustained energy from time to time. This energy accumulates during my long periods of complete idleness of body and mind and, on the whole, I am content that it should do so. What I found irksome was a daily and necessary routine intensified by calls at the door and on the telephone at hours I might reasonably expect to have to myself.

Calls out of hours are the bugbear of the general practitioner and a special technique has to be elaborated for dealing with them. I learned two separate methods very quickly. The custom of my predecessor was to answer a night call at once. If he had been taken from his fireside or his bed for something trivial or something to which he ought to have been called earlier in the day, he spent half an hour or so in exercising an acid and repetitive rhetoric of which he was a master. He left his persecutors badly shaken and, more often than not, in tears.

The other method was that used by my Uncle who practised in the same neighbourhood. He was the husband of my Aunt Maggie. He was a tall, bony, wiry man with strong white hair *en brosse* and a boyish manner. He was one of the Covenanting Howies— the toughest farming stock in the South West of Scotland. When he was on holiday, I acted for him and was immediately deluged by night calls. In the tradition of my practice, I responded at once and was met by astonished faces. My uncle had a game with his patients. If they rang him up, he said he would be round in the morning and hung up the receiver. This was the first round for the Doctor. A Messenger was then sent and my Uncle interviewed him from the first floor window. If the Messenger was an ill-informed neighbour-body, he was sent back for more detailed information and the Doctor won Round Two. Round Three was won if, on his return, the Messenger was content with a prescription. It took some force of dialectic and a deal of sincerity to get the Doctor to put on his coat and come out; for he did not come out unless his knowledge of Medicine, which was great, and his knowledge of human nature, which was profound, convinced him that it was necessary. He and his patients understood one another and he was immensely popular in a huge practice.

The practice I took over was much smaller. It was smaller still before I had been in it very long. At the end of the year, on an actuarial basis, it had dropped to one third of the value it had when I paid for it. This, I knew, was the way of the world. Choosing a family Doctor is a very difficult matter. It is also a very important matter. Once you have given your life and the life of your dependants into his hands, it is not easy or advisable to change. When the Doctor you have trusted leaves the district, it is safer to go over to a Doctor who is trusted by your neighbours than to take the old Doctor's word as to the merits of his successor. At least, that is what they thought in the South Side of Glasgow.

The faithful remnant formed a very nice practice indeed. My predecessor had been an idiosyncratic man and his practice had had time to sort itself out. His patients were nearly all intelligent, considerate people. The " panel," against which I had heard many diatribes from other Doctors, proved to be the most delightful section of my practice. They had not learned to regard their Doctor as a public official with a tendency to shirk his duty. Nor had they the pathetic air of people who are willing to pay extra if only they can get proper, non-panel, medical attention. They were clerks and artisans who understood the principles of insurance and behaved like civilised participants in a civilised contract. So did not the officials of the Approved Societies and my patients and I had many a merry battle with some of these ridiculous persons.

I did not like so much the patients from whom I felt justified in exacting seven and six or even half a guinea a visit; but then I have always disliked the rich. I have no prejudice against the poor devils, understand me. They cannot help being rich. They would be foolish to be anything else. But I don't like them and they don't like me and very few of my friends are even moderately well-to-do. On the other hand, very few of them are poor.

Be that as it may . . .

. . . .

I spent my mornings at the hospital teaching, visiting the sick and doing sporadic and ill-sustained bits of research. On some afternoons I attended the Sick Children's Hospital Dispensary to which I had been appointed an extra Physician, and on others I assisted at what was called the Bogey-Bogey Clinic. This was a Psychotherapeutic Clinic for shell-shocked War veterans.

Before I was allowed to tamper with the psyches of the veterans, I was attached to a young psycho-analyst for instruction. One incident in this instruction pleased me very much.

One man had a headache. He attributed it to the nipping of a portion of his brain between two pieces of bone. The young psychoanalyst was greatly shocked.

" My man," he said, " whoever told you that was telling you nonsense. Listen and I will explain to you what is the matter."

239

He drew the following diagram on a bit of paper:

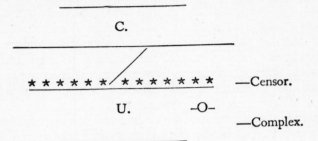

"Now, pay careful attention. It's all really very simple. This space labelled *C.* is your Conscious Mind. The thing you see me with and listen to me with and think with and so on. The space labelled *U.* is your Unconscious Mind. It is going on working all the time, only you don't know it. Why don't you know it? Why, because between it and your field of consciousness there is a Censor. I've showed that like a line of barbed wire entanglements passing right over the top of the unconscious part of your brain.

"Now, lots of things may happen in your Unconscious that the Censor doesn't want your Conscious mind to know about. And sometimes they impinge or bump into one another, so to speak. Two difficulties. Two opposing instinctive impulses. Two traumatic impressions. They fight each other for a bit and then they get walled off from the rest. They become encysted. You know what a cyst is? A thing like a balloon. Now they've got to pass through the wall of the cyst *as well as* forcing their way up past the Censor. So that, by the time they arrive at the level *C.*, they are distorted out of all recognition. They may take the form of a pain or a nightmare or both, don't you see?"

He made scribbling marks with his pencil to show the turmoil going on within the encysted complex and a shower of arrows bursting out of it to show how they became like barbed corkscrews by the time they reached the Conscious Mind. The man gazed like one bewitched.

" Do you think it'll require an operation, Doctor? " he said.

·   ·   ·   ·   ·   ·   ·   ·

I am utterly determined not to show disrespect to the Unconscious. I think nobly of the Unconscious; the more so that the Unconscious once gave me a poke in the eye at this very Bogey-Bogey Clinic of which I have been telling you. It was a very peculiar clinic. Patients were referred to it by neurological medical boards. One of the by-products of the war, besides the influenza epidemic, was a crop of neurologists. I do not know how the revelation came to these gentlemen, but the most unexpected people were endowed with neurology. Ex-Territorial colonels more military than the military would assure me, in response to some mild protest or other, that they were a bit of neurologists themselves. I suspect that Freud, Jung and Adler, that holy trinity, had made neurology easy for them. Be that as it may, there was an admirable single-mindedness about the post-war neurologists. This was exemplified by the number of patients suffering from general paralysis of the insane, disseminated sclerosis, locomotor ataxia and dementia praecox referred by the medical boards for psychotherapy and gladly accepted by the clinic. Don't misunderstand me. The officers of the clinic were very nice fellows. They talked peaceably and kindly to the poor jumpy souls who came to them for comfort, and they were very kind to me who belonged, perhaps, to a breed without the law. They explained to me that if I had been to Tooting I would be less uneasy about the clinic's methods and results. I respected their green turbans and scarlet beards, but stuck to what I believed to be the light of pure reason with occasional excursions into psycho-analysis, or what I understood to be psycho-analysis from my recollections of my early researches into Freud and my careful reading of *The New Age*.

It was during one of these excursions that the Unconscious poked me in the eye. One of my patients dreamt that he was marching along the pavé on his way to the line. He was carrying an enormous pack and was so tired that he had to keep going to prevent himself from falling down. I was lying on the grass by the side of the road and I motioned him to halt. I then handed him a bit of broken glass mirror and told him to shave himself with it.

Students of symbolism will readily understand what the Unconscious was getting at. Here is a key for the uninstructed.

The man's troubles were packed in his old kit-bag and they were pretty well as much as he could bear. It was easy enough for me. I had no troubles. I had only to loaf by the roadside. I checked his steady career into the unknown. I presented him with a fragmentary and irrelevant psychological instrument. It was intended to let him see himself, but it was only a bit of an instrument and it only showed a bit of him. He did not particularly want to see himself. He wanted to get on with his journey. But there was a lunatic connection between the fragment and a practical purpose; it was a piece of a shaving mirror. A razor was used for shaving, therefore the fragment was a razor. The Unconscious recognised the false syllogism at once and threw it back at me and at all psycho-analysts,

242

both those who had been to Tooting and those who had not.

It may well be that I have a very imperfect grasp of modern psycho-analytical practice. I am told that it takes at least three years to break down a personality thoroughly, and another two to build it up. I know nothing about breaking down personalities, but it seems to me that the building up is a job for Socrates, Christ and Confucius working in the closest collaboration. I should not care to entrust my personality, such as it is, to any individual of a lower intellectual and moral standard than that.

Some years later a young clerk came to see me. He had been misled by the advertising matter I had written about myself in the medical directory. I was only one call in a tour of specialists he was making. He said that the specialist who had done him most good was a psycho-analyst. He, the psycho-analyst, appeared to have hold of the right end of the stick and to have the root of the matter in him. The only trouble was that he, the clerk, felt too tired after a hard day's work to be psycho-analysed properly. I agreed with him that he was not an ideal subject for psycho-analysis. The ideal subject is a rich lady with nothing to do. I gave him the name of a general practitioner with a rosy face and a wide smile. I forecast the line of treatment I thought this practitioner would adopt, but I told him not to tell the practitioner what I had said. The practitioner ordered him a square meal a day and a five mile walk after tea. He was cured in three weeks of practically all the symptoms in the medical dictionary.

. . . .

I did not like being a general practitioner though the life had its compensations. I was conscious that I was learning a good deal. I learned how to talk to people and improved somewhat my technique in lying. I learned a little about human nature. I learned almost to a hair how much humbug is contained in the physician's alloy. I learned that, in women especially, invalidism is not so much an affliction as a powerful weapon. I learned that a doctor, unless he takes morphia, cannot starve. My practice grew steadily without any particular effort on my part. I learnt to distrust the opinion of doctors who work in offices or in laboratories. For example, a favourite article in the official doctor's creed is that the general practitioner is the spearhead or the infantryman or what have you of the army of public health. He is nothing of the kind. He is a person specially trained to look after the sick. He knows less about public health than a sanitary inspector. For another example, the laboratory physiologist is apt to turn dietician in his old age. Until he tells me how and at what point a dead rump steak turns into living cells I refuse to listen to his advice. In my practice I was accustomed to say " You must not take diet. You must eat food. If your wife is a good cook she knows what sort of stuff you ought to eat." This was the only great truth I discovered and enunciated during my seventh five year spell.

I learnt to appreciate courage and self-sacrifice in everyday life, and I learnt that sentimentality is a form of voluptuous cruelty. It is a complex of self-pity and delight in the sufferings of others.

It was pleasant to learn these things, but I did not look forward with any pleasure to a continuance of my state. I was restless and discontented. I hunted continually for a way out. I had thought no small beer of myself as an author. I wrote a great deal in the hope that I should be paid for it and gather sufficient money to subsidise a consulting practice. I earned, by my typewriter, something like seven pounds in three years. One thing I did not write for money. It was a three-act play and I wrote it to see whether I could write a three-act play. When I had finished it I sent it to Alfred Wareing for his opinion. His opinion was that it was very clever, but that no manager would risk a brace button on it. I accepted his verdict, put the play in a drawer and forgot all about it. It was called *The Switchback*.

I wrote a remarkable lot of rubbish considering the time I had at my disposal. Looking backwards I cannot see how I found any spare time at all, and yet I went a good deal to the theatre and the moving pictures and spent stretches of time at the Art Club, of which I had just become a member. It is said that nobody can become unhappy who has plenty to do. I had plenty to do and I was unhappy.

The hospital was a bright spot. I became secretary of the Staff Association. The Victoria Infirmary had the reputation of being a happy hospital, and certainly most of its visiting staff were on speaking terms with one another. I enjoyed going from ward to ward and hearing my friends vituperate against their colleagues. I know of no profession in the world whose members so denigrate and blackguard each other behind their backs as does the medical profession. Nor is there another profession so incapable of concerted action. Against these faults may be placed its capacity for pure altruism. It shares this capacity with no other body of men. The Victoria *was* a happy hospital. Its private and particular ray of sunshine was the Medical Superintendent, Duncan Otto MacGregor. I never met a merrier man within the limits of becoming mirth. He was a wit, a diplomatist, a procrastinator and a good companion. He amused himself with radiology as a side-line. He looked like a Scots terrier. He must have been about sixty years of age when I knew him first.

R

A patient of mine, a lad of eighteen, had swallowed something or other. I took him to the X-ray room and explained the circumstances to MacGregor. He appeared to be listening, but suddenly he turned round and barked at the boy.

" Can you turn a back somersault? "

" No," said the lad.

" I can," said MacGregor. " What were you saying, Mavor? "

He stopped a new probationer nurse in the corridor. He said,

" I haven't seen you before."

She said, " No, sir. I've just joined."

MacGregor said, " I hope you enjoy yourself here. Have you got an Aunt Maggie? "

The nurse was proud to meet the acquaintance of a relation and felt, moreover, her position in the hospital assured.

" Yes, I have," she said.

" Everybody's got an Aunt Maggie. It's a most extraordinary thing," said MacGregor, trotting away down the corridor.

As his summer holidays approached and Iona beckoned him [1] the arrears of work in the X-ray room began to mount up, and he used to spend days in the dark among crackling and disintegrating machinery, distracted nurses and bewildered, half-naked patients. To the lighted ante-chamber came Mr. Russell, a surgeon, Dr. Vost, the tall and grave senior anaesthetist, and Dr. Steen, the small and dapper House Surgeon. They waited for twenty minutes; then a nurse shot out of the sliding door to the dark-room with her cap awry and her hair dishevelled. They gave her a message and she returned to the chaotic inferno.

[1] He once wrote me a letter from Iona, " sitting," he said, " on pink rocks in a kilt."

246

" Mr. Russell, Dr. Vost and Dr. Steen," she said,
" have been waiting outside for the last twenty
minutes." MacGregor drew a line of sparks from an
overhead wire and said,

" Tell Russell and Vost they can go to hell, and
Steen can do as he pleases."

He was the best after dinner speaker I have ever
heard. On a very dignified occasion he began his speech,
" Ladies and gentlemen and gynaecologists . . . "

Sir James MacKenzie was brought by his friend
Ivy MacKenzie to inaugurate a new teaching and research scheme in the hospital. As Ivy MacKenzie
was my chief and as he was engaged in lecturing to his
students on the nictitating membrane or some such
thing—perhaps it was humming birds' hearts—I had
to show Sir James round the hospital. He was one of
the four great men I have met in my life. Marshal
Foch was not a great man. I met him in a newspaper
shop in Haazebrouck. I saluted him and he paid no
attention. The other great men were William Macewen, Rutherford and Bernard Shaw. He told me the
following story, with great wealth of detail.

Once upon a time there was a London Scot who was
afflicted with skin disease. He saw three or four
Harley Street baronets and knights about it, and his
own private doctor had a handle to his name. He got
no better. His titled doctor decided to call in all the
resources of modern science and he had a vaccine
made for the London Scot. This, with due estimations
of his opsonic index, he administered at regular intervals, for a fee suitable to the dignity of his establishment. After six months the London Scot was no
better and had to be given morphia to make him sleep
at nights. He told his doctor that he must have a
change. The doctor said that was an excellent idea
and suggested the south of France.

" No," said the man, " I have a feeling that I am going to die of this, and I am going to the Scottish east coast fishing village where I was born."

On the evening of the following day he arrived at his birthplace and immediately went to bed in the inn; but not to sleep. The vaccine seemed to have shot his nerves to pieces and, besides, his skin was agonising. He rang the bell and ordered the people of the inn to fetch half a grain of morphia from the local doctor. He told them not to disturb the good man; that he could administer the morphia himself. In a little while an aged gentleman with a waterfall moustache and hair growing out of his ears arrived at the inn and entered the suffering Scot's bedroom.

" Fat is 't ye want? " he asked.

The man explained the circumstances and recited the high sounding names and titles of the masters of medicine who had been, like the physicians on the tomb-stone, in vain. He politely invited the doctor to give him his soporific and be gone. The doctor replied by opening the man's pyjama jacket and peering at him through thick, steel-rimmed spectacles.

" Aye, mannie," he said, " ye've got the itch. I'll send ye round a pot of sulphur ointment. Ye'll be cured in four days."

He had. He did. He was.

. . . .

I do not know whether this story is calculated to shake or to confirm the faith of the public in the medical profession. If the public had a judicial mind it would see that the position is exactly as it was before the story was told. The two sides of the equation cancel out. But the public has not a judicial mind and is, I am told, greatly exercised and upset by stories of this sort, among which may be numbered Dr. A. J.

Cronin's book, *The Citadel*. In that story a young man of striking attainments, a prizeman in his year and, no doubt, the apple of his professors' eyes, neglects to ask their advice on the choice of a career. He takes up a blackleg practice in South Wales. He meets what he might have expected and migrates to London. In London he appears to be deserted by everything except his unerring clinical sense; for, you must know, this admirable young man never makes a mistake in diagnosis or fails to apply the correct treatment. He misbehaves himself badly in his private life, he gives his consulting work to a little ring of his fellow students, whom he well knows for idlers, wasters and ignoramuses. As a result of a difference of opinion with his hospital chief he hands over the daughter of a colleague to an unqualified quack for the operation of pneumothorax, though this operation could have been done for her by an expert at any nursing home or county council hospital. When he is very properly arraigned for this before the General Medical Council he harangues them like a fishwife. With excellent magnanimity they allow him to continue to practice and, I am happy to say, he settles down into a useful member of society.

I have no doubt this apparently incredible story is true in detail. I can almost identify the coven of warlocks to whom the hero entrusted his professional honour. I think it a pity, however, and I am sure Dr. Cronin thinks it a pity, that the story should have been taken by the public to prove something. If it proves anything it is the necessity for a disciplinary body within the medical profession. It suggests also, incidentally, the eternal simplicity, vulgarity, innocence and gullibility of the rich. I have known more than one pirate sail from Scotland to sack their harbours and singe the beard of the G.M.C. They did not belong to the higher grade of pirate quacksalver. To a member of that grade London is too easy. It is like hitting at a kid. There is honour among those who prey upon the sick.

.   .   .   .

This flat if not unprofitable patch in my life continued to the end of the statutory five years. My efforts to become an author had failed. It seemed as if, like Dr. Cronin's hero, I was fated to become a useful member of society. Then, as usual, things began to happen.

CHAPTER VIII

The Eighth Five

IN 1922, THOUGH MY body and mind were fully occupied, my soul was like a loose sheet flapping in the wind. In 1923 it was made fast. I got married. Up to that point I had an uneasy suspicion that life was meaningless.

" Why," asked the Mad Hatter, " is a raven like a writing desk? " and did not know the answer, for there was none. I became suddenly persuaded that the answer to all my riddles would appear in next week's issue, and that they could be solved if I had the wits to do it and the disposition to try.

A character in a forgotten play once said,

" You sort of change, like, oncet you've heard the old wedding march. You're never the same again. Some says better. Some says worse. I call it just different."

I felt suddenly comfort and confidence. My feet were on the ground. My bank balance was £13. 4s. 1d. on the credit side.

251

I bought a motor car that made a noise exactly like a distant machine gun. What with the motor car and the confidence, I put on two stones in weight in a very short time indeed. Life was not, however, without its vicissitudes.

My wife and I were driving in our brand new car up a steep hill in a suburb of Shawlands when I was confronted unexpectedly by a row of iron posts. I turned sharply to the right and pressed my accelerator instead of my brake. A lamp-post struck us right in the middle of the radiator. I had a charming sense of power as the lamp-post broke into three pieces and subsided into the street. From the naked pipe the gas whistled out merrily and the water dripped from my smashed radiator. We plugged the gas pipe with a handkerchief and I asked my wife to hold it down while I went for a policeman. The policeman I found took a cork out of his pocket and plugged the gas pipe. I suppose he kept it just for that purpose. How Lewis Carroll and his White Knight keep cropping up! No doubt the man had a bee-hive in his helmet.

A day or two later the insurance company asked for particulars of this policeman. It had not occurred to me to take his number, so I rang up the police station and asked. A West Highland voice at the other end of the line said,

" Well, now, who would that be? Stop you a moment, was it a big, tall man? "

I said yes.

" Ah, then," said the sergeant, " I know who it would be."

Now, the average height of the Glasgow Police Force is five feet eleven and three-quarters. I do not know how he knew who it would be.

The motor car was not my only step up in the social scale. One of the assistant physicians at the hospital

went to Zanzibar and I became an assistant physician
with the right to what is called consulting rank. I sold
my practice and, as they say, " blossomed out from a
struggling general practitioner into a full-fledged consulting physician." I rented a house on the edge of that
part of Glasgow known as the Valley of the Shadow of
Death because the specialists live there, and waited for
my general practitioner friends to invite my opinion.
They did not do so. I do not and did not blame them.
The consultants I had employed in my own practice
had nearly all been people I did not know and about
whose methods I had some curiosity. I made a hundred pounds in my first year, or, to be more exact, a
hundred and five pounds, mainly in sums of two
guineas. This was a fair start. I had every reason to
be hopeful. The darkest cloud on the misty horizon
was the fact that I had spent nearly all the money of
which I had robbed my successor in the Langside
practice. George Middleton had told me that it took
him ten years as a consultant to make more than a
hundred a year. I seemed to have begun where he
left off; but I had no guarantee that my income would
increase. I thought living on a hundred a year in an
expensive part of Glasgow would be rather difficult,
and, before my five-year cycle had ended, the arrival of
two sons promised to make it more difficult still.

I was never one to worry very much about money
matters. I left that first to my mother and then to my
wife. But it was just as well that other sources of
income began to appear. A huge hospital under the
governance of what was then the Glasgow Parish
Council wanted two consulting physicians, and I
applied for one of the posts. The honorarium was
small, but it was enough to pay my rent. The Parish
Council is dead and gone, but it may be instructive to
give a short and incomplete account of how I became

its employé. This will serve the double purpose of giving an insight into the workings of the democratic state and recording a vein of mulishness in the character of my hero.

The rumour was about that the Parish Council were proposing to transform their fine large hospital at Stobhill from a dump of human wreckage into something that could compare with the voluntary hospitals in Glasgow. It had something like thirteen hundred beds and seven hundred of these had been under the supervision of one physician. When this physician died I went to see those of my friends who were medical and surgical consultants to the Parish Council, and they told me that they had no objection to me as a colleague. They had a meeting and recommended to the council a short leet of four names to the two appointments. These names were, Dr. Smith, Dr. Jones, Dr. Robinson and Dr. Mavor. The Hospital Committee met and appointed Dr. Smith, who was a young man of brilliant attainments and a string of qualifications that reached almost from Glasgow to Edinburgh. The other three names they took to avizandum. I visited the Clerk to the Parish Council and the Superintendent of the Hospital and was advised to make myself known to members of the Committee. The first councillor I visited granted me an interview on a stairhead. I told him that I was not canvassing for his support, but that I thought it polite to let him see one of the candidates on whom he would later have to vote. He told me that there was some jiggery-pookery here. He told me the entire council was conducted on a system of jiggery-pookery. He told me that the post ought to and would be advertised in the newspapers and that he would be no party to jiggery-pookery of this sort. He told me he had never heard of me or of Jones or of Robinson. He told me that that was no bar to his favour, as he was

determined that an unknown man should make his
name at Stobhill hospital. He told me that in State
Medicine, as in every other public activity, a few powerful and predatory men gathered all the plums into their
own lap. He told me it was the same in the Labour
movement, where men like Maxton and Kirkwood
and Buchanan gathered all the limelight and considered that other workers should consider it a privilege
to be allowed to applaud them. He told me that he
had always set his face against this sort of thing and
that he would see that I got justice. By this time he was
in a crusading frenzy. He told me I would have the
Labour party solid at my back. If I gave him twelve
copies of my qualifications he would light such a
candle in the Parish Council as would never be put out.
He had reached this point before I was allowed to
speak and to reiterate what I had said at the beginning,
that I was not in any sense canvassing. He told me
that if I were blate I would never get anywhere and
that I must be prepared to fight with the gloves off if
I was to defeat the forces of reaction. I kept my gloves
on and moved on to the next Parish Councillor. He
was a Trades Union official, and I took my place in a
queue of dejected-looking men who were waiting at a
frosted glass door on which the councillor's name was
printed in large black letters. As the units in the
queue moved forward into the office others joined the
tail. The queue men who came out of the office looked
more dejected, if possible, than they were when they
entered it. Then a brisk man came out of the office
and cast a hard eye up and down the queue, muttering
" My God! " and pushing the first two back from the
door. His eye caught mine and he beckoned me in.
He was very businesslike and civil, and we had quite
a friendly chat. I could not rid myself of the impression
that he hated his employers who were lined up outside.

255

But he was a professional. I got on well with him. I could not away with the amateurs, or Members of the Moderate Group. I found they tended to be pompous, consequential and evasive, and I felt an almost overwhelming impulse to be rude to them. I soon sickened of the business. I broke off with more than half the committee still unvisited and awaited developments. I found that ten or a dozen consultants of all ages had applied for the post and I did not fancy my chances, especially as I had reason to believe that the Chairman of the Hospitals Committee was my enemy.

On the night of the afternoon on which the meeting was held I impudently rang the Chairman up and asked him what had happened. He was in a very bad temper. He said the appointment of Smith had been confirmed, but that the Bolsheviks and the Papists had taken great delight in the sound of their own voices, and that the meeting had adjourned without a further decision. I found, to my delight, that there had been jiggery-pookery. An attempt had been made quietly to foist on the meeting a fifth candidate who had not been on the consultants' short leet, and that my friend the demagogue had been as good as his word. He had thrown a spanner into the works. I suddenly grew very angry with my senior, Dr. X, who had suddenly appeared on my pitch with powerful backing behind him. I felt I had no quarrel with the other three members of the short leet, but that I must at all costs down him. I learned that the matter had been referred to a sub-committee of three of the most important members of all the Parish Council. I got my uncle to invite one to lunch, and discussed Art, Literature and the Future of Medicine with him for an hour and a half. I sent my Chief to the second and he employed all his eloquence on the Councillor, an old friend of his, for upwards of two hours.

I pulled a whole harpful of wires. I lobbied. I called out all my resources of low cunning. You see, I suspected Dr. X of jiggery-pookery and, if there was one thing I could not stand it was jiggery-pookery. Dr. X was mad with rage, but I was appointed unanimously. I am fully persuaded that it was a good appointment and that I did very well indeed at Stobhill. Dr. X and I are now fast friends.

At Stobhill I found the science and art of medicine laid out for me in neat row after neat row. The jigsaw puzzle was far from complete, but I could form some general impression of the design. In the voluntary hospital, if I wished to study rheumatoid arthritis I had to content myself with two or three patients, observed over a period of a few weeks. Beds were scarce and the hospital turnover a matter of importance. In Stobhill at any given time I might have thirty or forty cases and, as Stobhill was their last port of call, I could observe them indefinitely. I could assess also, in their unfortunate persons, the value of the " cures " to which they had been subjected in the voluntary hospitals.[1]

Smith and I enjoyed Stobhill tremendously. We were monarchs of all we surveyed, our right there was none to dispute. Our lords and masters, the Parish Council, interfered with us not at all, and our colleagues were our friends. They included one genius, Old Bill, who had been superannuated from the Royal Infirmary some years before, but who was so full of energy that he had to find some outlet for it. He was ostensibly specialist in diseases of the ear, throat, and nose; but the human subject was not to him like an elephant, all lugs and trunk. He had been for many

---

[1] This is not a medical text-book. Rheumatoid arthritis is not incurable ; but I learned to regard certain sensational processes in the treatment of the disease as very illusory indeed.

years a general practitioner in a mining town and he was a doctor first and a specialist second. I consider him the only man who has ever written common sense about asthma. He was also the worst and most dangerous driver of a motor car in the world. He used to drive round slippery corners with his foot on the accelerator and one arm reached well over into the well of the car, rummaging in an attache case for clinical notes, the while he argued furiously that cerebral abscess was one of the commonest sequels to bronchiectasis.

Even in the wards his impatience to be up and doing amounted almost to violence. After a consultation I asked the patient whether he would rather be examined by the Doctor or do three rounds with Elky Clark.

The man said, " Three rounds wi' Elky Clark, and I ken something about scrapping."

Old Bill's face creased like an old blanket ill laid up and he roared with laughter.

Another day he invited me to see a girl. She suffered from bronchiectasis, a condition in which one of the smaller bronchial tubes dilates till it becomes a cavity, and Bill proposed then and there to wash out this cavity through an enormous tube thrust down the girl's trachea. It is not a pleasant operation, and the girl was sitting in the theatre wrapped in a flowered dressing-gown and chittering with apprehension. While I was examining her chest I did my best to soothe her fears, but I only made matters worse. Bill, who had been bustling about the theatre, came up. He wore a long white pinafore and a head mirror. He said,

" What d'you think of it? It's a big one, isn't it? She's a fine pianist. Come on, my lassie, you'll play us yon Chopin Prelude."

He took her by the wrist and led her out into the

corridor and into the patient's concert hall. It was large and bare, with a battered grand piano on the platform. Bill and I and our satellites sat down in the front row, after Bill had escorted the girl to the platform, like Sir Henry Wood leading in Myra Hess. She played us a prelude, and Bill said,

" Thank you. That'll do. It's better than Cortot. You can hear the bass. Now come on and we'll wash out that bronchiectasis."

He took the girl by the wrist and led her back to the theatre. Her nervousness was gone and she mounted the operating table as if it were part of the joke.

.   .   .   .

In 1926 there was a General Strike. I saw little of it, and kept drifting between the Victoria, the Sick Kids and Stobhill in other people's motor cars without seeing much evidence that anything unusual was happening. One day, however, I met a friend of mine who was on temporary secret service. He asked me if I would like to see a riot, and I said yes. We got into a taxi and drove to the Townhead. A column of miners was expected to enter the city, break the police cordon and make a demonstration on Glasgow Green. As we came near to the Townhead, the driver told us that he had to think of his cab and could take us no further. We went the rest of the way on foot. The street along which the miners were expected to march was lined with people in cloth caps. They packed the pavements. They extended as far as eye could see. The police were dotted at intervals along the kerb, as if it had been a Royal procession. We moved about among the crowd as well as we could and talked to some of the people. This was not the Red Proletariat rising in its wrath. It was a quiet, well-behaved, sober, good-natured crowd of football spectators. We and

259

they waited for an hour to see the fun, but we waited in vain. The police told us that the miners had met superior forces two miles outside the town and had turned and gone home. We believed the police, and we too turned and went home. That is all I know at first hand of the General Strike.

．．．．．．．．．

As the eighth five years wore on, the ninth began to throw intimations across its path. I renewed acquaintance with a man who had been one of the dispensary surgeons at the Royal Infirmary when I was a houseman. He had given up his ambitions as a surgeon and was practising general medicine in the Hyndland district of Glasgow. He was a burly, rosy-faced man with white hair and a quiet voice. His name was John Brandane, though his patients knew him as John MacIntyre. His main interest at that time was a thing very grandly called The Scottish National Theatre Society. It had been sponsored by the St. Andrew's Society of Glasgow, and had fallen heir to what was left of the capital of the old Repertory Theatre. I was shamefully ignorant about its activities, but I knew that Brandane was an established Scottish novelist and had written one or two plays for the Society. I had seen none of those plays, but I had heard that one, *The Glen is Mine*, was regarded by good judges as the first great Scottish comedy.

Brandane took to me and I to him, and he asked me to join the board and help him to fight his battles. The battles were over a matter of general policy. There were three main trends of opinion. Brandane was for the pure milk of the Gospel. He considered that the Society should produce a Scottish drama by Scottish authors and, as there was no existing Scottish drama by Scottish authors, that the Society's sole

function was to evoke one. In this he had the support
of Gordon Bottomley, who lived in Cumberland but
who took the keenest possible interest in the movement. Another trend of opinion was expressed mainly
by the actors. They wanted to get their teeth into well-
carpentered professional work, and were inclined to
look down their noses at Scottish drama *per se*. A
third trend was just beginning to make its appearance.
A young professional producer had just been engaged.
He had been trained with J. B. Fagan's Oxford
Players, and had been with the B.B.C. at Belfast.
He was an Irishman of Scottish extraction, born at
Tunbridge Wells and educated at Wellington and St.
John's, Oxford. He was six feet four high and wore
a jersey and sandals. Brandane did not entirely
approve of him. He had a friend called David Cleg-
horn Thomson, who was Regional Director for Scot-
land of the B.B.C. The ideas of these two gentlemen
did not conform strictly to the canon laid down by the
St. Andrew's Society.

The name of the producer was Tyrone Guthrie, and
I need not tell any theatre-goer that the Scottish
National Players had got hold of a handful. His
predilections at this time ran somewhat in the direction
of song, mime and step-ladders; and Brandane,
Bottomley and Walter Buchanan of the St. Andrew's
Society regarded these things as dangerous innova-
tions, I think rightly.

The Society had some notable achievements to their
credit. Among them were Robert Bain's *King James*,
Brandane's *The Glen is Mine* and a gloomy play by
George Reston Malloch called *Soutarness Water*.
The most famous of all was the premier of Gordon
Bottomley's *Gruach*. Their actors were amateurs or
teachers of elocution, and a sufficient number of them
were almost constantly in practice and they reached a

very high standard indeed. Elliot Mason, James Woodburn and Morland Graham have gone on to make notable successes in London and America. There were at least half a dozen actors and actresses just as good, but these names will show that their strong suit was a fine sense of character. A number of them had already enchanted John Masefield and Gordon Bottomley by their skill in speaking verse. Brandane disliked seeing them prancing and leaping about in sham medieval costumes, intoning Hungarian nursery rhymes. On the other hand, Guthrie was able to point out that these entertainments took more money at the door than any kitchen comedy or tragedy, however subtle. A proportion of our playwrights found it difficult to get away from the farmhouse kitchen as their *mise-en-scène*. We had our eyes a good deal on the Abbey.

I was elected to the Board. The battle was not so bitter as John Brandane's Highland and bloody imagination had pictured it, although we recruited a red-headed, fiery specialist in diseases of children who had dandled David Thomson on his knee and was not prepared to stand any nonsense from him. My first step towards compromise was to write a play with almost everything in it but step-ladders. It was called *The Sunlight Sonata*, or *To Meet The Seven Deadly Sins*. Guthrie liked it. With magnificent courtesy and patience he helped me to iron out its amateur crudities. Brandane liked it, because, although it leaned over to the fantastic, it was as Scots as Freuchie. The Devil spoke from the top of Ben Lomond, addressing the Seven Deadly Sins in braid Scots hexameters, and the eight of them interfered in the private lives of a bunch of quite justly observed Glasgow citizens picnicking on the Bonnie Banks. Three pantomime fairies called Faith, Hope and Charity intervened. It was the last and only extant survivor of my morality play period, and I thought it very amusing. I wrote it on a Sunday and had to ring up a clergyman of my acquaintance to find out exactly who the seven deadly sins were. He did not know.

The play opened the ninth cycle, and I shall tell you what happened to it. In the meantime I had become a Professor in a curious old extra-mural school called the Anderson College of Medicine. It had been founded at the beginning of the nineteenth century by an eccentric called John Anderson, who was in revolt against the University. John had intended to endow it, but when his will came to be read it was found that he had practically no money at all. Strangely enough, his college survived, first as the Andersonian University and second as the Technical College and Anderson's College of Medicine. The Technical College is now an enormous affair with the title " Royal " in front of its name. The Medical College survives as a rather grubby building at the Western Infirmary gate. It had and still has a reputation for good, unorthodox teaching. Its most famous professor was Thomas Graham, the chemist, its most famous student was David Livingstone.

I was not a great success as a professor. I lectured daily to classes varying in number from six to twelve. Apart from the fact that they had to be given daily I enjoyed these lectures. My receipts as a consulting physician had risen to four hundred pounds a year. I had gathered in an insurance company and a tobacco factory, who paid me sufficiently for the services I was able to render. The eighth cycle closed on a cheerful note.

. . . .

Oliver Goldsmith sat down beside me.
" *You are about, I judge, to tell us how you came to be*

a writer of stage plays. That will interest me. I have been confused somewhat by the stories told me by Schiller, Chekhov, Schnitzler and Maugham. My own motives were, I confess, less complicated than theirs. I have always attributed this vice of mine to unsuitable company and the immoderate use of wine and spirits. With these others there appears to have been an element of paranoid dementia—of the hearing of voices."

"Indeed, Doctor," I replied, "I am afraid you will find little satisfaction to your curiosity in anything I am about to write on the intermediate steps between Doctor and Dramatist. I am inclined to put it down to sheer laziness."

"They say you write lazy plays," said the Doctor, mildly.

"Who say so?" I cried indignantly. "They lie. I may love and ensue idleness, but I am an artist. I have an artist's conscience. I will not suffer anybody to say that my work is influenced by sloth. Sacred name of a bomb..."

I found myself listening to somebody swearing in French. Our French Officer of the night before had joined the train and attempted to eject my gunner from his seat. I was in time to prevent bloodshed.

That night we arrived at the Somme and it was very noisy indeed.

I carried with me a reminder of the work of my Casualty Clearing friends in the form of a cyst in my lower jawbone. A series of my surgical and medical friends made painful jabs at it and, finally, I went into a Nursing Home to have it flattened.

I walked quite jauntily through the Stage Door. Things had come to pass. I had written plays and been paid for them. The facts of the case were now in the comfortable, intelligible, malleable Past. I was prepared to speak up to Goldsmith as a tradesman of his craft.

There was nobody there. I took up my story sadly and it was dull, dreadfully dull. This great adventure, this

Sindbadism of the Soul was no more lively a matter than collecting passports and tickets and insuring the luggage. I began to be glad that Goldsmith wasn't there. Still— there were the facts. I had promised the facts. I should not embroider them. I should set them down fairly, so that no Professor could possibly make a mistake. For why should I not be interesting to Professors some day when my spelling had become archaic and my jokes stale? I could not hope to make one of the weekly revivals in the Celestial Theatre, but there were always the Professors. I should not keep my Memoirs (as Mr. Home called them) for the eye of the Recording Angel's Department alone. I should sell them.

With this solid motive working within me I set solidly to work to set down solid facts solidly.

CHAPTER IX

The Ninth Five

THE SUNLIGHT SONATA WAS produced in the Lyric
Theatre, Glasgow, in March, 1928, and fittingly set
the new cycle bowling. Guthrie set and produced it
beautifully, Elliot Mason and Morland Graham were
funnier than I have seen them in anything else, and the
audience liked it. I had yet, however, to satisfy the
press.

We had a powerful school of dramatic critics in
Glasgow at the time. I like to think they sprang up in
response to our efforts. The model they chiefly
followed was Mr. St. John Ervine of *The Observer*.
His downright, forthright, plain man style was a very
suitable medium for the youths who were themselves
nothing if they were not plain men.

The notice that gave me most delight was that in
the *Glasgow Herald*. I had concealed my identity
under the name " Mary Henderson " and written the
following epilogue to the play which was beautifully

spoken by one of our best actresses, Jean Taylor Smith, in the character of ACCIDIA:

" I suppose, strictly speaking, I am the Author of this piece. But I feel very strongly that I must acknowledge my indebtedness to my little friends, Pride, Envy and Avarice, without whose continual encouragement this Play would never have been written. I cannot but refer, moreover, to that great Patron and Master of all young Dramatists, dear Beelzebub, without whose direct inspiration this Play might never have been written.

" This play is really a sort of propaganda play. In these days when all sorts of fancy and synthetic vices are being hourly imported from Europe and America, it is up to us to show by our enthusiastic support that Great Britain is still the best breeding ground for the good old-fashioned Sins that made our fathers what they were."

On the following morning I was encouraged to find the following in the *Glasgow Herald*:

" . . . The last play on the programme was *The Sunlight Sonata* by Mary Henderson. It was a somewhat extraordinary piece. In response to calls of Author, Miss Henderson said that it was intended to be a propaganda play and was designed to combat synthetic productions from Europe and the United States."

I was later to submit my work humbly to the approval of the best minds in London dramatic criticism, but this remains my favourite. They had more grace but he did it more natural.

The o'ercome of the song of most of the other young men of genius was that the first great Scottish play had yet to be written. In the meantime it was necessary for them to be very firm.

.   .   .   .

267

Brandane asked me why I had never written a full length play. I said I had and dug *The Switchback* out of its dusty drawer. He told me that he liked it and taught me how to write it properly. If anything comes of the Scottish Drama, John Brandane is its begetter. He spent more time driving technique, construction and common sense into raw young dramatists than he spent on work that might have made him famous. He is a most unselfish, great-hearted man, and he loves the theatre as it had been his son.

When *The Switchback* was clean, tidy and respectable he made me send it to Barry Jackson. Within a fortnight Barry Jackson said he would do it at Birmingham in the spring of the year. It was difficult to wait. I was not invited to rehearsals and could not have attended if I had been. But I dashed down to Birmingham, changed into a white dickie and made my way to the historic little lecture-hall-looking place which is the Birmingham Repertory Theatre. I was a little late, and Phillips and Turner shook hands with me and pushed me into a box. The curtain was up on a black stage and a telephone bell was ringing.

The play was about a doctor in practice on the Borders, who had discovered a cure for tuberculosis. He was exploited by a newspaper proprietor and a financier and struck off the Medical Register. At this point there was an impudent change of technique. For the first two acts the play had been plain sailing and naturalistic. In the third act it became a compound of Grand Opera and the Crazy Gang at the Palladium. The change over was made credible by the fact that the ruined doctor was steadily drunk and his last friend, an old aunt-housekeeper, was mad. I thought then, and still think, that I made a very exciting thing of that last act; but apparently it didn't conform to something or other. When the play was performed later at Malvern, with Cedric Hardwicke as the doctor, the last act proved to the Jews a stumbling block and to the Greeks foolishness. I was luckier at Birmingham.

At the first interval I was led to a neighbouring box and introduced to a tall man with long, grey curly hair and a taller lady with an indescribably detached air. They were Alan Parsons and Viola Tree. Alan Parsons was the critic of the *Daily Mail*. I had not expected to see anybody so important on my first professional night. After the second act I found the troglodyte Bache Matthews in the bowels of the earth, and he told me he was sorry Barry Jackson was not at home and showed me his theatrical library. We tried to find Ayliff, the producer, but for some reason or other he was nowhere to be found. After the play I went with Cyril Phillips and the Parsons to the Queen's Hotel, and we supped very pleasantly on point steak and Bollinger. Alan Parsons gravely approved of the play, and Viola Tree talked inconsequently of Ivor Novello. In the *Daily Mail* the next day Parsons announced that Barry Jackson had discovered a new dramatist. He was a good friend to me after that, and more than once fought St. John Ervine on my behalf.

In November of the same year, Barry Jackson put on another play by me. It was called *What it is to be Young*. It was not very good. Parsons came again to see it, but this time without his wife. At the play also was a tired looking, beautiful woman called Dorothy Massingham. Parsons was ill and Dorothy Massingham was depressed. Sir Barry had to go home early, and I had a pleasant party with Phillips, Alan King, a playwright and my first genuine man about town, and Phyllis Shand. We sat talking till four in the morning. I was already an infant of the theatre. These things could not be hid. The receipts from my consulting practice dropped promptly to two hundred, and from there to one hundred. They were never to surpass the latter figure again.

A new theatre had started in Glasgow. It was called the Masque Theatre. Their producer was called Claud Gurney. He was another of Fagan's young men, but he differed from Mr. Guthrie in many respects. He was dark and demoniac and was reputed to have a violent temper.

The easy-going couple who controlled the destinies of the Masque Theatre were standing with me beside a little hole in the wall we had in the Art Club, and they asked me whether I wouldn't like to write a play for them. I asked them if they would like a play about Burke and Hare, and they said yes. So I went home and wrote one. I felt very guilty about the Scottish National Theatre Society, so I wrote them a play too. It was called *The Girl who did not want to go to Kuala Lumpur*. Guthrie had gone by this time and had installed himself under Anmer Hall at the Cambridge Festival Theatre. *The Girl who did not want to go to Kuala Lumpur* was not a very good play. It was about a girl who fell in love with a postman and I laughed myself sick when I was writing it. The actors laughed themselves sick at rehearsals. It went on the stage with excellent prospects, but the audience were hardly quite so much amused, and the Glasgow dramatic critics not at all.

The Anatomist was produced by the Masque Theatre in Edinburgh in the summer of 1930. I could not attend its rehearsals either, but in the middle of the week before we opened I got a panic-stricken message from Gurney that he could not make head or tail of my script. I went through to Edinburgh and found that, indeed, the script did not seem to have much sense in it. I did not recognise it as my own, and we turned the Lyceum Theatre upside down looking for the original manuscript. We found it at last below a pile of press cuttings. Some person or persons unknown had been doodling over it with a blue pencil, and the typist had done her best. The unfortunate actors set themselves straight away to commit the more intelligible version to memory, and at quarter to eight on Monday night the curtain went up five minutes after the dress rehearsal had stopped.

The actor who played the leading part forgot altogether the two sets of words he had learned, but carried through the part with great verve by dint of shouting " God Almighty! " " Damn! " " Rot their souls! " and " Barbara Celarent! " at suitable intervals. His interlocutors gave him as many of his words as they could remember, but, as he was a little deaf, they very often had to speak the words themselves, prefacing them with " As you very truly observe," or " As you are never tired of remarking," or some such appropriate phrase. The performance was a great success and the dramatic critics of Edinburgh said that the first great Scots play had yet to be written. One of them said, quite truly, that I had a great deal to learn of the elements of my craft.

In the meantime the production of the Scottish National Players was being done by Elliot Mason. She was not yet a leading West End actress and we, in Glasgow, find it difficult to believe in an artist who has not been to London for a hall-mark. Apart from that, although she was a competent producer she was a very much better actress and it was a waste. We advertised for a professional producer, and were immediately snowed up by a heap of letters, most of them pathetic. Then Brandane and I had the thought of W. G. Fay, who, with his brother Frank, had been responsible for starting the great Irish theatre movement. A little later I wrote this about him:

" It was as if the L.M.S. in search of a managing director had suddenly heard the name of George Stephenson. The Abbey was our ideal, our star. It seemed to us to have been there since the beginning of time. It was incredible that one of its founders should still be alive and practising his art and kicking against the pricks. We found that such was the case and that we could just afford his fee. So it happened that John Brandane and I walked a rainy Sauchiehall Street with the impressario of Synge, Yeats, Russell and Lady Gregory. He was a wizened little man in a soaking mackintosh and insecure looking pince-nez. A wet cigarette hung from his expressive lower lip. We showed him the theatre where the Glasgow Repertory used to be. It is now the property of the Young Men's Christian Association. He looked dismally at the asbestos box which had been erected on the stage to prevent fire and the rapid change of scenery. ' The Lord look sideways on them,' he said. As cheerfully as an Old Contemptible moving up to the attack on Passchendaele Ridge he agreed to undertake our melancholy task. We felt ashamed of intruding on his sorrows, but later he went to tea at the Brandanes' and made them laugh till they cried."

He came with me to see *The Anatomist* and was entranced by it. He borrowed a script and sent it to Henry Ainley. Ainley liked it too. He went round a series of London managers with the script in his pocket. He read it to them in his golden voice and was told that he was mad to think that such nonsense would attract a cultivated West End audience.

Robert Lorraine came to Glasgow to play for the Masque Theatre in Strindberg's *The Father*. The Masque tried to get him to adopt *The Anatomist* and the part of Dr. Knox. But he thought nothing of it. I wrote another play. It was called *Tobias and the*

Angel, and I sent it to Tony Guthrie at Cambridge. Anmer Hall liked it. Guthrie wanted to play the Angel, and the production was entrusted to Evan John. In addition to his many other fine qualities Evan John writes a beautiful hand. His letters were like missals. Two other men who write to me sometimes—Gordon Bottomley and Macaulay Stevenson—make every page a picture. One can sit and look at their letters for hours from sheer delight at the lovely forms.

I went down to Cambridge for the dress rehearsal. An intelligent looking man in tweeds met me at the station, took my bag and trotted with it to a taxi. We had not got very far in our journey when I found that we were at cross-purposes in our conversation. He had expected to meet Dr. Somebody Else at the station and was filled with alarm and despondency when he found that I had not come to lecture but to witness a stage play. I took my bag out of the taxi, advised him to hurry back to the station and asked him to direct me to the Festival Theatre. He had never heard of the Festival Theatre and was in much distress till I ordered the taxi driver to drive away.

The Festival Theatre was an aged building with a modern stage and proscenium and an auditorium arranged in the antique English pattern. A rehearsal was in progress and I sat down beside Tobit who, I was charmed to find, was Anmer Hall himself, masquerading under one of his soubriquets. He had a delightful free and easy family party sort of company. One of them was a tall girl who reminded me of an Irish terrier. She went galloping about with cups of tea for the thirsty in one hand and a needle and thread for the ragged in another. All she had to do in the play was to sing a song; but she had constituted herself honorary maid of all work to the company and a general good influence. Guthrie whispered to me

273

" You must write a play for Flora Robson some day.
Nobody knows it but me, but she is going to be a great
actress." She had left the stage in despair a year or
two before, and I think it was Guthrie who persuaded
her to come back and give the Festival Theatre a
trial.

Tobias was a great success. It was played with an
artful simplicity to full houses for a fortnight. I came
back to Glasgow very pleased with myself and wrote a
play called *The Dancing Bear* for the Scottish National
Players. Fay helped me with it and produced it. It
was an interesting play. I made a huge tapestry of
talkative small parts and played out a little sentimental
comedy in front of it. Press notices showed a subtle
change. They ceased to be merely patronising and
stupid and attacked the play for all they were worth.
This pleased me, for we of the Bandar Log like to be
noticed. I felt that I had joined the noble army of
martyrs to the cause of Art. On the previous winter
the little chaps had maltreated a strong and beautiful
play by Neil Gunn, and I joined issue with them with
great delight. To tell the truth, *The Dancing Bear*
was no great matter, but it was good enough to fight
about and it displayed very well the remarkable acting
resources of the Society.

In August, 1931, Barry Jackson chose *The Switchback* to represent modern plays in a cycle of five centuries of English Drama at the Malvern Festival. My
experiences with my little Glasgow playmates had prepared me for the sterner stuff with which this play was
greeted by the London critics, and I was not much cast
down. Mr. A. K. Chesterton contributed an article to
the *Malvern Gazette* and proved to my satisfaction that
my critics were malignant dullards and dolts and that
the play was a great play. I went on to my London
début with a good heart, for Anmer Hall had promised

to open his new theatre, the Westminster, with *The Anatomist*.

Henry Ainley made a fine come-back in the part of Dr. Knox. A new and distinguished little theatre was added to the West End map. I made my first appearance in first class cricket and scored a century. It was rather a flukey century, but still it was a century. For those who are interested in such things, here is the Cast:

Dr. Knox.	Henry Ainley.
Dr. Anderson.	Carleton Hobbs.
Amelia Dishart.	Gillian Scaife.
Mary Belle Dishart.	Betty Hardy.
Jessie Ann.	Meg Buchanan.
Mary Patterson.	Flora Robson.
Davie Patterson.	Morland Graham.
Janet.	Joan White.
Augustus Raby.	Robert Eddison.
Nebby.	Craighall Sherry.
Burke.	J. O'Rourke.
Hare.	Harry Hutchinson.

The play was produced by Tyrone Guthrie and decorated by Molly Macarthur. The critics smiled on the play, with the notable exception of Mr. Agate, and all was gas and gaiters. *The Anatomist* ran for a hundred and twenty-seven nights, which was not bad for a new theatre a mile from Seven Dials. It was succeeded by *Tobias and the Angel* in March, 1932. Ainley played the Angel and Hermione Baddeley Sara. Oddly enough, this play did not do so well as *The Anatomist*. Ainley was terrific. The critics liked it better. It appeared to take a minor but quite definite place in the talk of the town. Repertories and amateurs have not tired of it yet, and it was revived in the West End last winter. And yet it ran for a paltry seventy performances and then fell down. It would be useful to employ—say at fifty thousand a year—a clairvoyant who could tell us what the London theatre-going public wants. Apart from some such method there is no way of knowing.

Anmer Hall, however, doggedly kept on presenting successes of esteem at the Westminster Theatre, losing many thousands of pounds in the process. One of these was my *Jonah and the Whale*, a little piece with an enormous cast. The Westminster Theatre weathered it for forty days, like the Ark but not so full.

At the end of 1932 I completed a play called *A Sleeping Clergyman*. I had been at it, off and on, for two years.

.   .   .   .

At the beginning of 1931 I found myself unable to pay my grocer's bill. I had stopped calling myself Mary Henderson and now called myself James Bridie, after my grandfather, James Mavor, and my great-grandfather, John Bridie, the sea captain. But the secret was out. Nobody who wrote plays could be expected seriously to apply his mind to consultations. Golf and bridge were permitted, but the playwriting was, as a relative put it, " apt to become too all-absorbing a hobby." Besides, it was a wee thing disreputable. So I had, as I say, some little difficulty in paying my grocer's bill. I solved the problem of the grocer's bill by carrying out one of the few really brilliant ideas of my life. I bought a new house. I recommend this method to anybody finding himself financially in a tight corner. A building society paid for the house, the bank furnished it and I lived on the proceeds of these crazy transactions for nearly a year.

CHAPTER X

The Tenth Five

I BEGAN THE LAST lap before the fifties in a very pleasant situation indeed. I was a respectable consulting physician and a sort of a professor. I lived in a genteel terrace house on the top of a hill. I could look from my windows over the nursing homes and over the river at twenty miles of green hill. I had a good family life and, that my father's prophecy might be fulfilled, I could " go and tell blue stories at the Art Club " whenever I liked. It is true that I was still in debt, but the angels bore me up and cut a bit off the over-draft every now and again. In an astonishingly short time I had reached a position of small but solid repute as a dramatist. I had no plays on the shelf awaiting production or acceptance. Every full length play I had written had found its way on to the stage. There had been no struggle. I had not fallen to rise, been baffled to fight better. It was all very satisfactory and dull.

In 1933 Shaw's new play was not ready for the Malvern Festival and I offered Barry Jackson *A Sleeping*

Clergyman. As this curious play was the nearest thing to a masterpiece I shall probably ever write, perhaps you will allow me to spend a little time on it.

The Anatomist was about Science. So was *The Switchback*. In the one case I considered the Scientist as Dictator and the other as Lost Sheep in the Wilderness. *Tobias* and *Jonah* were about God and the relation of the individual man to Him. These tremendous themes I treated in the only manner I had at my disposal—the jocular-conversational manner. Apart from the themes I had done everything I could to make the plays works of art. I used every trick I could find and a few I invented for myself. If the plays had been about nothing there would still have been something to have been said for them. They were neat and lively and kept the audience awake.

In *A Sleeping Clergyman* I attempted to combine my two main themes. I showed a wild horse after three generations or incarnations finally harnessing itself to the world for the world's good. God, who had set it all going, took his ease in an armchair throughout the play. The odd quality of the play made itself evident in rehearsal. The electricians, stage-hands, the wardrobe ladies, the charwomen in the theatre showed an interest in it from the beginning. I am told some of them wept. The company were awe-struck by this phenomenon. The first note of doubt was struck by Barry Jackson, who saw the dress rehearsal and decided that the play was too obscure and coarse in the grain for London. He was too disappointed to attend the first night, a Saturday. I sat beside Bernard Shaw and he calmed my fears by not discussing the play at all. He told me he had narrowly escaped being swallowed by a whale in Loch Fyne. I told him that that proved he wasn't a false prophet, and he said that might well be so. He told me not to bother about

London successes. He said a London success meant the moral, spiritual, intellectual and financial ruin of the unfortunate who attained it. He told me to wait patiently till the steady ninepence a week kept dropping in from the repertories and the amateurs. By that I should know I had arrived. He invited me to lunch with him on the following day.

The play made an impression. A Malvern audience is different from most kinds of audiences. A large proportion of most British audiences have no clearer impression of the meaning of what is going on in the illuminated area behind the frame than a dog has of a Velasquez. This seems a hard saying, but I have found no man of the theatre of any experience who can deny it. If a dramatist is writing for forty per cent. of his audience he is very lucky. The Malvern audience is a picked audience of Britons and Americans who have really learnt the complicated and difficult business of theatre-going. Their only fault from the author's point of view is an essential fault in people who know something about anything. They are over tolerant. The fact that they liked *A Sleeping Clergyman* was no indication that many others would. I placed my confidence in the stage-hands and charwomen.

I did not place my confidence in the dramatic critics. They were puzzled and a little angry. But most of them went again when the play reached London and more than one of them handsomely recanted. Mr. Ervine and Mr. Agate would have none of it; and I cherish a delightful criticism by Mr. Lionel Britton who at that time was an acknowledged representative of Left Wing Thought.

Mr. Robert Donat, Mr. Ernest Thesiger, Miss Dorice Fordred and Mr. Evelyn Roberts led a splendid company under the guidance of H. K. Ayliff. Paul Shelving's scenery was so adroit that nobody noticed the fact that not a door was opened or shut throughout the entire play. The scenery consisted of back-cloths and wings as it was in the days of old. I took a call and the curtain was rung down on my head. I went to see Barry Jackson on Sunday morning and found that a very distinguished gathering had arrived before me. Mr. and Mrs. Shaw, John Drinkwater, Lady Rhondda, Professor Cullis, Hugh Walpole, Mrs. Enthoven, Gordon Bottomley and the Allardyce Nicols were there with others of the great and famous. They were all praising the play as hard as they could. Shaw, perhaps, was an exception. A character in the play had been poisoned by prussic acid and Shaw said prussic acid was no good at all. He said he once had to destroy a sick cat with prussic acid. He had poured about an ounce of the deadly substance down a silver tube into the cat's mouth, and, for a while, he and his associates thought the cat was done for. In a few minutes, however, the cat got up and walked away.

Barry Jackson was at last convinced. He sent Cyril Phillips to London by the first train and told him to find a theatre. The Autumn season was crowded with plays and it was some time before he found a theatre. In the meantime the play went to Edinburgh, Birmingham and Glasgow. I followed it about, pulling out bits here and putting in bits there and learning to know and appreciate Ayliff. This tall, cadaverous, ingenious man has never had his fair share of glory in the theatre. He does not go to parties, he never takes a curtain call, he does not make speeches at luncheons on the future of the theatre. Actors and actresses of the first rank who owe their early training to him seldom mention him. They like to think that they sprang fully armed from the forehead of Jove, or, at least, that their genius grew from their early battles with misery and starvation. To remember the old school-master who taught them all they know blurs the beauty of these conceptions. In the early days, I am told, he had a tongue like a file, and this may explain why, from time to time, he has lacked advancement. Advancement or no advancement, he has cut his work deep in the history of the theatre and characteristically omitted to sign it. His latest feat was (in 1938) to produce five new plays by leading authors and *Saint Joan* with a great Continental star in the part of the Maid. These plays were all produced in a single week at the Malvern Festival. His past record includes *The Barretts of Wimpole Street*, *Back to Methuselah*, *Heartbreak House*, the first *Hamlet* in modern dress, *The Farmer's Wife*, and *The Apple-Cart*. In these days of brilliant and famous producers it is interesting to reflect that hardly anybody knows who directed these plays.

Edinburgh thought little of *The Clergyman*. Glasgow began warily as it invariably does with anything short of musical comedies on which it has been assured that at least £30,000 has been spent. It built quite pleasantly during the week, however, and I was delighted to find that the orchestra sat through every performance and that the reactions of the real people of the theatre were the same as they had been at the London rehearsals. The cloak-room lady went so far as to kiss me.

On Thursday night I entered the theatre by the stage door after the play had been in progress for some time. The sergeant said, " Very good house tonight, sir." And the next thing I met was Ernest Thesiger just coming off the stage. If I had not known him I should have thought he was drunk. He had tears streaming down his make-up and opened and shut his mouth once or twice like a goldfish before he could speak. I asked him what was the matter. He said, " Matter! Have you been in front tonight? " I said no. He said, " Never in my life have I experienced such an audience. They're hanging out of every crack in the ceiling. They're sending waves of emotion on to the stage that nearly split the scenery. It's terrific! I don't know if I can stand it." I went through the pass door to the upper circle and sat on the steps watching the audience. I cannot think such an audience happens more than once in a lifetime. So overwhelming was my love for them that I went home after the first act. It never happened again. We had plenty of people and plenty of enthusiasm in the remaining two nights in Glasgow, but not the time and the place and the loved ones all together. We found a home in London up a back street, one end of which was continually " up." The theatre was the Piccadilly, and we ran for nine months on a rather bare margin. The London public took to the play in steady but unsensational numbers. I am proud to think that Gracie Fields saw it four times; that Wee Georgie Wood saw it five; and that Noel Coward and John Van Druten made up a quarrel on the strength of it. It was not a masterpiece. The second act attempted an impossibility and failed badly. It takes a better dramatist than I shall ever be to show an apotheosis explicitly on the stage. But there was satisfaction in it. It was an honest piece of work, and it gave Robert Donat a chance of proving that he was the finest young actor in England. I cannot resist quoting my left wing critic, Mr. Britton. He was the author of a play in which, I believe, megaphones were freely used. He wrote about me as follows in *The New Clarion*.

" I haven't seen his other plays, so I can't talk about them. But after trying to sit out *A Sleeping Clergyman* I know why the clergyman slept. It would put anyone to sleep.

" The play opens in a pub with members discussing heredity and a clergyman snoring in an armchair. That's a sort of prologue, and then you go on to the play proper, which is supposed to illustrate the discussion, and then I believe you get back to the discussion and the clergyman still snoring at the end. If that is so I suppose it means that heredity is an important subject and religion doesn't take any notice of it. I didn't wait for the end, so I can't say for certain; I did my best but I really couldn't stick it out. It was a bit too thick. This sort of stuff may be all right for an obscure provincial town but it really ought not to be brought to London."

Mr. St. John Ervine, lest anyone should take Mr. Lionel Britton as a lone intellectual fighting against the degradation of our theatre, took an Indian Civil Servant to see the play, and neither of them could make head or tail of it. Mr. James Agate got himself intolerably tied up with genetics, and had clearly not been paying attention. I got to know both these gentlemen later on—not the Indian Civil Servant, but Mr. Ervine and Mr. Agate, and I found out that it was only their fun. Neither of them is a stupid man. Mr. Ervine is the only dramatist in England who knows his job thoroughly, though it took the London managements many years and two big successes to find this out. Mr. Agate is in the great line of English essayists. I cannot understand why either of them is regarded as a dramatic critic.

My next play had a back-stage history so outrageous that it is impossible to print it. It was called *Marriage Is No Joke* and was presented at the Globe Theatre, where it had a run of five nights. During these five nights I had the privilege of seeing my name in lights in Shaftesbury Avenue. They glowed rather sardonically on my fulfilled ambition. Even this defeat had its compensations. A little later I was working with Berthold Viertel on the script of a film. *Marriage Is No Joke* was about an adventurous Highland divinity student, who married the daughter of the landlord of a border pub, fought in the War, headed a revolution in North Persia, became a Shah and returned home to the larger adventure of Holy Matrimony and family life. Viertel said,

" I have seen some time ago the best play I have effer seen in my life. I was the only one of the twenty people in the theatre who thought so. I have forgotten its name or who wrote it, but it was about a priest who got drunk in a café and married the barmaid. . . ."

He went on to describe *Marriage Is No Joke* and my wounds were immediately healed.

I do not like first nights. Nobody does, except those who go regularly to see and be seen at them. There is no more disagreeable noise than the babel they set up in the foyer two minutes before the curtain is due to rise. But they are not so black as they are painted. I find that if I have a couple of whiskies and sodas I can sit through the piece in my stall with an impudent face and laugh brazenly at my own jokes. *Marriage Is No Joke* was an exception. I sat through the first act and heard my lovely lines falling like cold porridge on a damp mattress. I stood at the back of the dress circle and heard the second act open to the accompaniment of scattered hisses from the gallery. I then walked round to the Piccadilly Theatre where the *Clergyman* was still being performed. I met Pamela Carme on the stair. She said nothing, but led me into a dressing room where she gave me a third whisky and soda. This fortified me to explain the situation to Pamela, Isobel Thornton, Eileen Beldon and Phyllis Shand. I did this with a brave facetiousness, was generously comforted and returned to the

Globe to take what was coming to me. A miserable and ill arranged supper party followed, and some strain of masochism in me made me lie awake till the morning papers arrived. They were kinder than I had any reason to expect.

A little later Flora Robson came to afternoon tea. Her magnificent performance in *The Anatomist* had forced her on public attention and she was now flying in the first flight. She said she wanted a play, and that it must not be a play about a frustrated spinster with an evil mind. I wrote her a play about a woman pirate called Mary Read. I wrote a pure picaresque in emasculated Smollet, and then took fright. A play of this sort must be of the stage stagey, and I had not sufficient confidence of mastery in this vein. I called in a collaborator. Indeed, it had been suggested by my agent that I should do so; and he went the length of mentioning one or two names. I felt somewhat affronted to my dignity. I chose my own collaborator, one Claud Gurney, who had steadily blackguarded and denigrated all my works to that date except *The Clergyman*. There followed a series of long range battles. Sprochles had told me long before that I had no finer feelings, and I began to believe that this was true. Claud sent me insolent letters full of plain speaking and moral superiority. I thought, " Hello, this is a game," and replied with abuse. My one supreme gift is the art of writing abusive letters, and I was delighted to be in a situation to exercise it. Claud was cut to the quick and replied by retiring from the collaboration. This happened two or three times, and at last we produced between us a hideous conglomeration of nothingness with this to recommend it, that it had a simple coherent story and a part for Flora. After a week in a Manchester fog, during which Flora took ill, it was presented at His Majesty's Theatre, at

enormous expense, with a magnificent cast and staggering settings, under the auspices of no less a person
than Mr. Alexander Korda. Flora gave a terrific
performance and Robert Donat supported her in the
most thankless part of his life; for it was a composite
of two parts, and the joins showed up badly. It was
such a bad part that he established himself firmly as an
actor in his own right, for anybody can play a really
good part.

The best that can be said for *Mary Read* as a play
was that it was good fun. I met Mr. Wells on the
first night and was entranced by his resemblance to a
sparrow and by his silvery voice. The play had a
hundred and five performances, and lost a very great
deal of money.

. . . .

I have told you of Viertel and a film script. This
was my first film script, and I helped Viertel and
Bruno Frank to make it. We made it in three weeks.
At the end of that time Viertel stood up, raised his eyes
to heaven and said,

" We haf composed the first film masterpiece. I
shall be able to shoot this film vord for vord with the
same reverence as I would give to directing a play of
Shakespeare on the stage. And now you will stay for
a little and explain it to Micky Balcon."

I did not wait to see Mr. Balcon, but it was reported
to me that he summed up the script with the one word
" Lousy." I do not know whether this is correct, but
I heard no more of the script. Our efforts were not,
however, entirely of noneffect. Viertel said to Frank
that it was a great pity his comedy *Sturm im Wasserglas*
was impossible to adapt into the English idiom. A
fortnight later I had done an adaptation. A week later
my agent had sold it to the Haymarket Theatre. Six

months later it had not been produced, and the option of the Haymarket Theatre had run out. On February 5th, 1936, it was produced in Edinburgh in a snowstorm, on the night of the death of King George V. W. G. Fay was the producer, and he was confident that the King would not die and so ruin any possible chances of success for the play. He said it was clearly written in the stars that Edward VIII would not be crowned. He was right and he was wrong. The play after opening in such dismal auspices moved to the Royalty Theatre, where it was such a success that it was transferred to the Haymarket. So the stone which the builders rejected became the head of the corner. It ran for a year.

While the Haymarket was making up its mind about *Storm in a Teacup* I sat at a pleasant window in North Berwick writing a play that made me laugh very much while I was writing it. It was called *The Black Eye*. I sent it to my agent, and he was very melancholy about it. I sat in his office for half an hour listening to his woebegone prognostications. I bet him five pounds that I would sell it myself, and he took the bet. I got into a taxi and took the script round to C. B. Cochran. Cochran said that nobody ever sent him a straight play unless it was called *If Christ came to Blackpool* and had twenty-five performing elephants in the cast. I said I had a play with no performing elephants in it and gave him the script of *The Black Eye*. He bought it next day. It was done in October at the Shaftesbury.

C. B. Cochran has had his ups and downs, but he is a professional to the backbone. He has an office in which nobody is kept waiting. He can make a three-minute interview appear to last half an hour. He has no coloured lights on his desk, and he does not interrupt conversations to ring up Budapest. His face is divided neatly into four compartments with a different expression on each, and you can take your choice. He did not know Ayliff, but was willing to engage him to produce the play. Life was very happy during the rehearsals.

The melancholy Frank Collins came into the theatre one day with a brown paper parcel under his arm and sat down beside me. He said,

" I see from *The Daily Telegraph* we're doing six new productions this winter. First I've heard of it, and I suppose I'd better get down to them quick. That's his way, you know. . . . What's all this stuff I hear about Mr. Ayliff this and Mr. Ayliff that? I'm not used to it and I don't like it. I was in the City before I went into the show business and they all called me Mr. Collins or Collins and made me feel like a starched worm. My name's Frank. What does Ayliff's wife call him? "

I told him. " 'Arry," shouted Frank, " I've got that new dimmer you wanted."

I went to dinner with Cochran and sat talking of this and that till two or three in the morning. Just as I was leaving I suddenly remembered about *The Black Eye* and that, for part of the play, Stephen Haggard had to make speeches in front of a curtain that was picked out in two shades of bile. I said I hoped we would have new tabs in time for the first night. Cocky looked very glum. He said he feared it was impossible. The Shaftesbury was not his theatre and new tabs were very expensive.

Next morning I went to rehearsal at ten o'clock. Ayliff was wreathed in smiles.

" This is a good management," he said. " Frank has just arrived to tell us that we're to have new tabs and that he's got them already. He dug them out somewhere this morning.

At the dress rehearsal, Cocky was worried about rumbling noises during the changes. He made a beautiful speech to the cast at the end of the rehearsal, and then retired, still grumbling about the rumble. Next morning twenty men were to be seen laying the stage with felt and linoleum. But my favourite happening was this. One of the actors was uncomfortable about his part. What bothered him was the psychology, and, at rehearsal, he was giving a nervous, complicated performance far below his usual level. We had grave doubts about him. I made him a little happier by explaining to him that there was, in fact, no psychology in the part and that he must play it straight and for laughs, as he well knew how to do. Cocky, Ayliff and I then went into a huddle and decided that he was a fine enough actor to override his psychological nonsense. Cocky then climbed on to the stage and took the actor into a dark corner. " Mr. X," he said, "this is a very much more important part than I had imagined when I offered it to you."

He paused at this point and the actor's heart sank into his boots.

" I should, therefore," said Cocky, " feel eternally grateful if you would accept another three pounds a week."

It is not necessary to say that the actor gave a brilliant performance.

The first night was great fun. It was a minor Cochran masterpiece, but none the less a masterpiece for that. The audience were miraculously in their seats five minutes before the curtain went up. Cocky appeared in one box and was cheered. Bernard Shaw appeared in another and the audience roared. Elisabeth Bergner appeared in a third and they went quite mad. The curtain went up to an audience who felt they had had their money's worth already.

At the interval I went to pay my respects to Shaw. He was holding court in the little room behind his box. Peggy Ashcroft came in and was introduced as the new Juliet. Shaw said, " You can't play Juliet. You get away with it because you're young and beautiful, but you can't play Juliet because there's no part to play. All the pork butchers who had an interest in the play tried their hands at writing up the part, and now there's nothing left but nonsense."

As he was leaving the theatre Burnell Binnie politely opened the door of his taxi for him and said, " What do you think of the play, sir? " Shaw wagged his beard at him. " It'll never do," he said. " It'll never do."

He was quite right. It had a good start, but the general election came along and killed it.

Cochran asked me to do a musical comedy. It was to feature Renée Houston. I thought I should enjoy doing that and wrote a book of words. The theme was the life of Mary Queen of Scots. I have never met Renée Houston, but she sent me a post card with a picture of the Dorchester on one side of it. The post card said, " Doctor, for heaven's sake be careful. Remember you're writing for a Papist."

I wrote what I thought was a very good book of words. I made Mary Queen of Scots a hereditary secretary general of a Soviet Republic in South Russia. I began the play at her Embassy in London. Châtelard, an American college boy, followed her to Krasnyegrad. She got out of the train in a brilliant red cossack uniform to find that the town band had gone away for lunch and that the only occupants of the station were the station-master and his wife sitting on a broken barrow sharing a raw turnip and terribly depressed because the Registrar had taken measles and they couldn't get divorced. John Knox was a commissar, Rizzio was a hotel keeper, Bothwell was a cossack hetman. The town band wore mufflers and overcoats and could only play " The Red Flag " and the " Internationale." Darnley was a communist grand duke. The play rejoiced in the title of *Mary had a Little Elephant*. I went to see Cocky about it. He was lying in a beautiful great bed with pink bedclothes. All four quarters of his face had a mournful expression and he wagged his head sadly. He said he would like to submit the book of words to an independent referee and whom would I suggest? I suggested Noel Coward. He said all right, and I sent the book of words to Noel Coward. Noel Coward gave it a negative vote, on the ground that it was satire and the British public would never stand satire.

I do not know whether it was satire or not. I am not very clear what the word means. But I cannot help feeling that the theatrical superstition to which Mr. Coward gave voice is strikingly ill-founded. At the time of which I write, the D'Oyley Carte Opera Company was packing the Savoy Theatre to the doors with the Gilbert and Sullivan comic operas. If these operas are not satirical I don't know what they are. I am for ever running up against these theatrical *clichés*,[1] and I cannot understand them at all. The next musical

[1] I met a third of these *clichés* not long ago. It was during the tremendous run of a play called *The Amazing Dr. Clitterhouse* that I offered a play about a madman to a London manager. He said the public would not stand plays about madmen. Now, Dr. Clitterhouse was a madman, and the manager must have seen the eager crowds in the Haymarket struggling to get in to see the play. I met once a fourth *cliché*. This was that it was suicidal to open with a new play in September, because nobody was back in town. I made a table from Mr. John Parker's excellent book. I listed all the plays within the last ten years which had runs of over a hundred performances. I found that by far the greatest number had opened in the first week of September. The second largest number had opened in the second week. The scramble for theatres has killed this *cliché*, but commonsense could never have done it.

comedy I wrote for Cochran was a dream play. He wired back that he was afraid of dream plays. They were always dangerous and hardly ever successful. I asked my ten year old child if he knew the names of any dream plays, and he told me three. I wired Cochran the names of six, and I can think of a dozen more, all overwhelming successes. They range from *A Midsummer Night's Dream* to *Berkeley Square* and *Dear Brutus*. It was no good. Yet Cocky did not lose hope. He arranged that I should collaborate with A. P. Herbert on the book of a musical comedy for Gitta Alpar. This brought me the pleasure of the acquaintance of A. P. Herbert and little else. Musical comedy is not my *métier*.

It was not very easy to collaborate with Mr. Herbert. He was a very much occupied man. After a variety of attempts we decided to get together seriously. I was to meet him at The Seven Seas (the old ship at the Charing Cross Steps) and we were to sail up the river in his barge and put in a good solid day's work at his house at Hammersmith. He would ring me up at about nine in the morning so that we could make a reasonably early start. By eleven o'clock he had not rung me up, and I went out to do some business. When I got back at twelve I found an urgent message waiting for me that I must hurry up or we should not catch the tide. I taxied down to the Seven Seas and found Mr. Herbert playing darts. He suggested that we should lunch on the ship, as there was very little time to spare. At about quarter to three we boarded the barge accompanied by a dirt track racer who wanted a lift to Hammersmith. The wind was piping loud in sheet and stay, and the waves were mountains high. At Battersea Bridge we lost the dinghy and had to turn back for it, at imminent danger of shipwreck, against the pillars of the bridge. We retrieved the dinghy and I was wet to the skin. I put on Herbert's pilot jacket and sat shivering on the roof of the cabin. When we made Hammersmith Reach the dirt track racer leapt ashore and we steered for our anchorage. But it was to be some time before we reached the desired haven. There was a regatta of little sailing boats in progress and, under some trailing willows, we found one such vessel lying on its side and its crew swimming about in the muddy water. Another little sailing boat was standing by in a helpless sort of fashion, buffeted by wind and tide. Herbert and I rescued the mariners, who had been in the water for half an hour and were bright blue with cold. The wreck and her consort were fastened to us with ropes and we began to yaw about in the fairway, interrupting the whole traffic on the Thames. I wrapped the mariners in blankets and tried to light the stove; but the only fuel I could find was about a thousand Sunday papers. Herbert said there was no whisky on board, but my Scotch nose smelled out the heel of a bottle and the lives of the drowned men were preserved. At this point a very excited motor launch drew alongside and shouted repeatedly for a bucket. I thought they were going to help to salve our wreck and gave them a bucket, whereupon they racketed away up-river at a great pace and were never seen again. Somehow or other we managed to get to the yacht club jetty, which was full of untidy women in long trousers and bearded men in short trousers. We left the salvage to the experts and went into the club for a drink. At about seven o'clock we pulled up in the mud opposite Herbert's house and went ashore.

Before we could get down to work a rite had to be practised. We had to visit the local public house for half an hour's conversation with prominent residents, a game or two of skill and chance and a glass of brown

sherry. We sat down to supper with two of Mr.
Herbert's delightful daughters at eight o'clock, and at
nine o'clock I had to leave to keep an appointment with
Auriel Lee in the Savoy Grill.

On Sunday I returned, this time by the under-
ground, and we collaborated to some extent. Our
only further meeting was at the House of Commons.
We were to lunch there and work furiously for an hour
or so in some secluded corner of that vast pile. At
lunch we were joined by a charming legislator called
Mr. Seymour Cocks. In the middle of the meal the
Tithes Bill suddenly called for Mr. Herbert. He shot
rapidly from his seat and did not reappear. Mr.
Cocks and I sat for some time drinking House of
Commons port and discussing the art of poetry. We
then adjourned to the smoking room, which was
occupied by a very pleasant group of Clydeside Reds.
I talked to them till half-past five and then went away.
I have not seen Mr. Herbert since, and the collabora-
tion was, from a worldly point of view, a failure.

At about this time other forces besides Cocky
attempted to divert me from that path of least resistance
to which the Lord had called me. Mr. Ramsay
MacDonald had been heavily defeated in his constituency. It was understood that he would be offered
the first safe seat that fell vacant after the general
election of 1935. The first safe seat was the Scottish
Universities. The Scottish Universities are not particularly politically minded; but even the dozen or so
enthusiasts who, in each university, constitute the
Unionist Association were shocked at the peremptori-
ness with which they were instructed to put forward
Mr. MacDonald as their candidate. The constituency
was a special kind of constituency. Its members had
been a distinguished historian and novelist, a celebrated
biologist and a leading educationalist. Each of these

294

had been elected and made his contribution to public
policy without interference from the party machine.
Mr. Ramsay MacDonald in his socialist days had
declared himself strongly against the system of
University representation and had even promised a
measure to abolish it. Many members of the University, and among them staunch Unionists and supporters of the National Government, could not help
feeling that this was a bit thick. One day I decided
to stand as an independent candidate against Mr.
Ramsay MacDonald. A few days later I decided not
to, but the fat was in the fire and the beans spilt.
I had fled to North Berwick, but my telephone bell
rang all day and the telegraph boy was continually
on the trot. The personal and public enemies of
Mr. MacDonald were prepared to look upon me as the
saviour of my country, and to support me in this
capacity with all the resources of their talents and bank
balances. I was swept to the surface of a very pretty
revolt before I knew what I was doing. When I had
time to examine the position I found a hundred practical reasons that unfitted me for the roll of saviour to
my country and, with my supporters, I set about
trying to find a candidate who would have a fair
chance of beating Mr. MacDonald. We failed.
Mr. MacDonald was elected by an enormous majority
with the machine going full blast behind him. We
had the minor satisfaction that it cost him seven hundred pounds in election expenses, whereas his predecessor, Mr. John Buchan, had paid twenty-five
pounds for the same majority; and to the Scottish
National candidate there accrued five thousand votes
which he himself could hardly claim to have been cast
for his policy. The late Lady Houston sent me a
telegram accusing me of black treachery, the tumult
and the shouting died, and I retired, as they say,

to the obscurity from which I should never have emerged.

If it had been intended that this sparrow should fall to the ground, that this lily should change its garment, the appropriate season would have been chosen. I should have become a Member of Parliament or a musical comedy millionaire at the beginning or at the end of one of my fateful quinquenniads. At the beginning of my second I changed from a countryman to a townsman. At the end of my second I cast out fear and embraced derision. At the beginning of my fourth I became a man. At the beginning of my fifth I became an author and an arbiter. At the beginning of my sixth I became a doctor and a soldier. At the beginning of my seventh I left wars behind and began to earn my living. At the beginning of my eighth I became a married man. At the beginning of my ninth I became a writer of plays. At the beginning of my tenth I became a West End dramatist. At the end of my tenth I laid down the toga and the stethoscope, moved into the country and closed one half of my double life. I had reached, on the surface at least, the position my father had wished for me, in that I had become a visiting physician in a teaching hospital. It, the Victoria Infirmary, was the smallest of the three Glasgow teaching hospitals. But to be a physician to it carried the same rank, honour and dignity as in any of the others. On the other side I had fulfilled my own early ambition, if such a tepid preference could be called an ambition. I had become a sort of an artist. If I have not made clear to you how these heights of fulfilment had been reached, it is because I do not know myself. If I appear to you a little smug and complacent, it is because I am smug and complacent. These adjectives, like the word hypocritical, are only terms of abuse used by those who are not virtuous to

describe certain virtues; for smugness is Faith, complacency is Content and hypocrisy is the nearest an
average man can get to goodness. " Goodness and
mercy all my life have surely followed me," say the
Metrical Psalms. That is smug. That is complacent.
That is true. I have lain back on a taxicab seat and
gone to sleep, trusting myself gladly to the extraordinary adroitness and nerve of the driver to take me
through the traffic in the highways and the byways.
I have wakened from time to time to shout a direction
and have fallen again on sleep, knowing that my
direction would be obeyed. And you must not blame
me for not sitting on tenterhooks with one eye on the
taxi-meter and another on the road in front, gripping
an imaginary steering-wheel, stamping on imaginary
controls. You must not blame me, either, for giving
you a vague account of the journey. Who are you to
blame anyone? Who *are* you anyway?

. . . .

*The Recording Angel turned over the pages rapidly,
raised his eyebrows at the final insult and handed them
back to me.*

" *I don't think much of this," he said.*

" *But," I said, " if I'd been made differently I'd have
behaved differently. And even if I hadn't been made
differently but had pulled myself together or taken advice or
what not and had contrived to behave differently I shouldn't
have been the same person, should I? I mean to say,
there, but for the grace of God, if you see what I mean . . .
I mean to say, I might have had a different kind of breakfast one day and swallowed a fish-bone and died and that
would have been the end of me and no story to tell and no
amusing plays and nothing whatever."*

" *Amusing? " said the Recording Angel.*

" *Well, they are," I said. " I know what you're*

going to say about them, but I don't agree with you. I make patterns. I'm a carpet playwright. I weave. If you cannot follow the lines of my design; if you cannot read the Great Names of Allah woven among olive trees and the scorpions and the stags, at least I hope you will like the gaiety of the colours and the variety of the shapes. Tread lightly on my Berlin Persians, on my quaint linoleums, for you tread on my dreams."

"That is all very well," said the Recording Angel when he had read my plays, " but . . ."

"Just a minute," I said. "Listen to this. ' She came downstairs. She went to an office and sat there all day. She went back to her divan room at six-thirty and stayed there reading library novels. She had no friends and no money to spend.' . . . If I make her alive then I have told a story, a story out of which you can take your own meaning, a story you can round off with your own moral. If I put in a murder in the next flat, a love affair with her employer or any such miserable incident I put it in because otherwise no one would buy this story. But they are not the story. The story is the girl herself, coming to life, reaching to you over the footlights and telling you that you are not alone in the world; that other human beings live, suffer, rejoice and play the fool within the same limitations that bind you. And all this nonsense about last acts. Only God can write last acts, and He seldom does. You should go out of the theatre with your head whirling with speculations. You should be lovingly selecting infinite possibilities for the characters you have seen on the stage. What further interest for you have they, if they are neatly wrapped up and bedded or coffined? It makes me angry to hear these doctrinaire duds. . . ."

"Yes, yes, yes, yes, yes," said the Recording Angel. " But up here we know something about the Absolute. We keep it at headquarters. We measure everything against it. We can tell at a glance how good or how bad or how *neutral anything is. Now, you are not very good. You must go back to earth and try to work a little harder."*

" I can ask for nothing better than to go back to earth," I said. " But as for working a little harder . . . I wish you would let me make a play of this. I think I could have shown you something."

" No doubt, no doubt," said the Recording Angel, and occupied himself with other matters.

PRINTED IN GREAT BRITAIN
BY ROBERT MACLEHOSE AND CO. LTD.
THE UNIVERSITY PRESS, GLASGOW

JAMES BRIDIE'S PLAYS

library editions (cloth) per vol. 7s. 6d. net

THE KING OF NOWHERE: AND OTHER PLAYS
Containing: The King of Nowhere—Babes in the Wood—The Last Trump.

COLONEL WOTHERSPOON: AND OTHER PLAYS
Containing: Colonel Wotherspoon—What it is to be Young—The Dancing Bear—The Girl Who did not want to go to Kuala Lumpur.

A SLEEPING CLERGYMAN: AND OTHER PLAYS
Containing: A Sleeping Clergyman—The Amazed Evangelist—Jonah and the Whale—Tobias and the Angel—The Anatomist.

THE SWITCHBACK: AND OTHER PLAYS
Containing: The Switchback—The Pardoner's Tale—The Sunlight Sonata.

MORAL PLAYS
Containing: Marriage is no Joke—Mary Read (*with Claud Gurney*)—The Black Eye—and a Preface.

separate editions (wrappers) per vol. 2s. 6d. net

THE KING OF NOWHERE	TOBIAS AND THE ANGEL
BABES IN THE WOOD	THE SWITCHBACK
THE LAST TRUMP	THE ANATOMIST
STORM IN A TEACUP	COLONEL WOTHERSPOON
MARRIAGE IS NO JOKE	MARY READ
A SLEEPING CLERGYMAN	(*with Claud Gurney*)
JONAH AND THE WHALE	THE BLACK EYE
WHAT SAY THEY?	

Birmingham Post: "Mr. Bridie is a writer of great individuality. He writes like an educated man and for the theatre of educated people; he does not place the current low value on human intelligence. Perhaps if he had, he might have been a millionaire-playwright."

Published by CONSTABLE LONDON

JOHN BRANDANE'S PLAYS

¶ *See page* 260 *et seq. of* " *One Way of Living* "

library editions (*cloth*)

THE TREASURE SHIP. 6s. net

THE INN OF ADVENTURE *and*
HEATHER GENTRY. 7s. 6d. net

theatre editions (*wrappers*)

THE GLEN IS MINE. 2s. 6d. net

RORY AFORESAID *and*
THE HAPPY WAR. 2s. net

THE INN OF ADVENTURE. 3s. net

HEATHER GENTRY. 3s. net

———————

" John Brandane has been established for many years as Scotland's leading native dramatic author. He is original in that he derives from nobody but himself, and takes his material direct from the kind of life he knows. An audience can smell the heather-honey and the peat and hear little waterfalls in every line. Brandane is not only a spontaneous but a conscientious artist. There are no slipshod, amateurish passages in a Brandane play. His construction is as strong as a Cathedral's."

JAMES BRIDIE

Published by CONSTABLE LONDON

GORDON BOTTOMLEY'S PLAYS

¶ *See page 260 et seq. of " One Way of Living "*

CHORIC PLAYS
Wrappers 6s. net

KING LEAR'S WIFE
AND OTHER PLAYS
Cloth 7s. 6d. net

GRUACH AND BRITAIN'S DAUGHTER
Cloth 7s. 6d. net

A VISION OF GIORGIONE
Cloth 10s. 6d. net

SCENES AND PLAYS
Wrappers 6s. net

LYRIC PLAYS
Wrappers 5s. net

THE ACTS OF ST. PETER
Wrappers 3s. 6d. net

" Dr. Bottomley has contributed more than any other man to the establishment of poetic drama . . . He has come to know more, probably, than anyone else in Great Britain about the art of writing dramatic dialogue in verse."   MARTIN BROWNE (*The Scottish Stage*)

" There is little anywhere else in English verse to set beside Mr. Bottomley's unfailing ability to express first things in noble and restrained cadence."

HUMBERT WOLFE

Published by CONSTABLE LONDON